HYBRID METAHEURISTICS

Research and Applications

SERIES IN MACHINE PERCEPTION AND ARTIFICIAL INTELLIGENCE*

ISSN: 1793-0839

Editors: **H. Bunke** (University of Bern, Switzerland)
P. S. P. Wang (Northeastern University, USA)
Joseph Lladós (Autonomous University of Barcelona, Spain)

This book series addresses all aspects of machine perception and artificial intelligence. Of particular interest are the areas of pattern recognition, image processing, computer vision, natural language understanding, speech processing, neural computing, machine learning, hardware architectures, software tools, and others. The series includes publications of various types, for example, textbooks, monographs, edited volumes, conference and workshop proceedings, PhD theses with significant impact, and special issues of the International Journal of Pattern Recognition and Artificial Intelligence.

Published

Vol. 84: *Hybrid Metaheuristics: Research and Applications*
by Siddhartha Bhattacharyya

Vol. 83: *Data Mining in Time Series and Streaming Databases*
edited by Mark Last, Horst Bunke and Abraham Kandel

Vol. 82: *Document Analysis and Text Recognition:*
Benchmarking State-of-the-Art Systems
edited by Volker Märgner, Umapada Pal and Apostolos Antonacopoulos

Vol. 81: *Data Mining with Decision Trees: Theory and Applications (Second Edition)*
by L. Rokach and O. Maimon

Vol. 80: *Multimodal Interactive Handwritten Text Transcription*
by V. Romero, A. H. Toselli and E. Vidal

Vol. 79: *Document Analysis and Recognition with Wavelet and Fractal Theories*
by Y. Y. Tang

Vol. 78: *Integration of Swarm Intelligence and Artificial Neural Network*
edited by S. Dehuri, S. Ghosh and S.-B. Cho

Vol. 77: *Graph Classification and Clustering Based on Vector Space Embedding*
by K. Riesen and H. Bunke

Vol. 76: *Automated Database Applications Testing:*
Specification Representation for Automated Reasoning
by R. F. Mikhail, D. Berndt and A. Kandel

Vol. 75: *Pattern Classification Using Ensemble Methods*
by L. Rokach

Vol. 74: *Wavelet Theory Approach to Pattern Recognition (Second Edition)*
by Y. Y. Tang

*The complete list of the published volumes in the series can be found at
https://www.worldscientific.com/series/smpai

Series in Machine Perception and Artificial Intelligence – Vol. 84

HYBRID METAHEURISTICS

Research and Applications

Siddhartha Bhattacharyya

RCC Institute of Information Technology, India

W **World Scientific**

NEW JERSEY · LONDON · SINGAPORE · BEIJING · SHANGHAI · HONG KONG · TAIPEI · CHENNAI

Published by

World Scientific Publishing Co. Pte. Ltd.
5 Toh Tuck Link, Singapore 596224
USA office: 27 Warren Street, Suite 401-402, Hackensack, NJ 07601
UK office: 57 Shelton Street, Covent Garden, London WC2H 9HE

Library of Congress Cataloging-in-Publication Data
Names: Bhattacharyya, Siddhartha, 1975–   author.
Title: Hybrid metaheuristics : research and applications / by Siddhartha Bhattacharyya,
    RCC Institute of Information Technology, India.
Description: New Jersey : World Scientific, [2018] | Series: Series in machine perception and
    artificial intelligence ; volume 84 | Includes bibliographical references.
Identifiers: LCCN 2018029187 | ISBN 9789813270220 (hc : alk. paper)
Subjects: LCSH: Heuristic programming. | Metaheuristics.
Classification: LCC T57.84 .B43 2018 | DDC 006.3--dc23
LC record available at https://lccn.loc.gov/2018029187

British Library Cataloguing-in-Publication Data
A catalogue record for this book is available from the British Library.

For any available supplementary material, please visit
https://www.worldscientific.com/worldscibooks/10.1142/10989#t=suppl

Desk Editor: Herbert Moses

Typeset by Stallion Press
Email: enquiries@stallionpress.com

Printed in Singapore

To my Late Father Ajit Kumar Bhattacharyya, my Late Mother Hashi Bhattacharyya, my beloved wife Rashni, my cousin brothers-in-law Rasaraj and Sabyasachi

Preface

A metaheuristic is a higher-level procedure designed to select a heuristic (partial search algorithm) that may lead to a sufficiently good solution to an optimization problem, especially with incomplete or imperfect information. The basic principle of metaheuristics is to sample a set of solutions which is large enough to be completely sampled. As metaheuristics make few assumptions about the optimization problem to be solved, they may be put to use in a variety of problems. Metaheuristics do not, however, guarantee that a globally optimal solution can be found on some class of problems since most of them implement some form of stochastic optimization. Hence, the solution found is often dependent on the set of random variables generated. By searching over a large set of feasible solutions, metaheuristics can often find good solutions with less computational effort than optimization algorithms, iterative methods, or simple heuristics. As such, they are useful approaches for optimization problems. Even though the metaheuristics are robust enough to yield optimum solutions, yet they often suffer from time complexity and degenerate solutions. In an effort to alleviate these problems, scientists and researchers have come up with the hybridization of the different metaheuristic approaches by conjoining with other soft computing tools and techniques to yield failsafe solutions.

A hybrid metaheuristic is essentially a technique that results from the combination of a metaheuristic with other techniques for optimization. In a recent advancement, quantum mechanical principles are being employed to cut down the time complexity of the metaheuristic approaches to a great extent. Thus, the hybrid metaheuristic approaches have come a long way in dealing with the real life optimization problems quite successfully.

This volume comprises 10 contributed chapters devoted to report the latest findings on hybrid metaheuristics and their applications to different engineering problems apart from an introductory chapter and the conclusion.

The action of combining the components from various algorithms is presently the utmost successful and effective trend in optimization. The foremost motivation behind the hybridization of diverse algorithmic ideas is to acquire better performing systems, which exploit and coalesce benefits of the different pure approaches, that is, hybrid systems that are supposed to be benefited from synergy. The hybridization of popular metaheuristics like particle swarm optimization, evolutionary algorithms, simulated annealing, variable neighborhood search, and ant colony optimization with techniques from other fields like artificial intelligence and operations research forms the basis for evolving more efficient and failsafe solutions. Chapter 1 provides an overview of the different hybrid metaheuristics which have been evolved till date with notable reference to the robust and failsafe incarnations.

Chapter 2 introduces a new hybrid metaheuristic optimization algorithm (TLBOGSA) with the incorporation of teaching learning based optimization (TLBO) and gravitational search algorithm (GSA) for solving the unconstrained or constrained optimization problems. The main purpose of this chapter is to alleviate the convergence of hybrid metaheuristic algorithm and reduce the computational overhead involved in solving benchmark optimization problems.

Of late, major areas of application such as forensics, government and commercial domain demand higher accuracy and reliability to identify individuals in real time. Biometrics is the automated measurement of ubiquitous and unique characteristic of an individual which can distinguish an individual from the mass. The design of a multi-biometrics system in real-time applications is an exciting research due to the limitations of unimodal biometric systems. The risk of attack to multi-biometric framework keeps on varying from time to time and hence adaptive systems are needed which can adapt to these varying security levels. Chapter 3 provides a review of the applications of metaheuristics techniques like ant colony optimization (ACO), particle swarm optimization (PSO), genetic algorithms (GA), hybrid GA-PSO, and quadrature programming (QP) optimization for optimizing support vector machines in developing real time multi-biometric authentication systems.

Automatic generation control (AGC) is a tool which helps the system to maintain the frequency within its targeted value by balancing the active power in the system. In Chapter 4, the authors propose a novel membrane computing inspired Jaya algorithm (MCJA) and applied to tune the controller parameters for AGC of multi-area interconnected system. The proposed algorithm is designed by incorporating the concept of membrane computing in basic Jaya algorithm (JA). A two area non-reheat thermal plant is considered for AGC in this study.

Underwater image edge detection becomes a difficult and challenging task due to various perturbations present in the water. Edge detection is a primary and important task in image processing. In Chapter 5, the authors introduce a novel edge detection method for underwater images. The method is based on human psycho visual (HVS) phenomenon. The HVS imitates the original visual technique of a human being and it is used to divide each sub-band into the Weber, De-Vries Rose and Saturation regions. The proposed methodology automatically detects the De-Vries Rose, Weber and Saturation regions in an image as an HVS system, based on image statistics using Mean particle swarm optimization algorithm (MeanPSO).

In Chapter 6, the authors present a new quantum-behaved multi-objective metaheuristic method for multi-level image thresholding. This method exploits the fundamentals of quantum computing by using a popular multi-objective framework, called NSGA-II for better usability and efficiency. A number of conflicting objective functions are employed to determine the set of non-dominated solutions. Subsequently, these solutions are used by a popular thresholding method, called Kittler's method for different levels of image thresholding.

In Chapter 7, support vector regression and whale optimization algorithm are presented for long-term prediction of wind speed. The whale optimization algorithm (WOA) is adapted for optimizing the support vector regression (SVR) parameters so that the prediction error can be reduced. The rendering of the proposed algorithm is evaluated using three different measurements including forecasting based measurements, statistical analyses, and stability. The daily average wind speed data from space weather monitoring center (SWMC) in Egypt was selected in the experiments. The experimental results showed that the suggested WOA algorithm is eligible for finding the best values of SVR parameters, avoiding local optima issue and it is competitive for wind speed forecasting.

In Chapter 8, the authors propose a hybrid classification approach using the gray wolf optimizer (GWO) integrated with support vector machines (SVMs) to automatically detect the seizure in EEG. The discrete wavelet transform (DWT) was utilized to decompose EEG into five sub-band components. The SVM classifier was trained using various parameters that were extracted and used as features. GWO was used to select sub-features. As the EEG signal rating depends on the optimal parameters that have been selected, it is also integrated with SVM to obtain better resolution of the classification by selecting the best tuning parameters SVM.

Chapter 9 introduces the application of a hybrid metaheuristic algorithm to the optimization of recurrent neural networks (RNNs) in generating forward walking gait of a hexapod robot. The algorithm used is the evolutionary group-based particle swarm optimization (EGPSO), which creates new solutions through the hybrid of group-based genetic algorithm (GA) and particle swarm optimization (PSO).

Chapter 10 presents an application of a hybrid optimization technique combining particle swarm optimization (PSO) with ant colony optimization (ACO) in finding economic load dispatch (ELD) of large scale thermal power system. The proposed PSO–ACO algorithm is tested on standard 40-generator system simulated in MATLAB. The test results in terms of total cost of power generation, transmission loss, and convergence characteristics strongly attests the viability of the algorithm for addressing large-scale economic dispatch in actual power generation scenario.

Chapter 11 draws a line of conclusion to the volume with future avenues for research.

This volume is intended to be used as a reference by undergraduate and post-graduate students of the disciplines of computer science, electronics and telecommunication, information science, and electrical engineering for some part of their curriculum as well as professionals, researchers, and academics.

The editor would like to take this opportunity to render his heartfelt thanks to Ms. Tegikuppe Narasimhaiah Sowmya, Editorial Contact and Mr. Steven Patt, Editor, World Scientific Publishing Co. Pte. Ltd., Singapore for the constant support and encouragement during the tenure of the book project.

Siddhartha Bhattacharyya
March, 2018
Kolkata, India

Contents

Chapter 1

Introduction to Hybrid Metaheuristics

Sandip Dey

Department of Computer Science & Engineering,
OmDayal Group of Institutions, Birshibpur,
Howrah-711316, India
dr.ssandip.dey@gmail.com

Sourav De

Department of Computer Science & Engineering,
Cooch Behar Government Engineering College,
Cooch Behar, India
dr.sourav.de79@gmail.com

Siddhartha Bhattacharyya

Department of Computer Application,
RCC Institute of Information Technology,
Canal South Road, Beliaghata, Kolkata-700015, India
dr.siddhartha.bhattacharyya@gmail.com

The action of combining the components from various algorithms is presently the utmost successful and effective trend in optimization. The foremost motivation behind the hybridization of diverse algorithmic ideas is to acquire better performing systems, which exploit and coalesce benefits of the different pure approaches, that is, hybrid systems that are supposed to be benefited from synergy. Actually, taking a suitable amalgamation of multiple algorithmic notions is often the key to achieve highest performance in solving number of hard (complex) optimization problems. Nonetheless, evolving an exceedingly effective hybrid method is not a simple task at all. The hybridization of popular metaheuristics like particle swarm optimization, evolutionary algorithms, simulated annealing, variable neighborhood search, and ant colony optimization with techniques from other fields like artificial intelligence, operations research forms the basis of evolving more efficient and robust solutions.

1

Keywords: Hybrid metaheuristics, quantum computing, metaheuristics, optimization, and advanced hybrid metaheuristics.

1. Introduction

Optimization is required in different fields of engineering such as mechanical engineering, civil engineering, mining engineering, nanoscience and nano-engineering, computer, communication, networking and information engineering, bioinformatics and biomedical engineering, etc. to obtain better solutions. To solve optimization problems practically in those above mentioned fields, some efficient and effective computational algorithms are very mush essential. The foremost objective of the optimization is to derive the optimal solution for a given problem. An optimization problem is determined as: deriving values of the variables that maximize or minimize the fitness (objective) function(s) in line with the constraints.[1] These kinds of problems are based on three factors: firstly, they solve some minimization/-maximization objective function(s), secondly, a set of unknown variables those are involve in the objective functions and thirdly, a set of constraints that permit the unknowns for taking some specific values but exclude others.[1]

Most of the optimization problems may have more than one local solutions. In this circumstances, choosing of the optimization method is very much important. The optimization method must not be greedy and the searching process will not be localized in the neighborhood of the best solution as it may stick at a local solution and that will misguide the search process. It should be observed that the optimization algorithm should make a balance between global and local search. Both the mathematical and combinatorial types optimization problems can be solved by different methods. The optimization problems that have large search space or more complex in nature will become difficult to solve using conventional mathematical optimization algorithms. Here is the utility of the metaheuristic algorithms. Different metaheuristic optimization algorithms, present in the research arena are very much capable to solve difficult optimization problems.

A heuristic method can be noted as the way of solving, leaning or discovery of a problem using practical methods and ultimately, will derive immediate near optimal results rather than exact results. Basically, a metaheuristic is an iterative generation procedure to solve a subordinate heuristic by syndicating intelligently different concepts to explore and exploit the search space, learning strategies are applied to structure information in order to find efficiently near-optimal solutions.[2] The main objective of metaheuristic is to derive a set of optimal solutions which is large enough to be completely sampled. The popularity of using metaheuristic techniques on a variety of problems is due to the fact that any conventional algorithm cannot manage many real world problems, in spite of the raising computational power, simply due to unrealistically large running times.[3] These algorithms make few assumptions to solve the optimization problems. It is not guaranteed that the metaheuristics may generate globally optimal solutions to solve some class of problems since most of the implementations are some form of stochastic optimization and the resultant solutions may dependents on the set of generated random variables. Metaheuristic algorithms are advantageous over optimization algorithms, simple heuristics, or iterative methods as they often determine good solutions with a lesser computational effort by exploring a large set of feasible solutions.

Most well-known metaheuristic algorithms are Genetic algorithm (GA),[4] simulated annealing (SA),[5] Tabu search (TS)[6–8] and different types of swarm intelligence algorithms. Genetic algorithm (GA) works on the principle of the evolutionary process in nature. Tabu search applies the memory structure in living beings, whereas simulated annealing imitates the annealing process in crystalline solids. Some well known and recognized swarm intelligence algorithms are particle swarm optimization (PSO),[9] ant colony optimization (ACO),[10] artificial bee colony optimization (ABC),[11] differential optimization (DE)[12,13] and cuckoo search algorithm,[14] etc. More swarm intelligence based optimization algorithms are coming out in research arena day by day like, Egyptian Vulture Optimization Algorithm,[15] Rats herds Algorithm (RATHA),[16] Bat algorithm,[17] Crow search algorithm,[18] Glowworm Swarm Optimization (GSO),[19] etc. are working efficiently.

Though the metaheuristic algorithms are robust enough to afford optimum solutions, these algorithms often suffer from time complexity and degenerate solutions. Facing problems to solve complex problems by any particular metaheuristic algorithm, scientists and researchers have come up with the hybridization of the different metaheuristic approaches. Different soft computing tools and techniques are hybridized with the metaheuristic algorithms to get failsafe solutions.[20,21]

A metaheuristic algorithm in the combination with other techniques, applied for optimization is known as hybrid metaheuristic algorithms that may become more effective to handle the real life optimization problems quite successfully. In a recent advancement, quantum mechanical principles are being employed to cut down the time complexity of the metaheuristic approaches to a great extent.[20,21]

The chapter is organized as follows. Section 2 presents an overview of metaheuristics. Some popular fundamental metaheuristics are elaborately described in this section. A number of recent metaheuristic algorithms are described and presented in Section 3. Section 4 presents the shortcomings of stand-alone metaheuristics. A number of limitations of using stand-alone metaheuristics, are listed in this section. In Section 5, the overview of hybrid metaheuristics is presented here. Some important research works are also reported in this section. In Section 6, some advanced hybrid metaheuristics techniques are presented. A number of quantum inspired techniques proposed by different researchers, are presented in this section. A group of recent quantum inspired metaheuristic algorithms are elaborately described in this part. The features of a number of hybrid metaheuristic algorithms are compared and presented in Section 7. Finally, the concluding part of hybrid metaheuristics are drawn and given in Section 8.

2. Overview of Metaheuristics and Their Applications

Metaheuristics are well-known techniques, introduced to describe and define different heuristic techniques that can be applied to an extensive range of diverse problems. Alternatively, a metaheuristic is also can be depicted as a general algorithmic structure which is suitable to solve different optimization problems. In such cases, relatively no or a very few modifications may be required to adapt it for specific problems. The typical representatives of its kind may be exemplified as genetic algorithm, evolutionary algorithms, simulated annealing, particle swarm optimization, tabu search, ant colony optimization, and iterated local search to name a few.

Each algorithm possesses a specific historical background, follows certain rules and ideas, and puts some individual strategies in the foreground.[20,21] A comprehensive overview of metaheuristics can be found in the literature.[22] This section is populated with some standard and popular metaheuristics as follows.

2.1. *Genetic and Evolutionary Computation*

Evolutionary Computation (EC) is referred to as the biology inspired technique used to solve problems. EC can be seen as an abstraction from the notion of biological evolution, which is basically applied to create numerous optimization methodologies, that are effectively used to solve various kind of problems. EC has two components.

(1) Genetic Algorithms (GA): It was first introduced by John Holland.[4]
(2) Evolution Strategies (ES): Ingo Rechenberg first developed ES.[23]

A GA is described by a population of candidate solutions. It has two different operators, viz. reproduction and evolution. The first one is directed by a selection strategy. The evolution operator has two components, viz., crossover and mutation. The GA is run for a number of generations for optimality. Each generation creates a new solution space. The parent chromosomes are selected from the pool of chromosomes to fill the population for the next generation. The selection is done by employing a figure of merit, called objective/fitness function, which computes the fitness value of each chromosome.[4] Few discrete components should be address while describing GA.[4,24] These are (i) chromosome encoding: it means encoding the chromosomes for replicating the solution space; (ii) fitness evaluation: it means evaluating chromosomes to determine the suitability of a chromosome; (iii) selection: it is a genetic operator used to fill population with the fittest individuals. The selection is done using different selection strategies viz., Boltzmann selection, roulette wheel selection, or rank selection methods; (iv) crossover: This operator is encountered for crossing over parent individuals to create new offspring; (v) mutation: This operator induces the population diversity by changing the value at some particular positions at random. The GA is described through the following pseudo-code.[4,24]

```
begin
    itn= 1;
    initialpop P(itn);
    compute P(itn);
    repeat
        Q := selectparent P(itn);
        crossover Q(itn);
        mutate Q(itn);
        compute Q(itn);
        P = selectsurv P, Q(itn);
        itn= itn + 1;
    until itn>mxgn
end
```

Here, **initialpop** function generates the population of starting (candidate) solutions (**P**) at random. Later, **compute** function computes the fitness of each individual in **P**. The **selectparent** function produces its successor (**Q**) using a selection strategy. Thereafter, recombine and mutate are consecutively applied for getting population diversity. Then **compute** function computes the fitness of each member in **Q** for selecting the best survivors. This method is run for a predefined number of generations (**mxgn**).

2.2. *Ant Colony Optimization*

Ant Colony Optimization is a popular example to design metaheuristic methods for solving various combinatorial optimization problems. In 1991, Dorigo *et al.*[10] presented the premier method which can be grouped within this structure and, since then, number of researchers has presented many dissimilar variations of the basic principle in the literature. The foremost underlying principle, inspired by the foraging behavior of real ants struggling for collecting food helped to get the concept of ACO. The real ants have no sharp vision. The real ants try to discover the shortest path from their nest to the food source. They squirt a chemical, known as "pheromone on the ground in order to exchange information about the source of food between themselves. If any particular ant selects the same path to follow, it squirts more chemical on that path, resulting stronger path, which motivates others to follow the similar path. The ACO is implemented through the pseudo-code as given below.

```
begin
  itn:= 0;
  initialPheromone B(itn);
  initialPopulation A(itn);
  evaluate P(itn);
  repeat
    itn := itn + 1;
    A: =updatePopulation A(itn);
    evaluate P(itn);
    B: =updatePheromone B(itn);
  until itn>MG
end
```

At initial, **initialPheromone** and **initialPopulation** are invoked to randomly initialize the pheromone matrix (B) and the staring population (A), respectively. Thereafter, the fitness of each member of A is evaluated. The **updatePopulation** and **updatePheromone** functions are used to update the A and B matrix, respectively at every generations. This process is executed for MG number of generations.

2.3. *Particle Swarm Optimization*

Particle swarm optimization is a very popular population-based, nature-inspired stochastic search procedure, originally developed by Eberhart and Kennedy in 1995.[9] The inspiration behind the development of PSO is the communal behavior and movement dynamics of fish, insects or birds. PSO is suitable and effective for solving continuous variable problems. This metaheuristic is simple for implementation and is derivative free. It handles very few parameter set for making its population diversity. It starts working with randomly distributed particles set, sometimes called potential solutions, the metaheuristic tries to improve the quality of solutions on the basis of a quality measure, called fitness function. The improvisation is accomplished through the movement of participating particles around its search space by dint of few simple mathematical expressions. Generation wise, PSO advocates the particles own best position (experienced by that particle) and the best position of swarm so far. The idea is to let the birds, insects or fishes find an unidentified favorable place in the whole search space through exploiting on one others knowledge. The position of each particle in the search space is updated using the following rule:

$$v_{k+1}^i = v_k^i + \varrho_1 r_1 (p_k^i - y_k^i) + \varrho_2 r_2 (p_k^i - y_k^i) \tag{1}$$

$$y_{k+1}^i = y_k^i + v_{k+1}^i \tag{2}$$

where, y_k^i and v_k^i represent particle position and particle velocity p_k^i and p_k^g are the particle position (best "remembered") and swarm position (best "remembered"). ϱ_1 and ϱ_2 signify the cognitive and social parameter. r_1 and r_2 randomly generated numbers between (0,1).

The pseudo-code of PSO is described as follows.

```
begin
  itn:= 0;
  initialSwarm Q(itn);
  evaluate Q(itn);
```

```
  repeat
    begin
    itn:= itn + 1;
    sltPbst Q(itn);
    sltGbst Q(itn);
    calpVelocity Q(itn);
    updatePosition Q(itn);
    evaluate Q(itn);
    end
  until itn >MxGen
end
```

The **initialSwarm** function is used to randomly generate the swarm of trial solutions (Q). Then, evaluate function finds the fitness value of each particle in Q. The **sltPbst** and **sltGbst** functions are used to find best fitness of each particle and the best fitness value of swarm so far. **calpVelocity** and **updatePosition** functions are used to modify the position of each particle in the search space. This procedure is run for **MxGen** number of generations.

2.4. *Differential Evolution*

Differential Evolution is a popular population-based optimization method proposed by Rainer Storn and Kenneth Price.[12,13] This method has been designed for optimizing problems whose solution are found in continuous domains. DE is robust, simple and easy to use. It has a simple framework. DE is basically a genetic type method which uses real valued variables to solve problems. DE is a design tool which has been successfully used to access practical applications in several science and engineering domain. If it requires for a system to be rationally evaluated, Differential Evolution perhaps be the best choice among other methods, which can extract the best possible solution from it. DE successively uses two genetic operators, called mutation and crossover as a search mechanism and it directs the searching toward the potential regions. The DE is implemented through the following pseudo-code.

```
begin
    itn := 0;
    initialPopulation A(itn);
    evaluate A(itn);
```

```
repeat
  A := mutate A(itn);
  A := crossover A(itn);
  A := selectparents A(itn);
  itn := itn + 1;
  evaluate A(itn);
  until itn>MG
end
```

At initial, **initialPopulation** function is used to randomly generate the initial population of trial solutions (A). Thereafter, **evaluate** function finds the fitness value of each member of A. Then, two genetic operators, viz., **mutate** and **crossover** are successively used in (A) to get the population diversity. Finally, **selectparents** function is invoked to select the best individuals from A to make the population for its subsequent generation. These three functions are being executed until the stopping criterion is reached.

2.5. *Simulated Annealing*

Annealing is process of tempering certain metallic substance, crystal or glass by heating beyond its melting point. In its process, it holds its temperature, and thereafter cools it very gradually until it reaches at solid state to form a crystalline structure. This process basically yields high-quality material substances. The simulation of this annealing process is referred to as simulated annealing. It was invented by Kirkpatrik *et al.*[5] SA is fundamentally experiences two different stochastic processes. The first process generates solutions while the other one accepts these solutions. The temperature causes to correlate the generated probing solutions with the original solution. SA explores its parameter space at very high temperature, but it restricts its exploration when the temperature becomes low. If cooling is adequately slow, SA reaches at its global optima. The following pseudo-code demonstrates the executional steps of SA.

```
begin
  initialSolution ya;
  initialize tmax,tmin,mxitr,r;
  evaluate ya;
  tma= tmax;
  S=xa;
```

```
repeat
   begin
      repeat
      itr := 1;
      yf :=neighbor(ya)
      d=Fn(yf)-Fn(ya);
      if(d<0)
      ya=yf;
      else if(rand(0,1)<power(e,(-d/tma)))
      ya=yf;
      update S(itr);
      itr:= itr + 1;
      until itr> mxitr
      tma=tma*r;
   end
until tma>tmin
end
```

Initially, the **initialSolution** function is used to generate a trial solution (**ya**) at random. Then, the parameters like initial and final temperature, number of iterations for running the inner loop and reduction factor are initialized at earlier. Afterward, the fitness of **ya** is evaluated. SA stops its execution when it reaches at final temperature (through outer loop). The neighbor solution of ya is explored at each iteration and the best solution is saved on the basis of a certain criterion, **update** function is employed to update the global best individual.

2.6. *Tabu Search*

Tabu search is basically a popular local search procedure which has a flexible memory structure. The basic method of Tabu Search has been originated on thoughts introduced by Fred Glover.[6] TS is designed in such a way that it can overcome boundary limits of feasibility or/and local optimality, rather than considering them as barriers. TS is designed in such a way such that it can adapt intelligence, if required to solve certain kind of problems. TS has the adaptive memory feature that helps to implement processes which is capable to search the solution space effectively and economically. In TS, local choices are dependent on the information gathered during its searching operation.

Some important parts of TS can be termed as follows:

(1) Neighborhood: It contains an assortment of adjacent solutions which can be derived from the present solution.
(2) Tabu: To use memory in tabu search that is to categorize in neighborhood as access in tabu list.
(3) Attributes: It is can be coined as classification based on the recent history.
(4) Tabu list: saves the forbidden moves, called tabu moves.
(5) Aspiration criterion: If the tabu classification is required to be overridden using some applicable condition, it is known to be aspiration criterion.

TS is described though the pseudo-code as given by

```
begin
    itn= 0;
    initialSolution ya;
    initialTM POP :=null;
    Compute ya;
    S=ya;
        repeat
        itn=itn +1;
        nbs=neighborSet(ya)
        b=findBst nbs (itn);
        update POP(itn);
        S=b;
        itn=itn + 1;
        until itn >mxit
end
```

The **initialSolution** function randomly generates a single trial solution (ya). Initially, the **initialTM** function is invoked to initialize the Tabu memory (POP) to null. Next, Compute function is used to evaluate the fitness value of ya. Then, a solution set (neighbor solutions) is found using **neighborSet** function. The function **findBst** determines the best individual among these solution sets. The **update** function is used to update POP. This process stops executing when **itn** reaches the predefined value, **mxit**.

2.7. *Variable Neighborhood Search*

Variable neighborhood search (VNS) is a popular metaheuristic, basically appropriate to solve global and combinatorial optimization problems, introduced by Mladenović and Hansen about two decades ago.[25] The basic thought for developing VNS is that a systematic change of neighborhood is performed. It selects the non-decreasingly neighbors of the imperative solution and explores them. In this way, it searches for betterment, and if it finds and improvement, this solution is jumped to another one. In such a way, good (optimal or near optimal) variables are kept in the incumbent and attains encouraging neighbors. Thereafter, VNS applies local search procedure to acquire local optima from these neighbors. The executional steps of VNS is demonstrated through the following pseudo-code:

```
begin
    initialSolution, s0;
    neighborhood operators,{Ni} for i=1,2,...,imx;
    local search process (using neighborhood operators), LS;
    fitness function, fn
    curr= s0;
repeat
    begin
        repeat
        i= 1;
        s1=a randomly generated solution in Ni;
        s2=LS(s1);
        if(fn(s2)<fn(curr))
        curr=s2;
        i=1;
        else
        i=i+1;
        until i<imx
    end
until stopping condition not encountered
end
```

Initially, the **initialSolution** generates a trial solution (**s0**) at random. Then, a local search procedure (LS) is encountered using a set of neighborhood operators, (Ni). VNS runs until stopping condition not encountered.

3. Recent Metaheuristic Algorithms

In this section, we will throw some light on few recent metaheuristic algorithms.

3.1. *Egyptian Vulture Optimization Algorithm*

Compare to the other birds, Egyptian vulture is capable of the natural and phenomenal activities, intelligence and unique perceptions for leading lifestyle and acquisition of food. Taking inspiration from these habits of the Egyptian vulture, a nature-inspired metaheuristic algorithm named Egyptian Vulture Optimization Algorithm (EVOA) proposed by Sur *et al.*[15] in 2013. The dexterous capabilities to handle tough challenging problems and having the weakness finding ability and force makes the Egyptian vulture a unique from other birds. Mainly, two features of this method are capable of breaking eggs using pebbles and the ability for rotating objects using twigs. The multistep procedures like, graph-based problems and node based continuous search can be handled easily by EVOA. The steps of EVOA follows as:[15,26]

(1) Initialize the set or string of solutions which represents the parameters in variable form.
(2) Tuned the variable representatives by checking of the superimposed conditions and constraints.
(3) Tossing of Pebbles at random (or selected) points.
(4) Rolling of Twigs on the whole (or selected) string.
(5) Changing angle through selective part reversal of solution set.
(6) Evaluation of fitness.
(7) Check the stopping criteria.

3.2. *Rats Herds Algorithm (RATHA)*

Based on the social behaviour of Rats Herds, Ruiz-Vanoye and Daz-Parra[16] suggested a new metaheuristic algorithm, named Rats Herd Algorithm (RATHA). General intelligence and learning ability by simple avoidance conditioning are the behavioral property of the rats. Avoidance conditioning is the behavioral pattern of a subject when it develops awareness of an imminent adverse situation that is to happen.[16] From the past experience, the subject adopts the experience and become capable to avoid the said averse state and averts it from affecting its own functioning. In other words, when someone faces some unfavorable situation that may happen in the near future, that person tries to avoid that particular unfavorable event by taking some solution of his past experience. The following algorithm shows the RATHA algorithm:[16]

- Supplied N of rats as input.
- Initialize the rats population with x_{ij} random solutions.
- Repeated the total number of rats by parallel and/or distributed processing.
- Initial locations (x) of the rats (N) generated.
- Use avoidance conditioning to generate new solutions and update thereafter it update locations (x).
- Find the current best Solution and Rank the rats.
- Best solution (S) selected.
- Store the best food source position achieved so far.
- while $(N$ total of rats$)$.
- Best solution reported.

3.3. *Bat Algorithm*

Bat algorithm,[17] taking inspiration from the research on the social behavior of bats is a bio-inspired metaheuristics method for solving hard optimization tasks. This algorithm formed on the basis of the echolocation behaviour of bats.[16,17] A very loud sound pulse is emitted by the microbats and the echo that bounces back from its surrounding objects has also listened to them. They apply these properties for detecting prey, avoiding obstacles, and locating their roosting crevices in the dark. Different properties based pulses can be interrelated with their hunting policies, depending on the species.[16,17,27] Xin-She Yang nominates the Bat algorithm on the basis of the above-mentioned description of bat process.

Every single bat constitutes one solution in N-dimensional search space in which optimization takes place. A fitness function is provided to evaluate the fit value of the individual solutions. Two real-values N-dimensional vectors are linked with each bat in population. First one is the real valued vector representing position of a bat in solution search space, known as position vector and the real valued vector representing velocity in each of N-dimensional directions, recognized as velocity vector is the other one. At the beginning of the algorithm, these two vectors are initialized randomly. Basically, it is a iterative process to derive the solution. In every iteration, each member of the population is assessed by the provided fitness function and the relative distance from best and current solution in population applied to calculate the new velocity vector. Accordingly, the velocity vector is updated by the position of the individual bat. At the end of each iteration, the best solution is compared with the previously stored best solution and the new best one is updated. This search process continues until the predefined number of iterations reached or improvement of the best solution is very negligible. The pseudo code of this algorithm is presented in Algorithm 1.[17,27]

Algorithm 1. Steps of BAT Algorithm

1: Initialize position po_i and velocity ve_i of ith bat in population randomly.
2: Initialize pulsation frequency $PF_i \in [PF_{min}, PF_{max}]$, pulsation r_i and loudness A_i of ith bat in population.
3: **while** until termination conditions are satisfied **do**
4:    **for** individual bat in population **do**
5:       $ve_i(t) = ve_i(t-1) + Q_i(x_i(t-1) - rx^*)$
6:       $rx_i(t) = rx_i(t-1) + ve_i(t)$
7:       **if rand(0,1)** $> r_i^t$ **then**
8:          Generate new solution around selected best solutions.
9:          Generate new solution by flying randomly.
10:          **if rand(0,1)** $< A_i^t$ **and** $f(x_i) < f(x^*)$ **then**
11:             Accept new solution and update pulsation and loudness factors r_i^t and A_i^t as:
12:             $A_i^{t+1} \leftarrow \alpha A_i^t; r_i^{t+1} \leftarrow r_i^t(1 - \exp(-\beta t))$.
13:          **end if**
14:       **end if**
15:    **end for**
16: **end while**
17: Evaluate bats population using fit function f.
18: Find best bat in population and mark him as rx^*.

---

where $ve_i(t)$ and $rx_i(t)$ are the real valued velocity vector and position vector of ith bat, PF_i is the pulsation frequency of the ith bat. α and γ are two constants.

3.4. *Crow Search Algorithm*

Crow search algorithm, inspired by the intelligent behaviour of crows is a recently proposed metaheuristics search algorithm by A. Askarzadeh.[18,28,29]

Basically, the behaviour of the crow is to save and hide their excess food for future usage and retrieve it when required. Crows are noted as the most intelligent birds and it has been observed that their brain-to-body ratio is nearer to the one in human.[29] By remembering the faces of the other crows, they prevent the foods from the unknown crows when they try to approach it. They find out the food locations of other birds and steal when there are no birds at that place.

Assume that N number of crows are present in the environment and the position of the ith crow on the jth generation is denoted as $p_{i,j}$ and the maximum number of iteration is referred as j_{max}. Each ith crow may have a memory of their food hiding position i.e. $m_{i,j}$. The best derived position of the crow is saved by the memory locations. Mainly, crows follow other crows for the allocation of places to hide their food and hunt it. Based on this strategy, the qth crow wants to go to its food hiding location, $m_{q,j}$. Two cases can arise in that iteration, when i^{th} crow decides to follow the qth crow to approach the ith crow food hiding place.[28]

Case 1: q^{th} crow does not aware that i^{th} crow is following. Thus, it will be easy for the ith crow to find the hidden food and easily change its position to a new one as given in Equation

$$p_{i,j+1} = p_{i,j} + r_i \times f_{i,j} \times (m_{q,j} - p_{i,j}) \geq PR_{q,j} \qquad (3)$$

where $r_i \in 0, 1$ is the random number and $f_{i,j}$ is the flight length of ith crow at j^{th} iteration. Larger values of the flight length is desireable as smaller value of that may face the problem of local optima.[18,28] At j^{th} iteration, PR_j is the awareness probability of the jth crow.

Case 2: In opposite, if q^{th} crow knows that i^{th} crow is following, q^{th} crow mislead the ith crow by moving to another place in the search space. Thus, i^{th} crow will have to find another crow to follow and will reach to a new random position.

$$p_{i,j+1} = a\,random\,position \qquad (4)$$

3.5. *Glowworm Swarm Optimization Algorithm*

Glowworm Swarm Optimization (GSO)[19,30,31] is another nature-inspired optimization algorithm that imitates the behavior of the lighting worms. A swarm of glowworms, treated as a population of solutions are disseminated randomly in the search space of the solutions. Each glowworm has a luminescence quantity, called luciferin along with them. Each glowworm applies a probabilistic mechanism for moving towards a brighter neighbor. The swarm of glowworms divides themselves into a number of disjoint subgroups, which in time converge to numerous local optima of any given multimodal function.[32] The fitness of their current locations is evaluated by the glowworms luciferin intensity. In the search space, the better quality of the location of the glowworm is determined by the higher intensity of luciferin.[32] The luciferin value in each iteration updates when the positions of all glowworms change. The luciferin updating happens in each iteration and it is followed by a movement-phase based on a transition rule.

(1) Luciferin-update phase: Assume, at an instance t, $p_i(t)$ is the location of the ith glowworm and the corresponding value of the objective function at that location and at same time is denoted as[19,30,31] $J(p_i(t))$.[32] The luciferin level ($lu_i(t)$) associated with the ith glowworm is presented as

$$lu_i(t) = (1 - \beta) \times lu_i(t - 1) + \rho \times J(p_i(t)) \tag{5}$$

(2) Movement phase: For each ith glowworm, the probability of moving towards a neighbor j^{th} glowworm is represented as[19,30,31]

$$p_j(t) = \frac{lu_j(t) - lu_i(t)}{\sum\limits_{k \in N_i(t)} lu_k(t) - lu_i(t)}, \tag{6}$$

where $j \in N_i(t)$, $N_i(t) = j : d_{i,j}(t) < r_d^i(t); lu_i(t) < lu_j(t)$, t is the time or step index, $d_{i,j}(t)$ denotes the euclidian distance between glowworms i and j at time t, $lu_i(t)$ indicates the luciferin level associated with glowworm j at time t, $r_d^i(t)$ denotes the variable local-decision range related to glowworm i at time t and r_s represents the radial range of the luciferin sensor. Let the ith glowworm select a $j \in N_i(t)$ glowworm with $p_j(t)$ (given in equation 6). Then the discrete-time model of the glowworm movements can presented as[19,30,31]

$$x_i(t + 1) = x_i(t) + s\left(\frac{x_j(t) - x_i(t)}{||x_j(t) - x_i(t)||}\right) \tag{7}$$

where s is the step size.

(3) Local-decision range update rule: The neighborhood range is updated as[19,30,31]

$$r_d^i(t + 1) = minr + s, max0, r_d^i(t) + \gamma(n_t - |N_i(t)|) \tag{8}$$

where, γ is a constant parameter and r_d^i changes dynamically ($0 < r_d^i \leq r_s^i$).

4. Demerits of Stand-alone Metaheuristics

Metaheuristics are mainly acknowledged as one of the successful approaches for solving combinatorial problems. As opposed to the early days research in metaheuristic domain, a large number of researchers have developed lots of algorithms since the last few years that cannot be categorized into a single metaheuristic group. The metaheuristics can be categorized in different ways. Each algorithm has its own strengths and limitations. Metaheuristic algorithms have the potential to yield good set of solutions in small time frame if used appropriately. The foremost shortcoming for these kinds of algorithms is addressed below.[20,21]

(1) The solutions (best) obtained by metaheuristic algorithms may not be always the optimal solutions.
(2) Generally, the performance of optimization is exceedingly depends on fine (proper) parameter tuning.
(3) They usually do not possesses "sound mathematical basis", while comparing with more traditional methods.
(4) Optimality cannot be established using metaheuristic algorithms.
(5) The search space also cannot be reduced using metaheuristic algorithms.
(6) There is no guaranteed to have repeated optimized results when the metaheuristics are executed number of times having similar initial criteria settings.

The initial formulations have been focused on single-objective optimizations. Many researchers has extended the band of research work from mono-objective optimization to multi-objective domain, but each formulation has exhibited precise advantages and boundaries, in general, over some specific problems. Hence, it is hard to presume the existence of "best multi-objective metaheuristics".[20,21]

5. Hybrid Metaheuristic Algorithms

The procedure of combining a metaheuristic method with other methods optimization is known as hybrid metaheuristics. Hybrid metaheuristic algorithms recognize a new line of research in the current age. The motive of developing hybridization of various algorithmic ideas is to acquire better-performing structures that exploit and associated benefits of the distinct pure strategies. Hybrid systems are thought to be benefited from synergy. As opposed to the early days' research in metaheuristic domain, a large number of researchers have developed lots of algorithms since the last few years that cannot be categorized into a single metaheuristic group. A few hybrid algorithms presented by different researchers are reported in this section.

Ojha *et al.*[33] presented a good literature survey report on the betterment of the feedforward neural network (FNN) optimization using different metaheuristic algorithms. A hybrid optimization method of back propagation (BP) neural network and genetic algorithm (GA) is applied for optimizing the process parameters during plastic injection molding (PIM) on the basis of the finite element simulation software Moldflow, BP neural network Orthogonal experiment method as well as Genetic algorithm.[34] The metaheuristic algorithms are blended with the greedy gradient based algorithms to get the hybrid improved opposition based particle swarm optimization and a back propagation algorithm with the momentum term.[35] This hybrid algorithm is utilized to improve the performance of prediction model based artificial neural network (ANN) training. Two efficient metaheuristic algorithms, *i.e.* GA and PSO is applied for the learning process of the recurrent neural network.[36] In this process, the same population is optimized by both GA and PSO algorithm. A hybrid genetic algorithm (GA) based artificial neural network (ANN)algorithm is applied for permeability estimation of the reservoir.[37] The local searching ability of the gradient based back-propagation (BP) strategy is combined with the global searching ability of genetic algorithms in this algorithm. To derive the initial weights efficiently, a real coded GAs are employed to decide the starting weights of the gradient decent methods. An efficient GA is applied to determine parameters of the feed-forward Neural Networks (NNs) and the iterative computation time to enhance the training capacity of NN is also reduced by this hybrid approach.[38] In this GA approach, a column-wise and a row-wise crossover operators are employed on the matrix-based representation of weights. Different real-world applications are solved by the GA-based real coded weights optimization methods.[39]

The multilevel gray scale images segmented efficiently in multilevel by the GA enabled multilevel self-organizing neural network (MLSONN).[40–43] In this method, the activation function of the MLSONN, *i.e.* the optimized multilevel sigmoidal (OptiMUSIG) activation function[40–43] is generated with the help of single objective function based GA. De *et al.* overcame the drawback of the single objective based OptiMUSIG activation function and presented multi-objective based OptiMUSIG activation function[44] and NSGA II based OptiMUSIG activation function.[45] The GA is combined with the multilevel self-organizing neural network (MLSONN) to segment the true color images.[46–48] The levels of the activation function, *i.e.* the parallel optimized multilevel sigmoidal (ParaOptiMUSIG) activation function[47,48] of MLSONN are generated by the GA. Not only with the single objective function, this activation function is designed with help of multi objective function.[44] De *et al.*[45,49,50] presented NSGA II based ParaOptiMUSIG activation function incorporating the multi-criterion to segment the color images.

Simulated Annealing is applied on FNN for weight optimization and it is found that the combined approach performed better in comparison to conventional approaches.[51] Differential evolution (DE) algorithm is also applied to solve real world complex continuous optimization problems. It was found that DE algorithm performed efficiently for real-valued weight vector optimization.[33,52,53] The PSO algorithm is hybridized with back-propagation (BP) algorithm and this PSO-BP algorithm is applied to train the weights of feedforward neural network (FNN).[54] This hybrid algorithm improved the global searching ability of PSO and the local searching ability of the BP algorithm. The PSO-BP algorithm proposed to transform from particle swarm search to gradient descending search.[54] In Refs. 55 and 56, the population of the FNN weight vectors are guided by PSO towards an optimum population. Al-kazemi and Mohan[57] proposed a multi-phase particle swarm optimization algorithm (MPPSO). In this algorithm, the updating of a particle position is done on the basis of the improved location of the particle otherwise, the particle position will remain same into the next generation. A hybrid of cooperative particle swarm optimization and cultural algorithm, named cultural cooperative particle swarm optimization (CCPSO), applied on a collection of multiple swarms that increase the global search capacity using the belief space.[58] To optimize the fuzzy neural network, the CCPSO gives a better result than BP and GA. In the same fashion, a beta basis function of neural network developed with the help of the hierarchical particle swarm optimization.[59]

Ozturk and Karaboga[60] proposed a hybrid algorithm *i.e.* artificial bee colony (ABC) algorithm with Levenberq-Marquardt (LM) algorithm, to train the ANN and this algorithm tried to overcome the local minima and global minima problem. They tried to derive the optimal weight set of the network to train the network. An improved version of the tabu search employed to optimize FNN weights and they outperformed the hybrid SA and BP algorithm.[61] Other metaheuristic algorithms, like, Harmony Search (HS),[62] Firefly (FF),[63] Cuckoo Search (CS),[64] Gravitational Search Optimization (GSO) algorithm,[65] Bacterial Foraging Optimization (BFO) algorithm,[66] etc. are hybridized with different types of neural networks to solve different types of real life application.

Due to a varied amount of uncertainty and vagueness manifested in the real life applications, most of the real life problems can be efficiently tackled by fuzzy set theory and fuzzy logic. The limitation of the fuzzy can be overcome if any problem can handle by the combination of fuzzy and metaheuristic algorithms. Single-period problem (SPP), a classical stochastic inventory model, tackled with the help of a hybrid fuzzy-metaheuristic model.[67] The authors proposed five hybrid intelligent algorithms based on fuzzy simulation (FS) and metaheuristic methods and among them, it had been proved that the hybrid bees colony optimization (BCO) and fuzzy simulation (FS) approach outperforms other four hybrid methods. The hybrid algorithm, GA and PSO coupled with fuzzy logic control is capable to handle flow shop scheduling problem.[68] It had been observed from the result that the performances of both genetic and particle swarm optimization algorithms improved with the help of fuzzy logic control. The recent advancement in the field of fuzzy logic in combination with nature-inspired optimization metaheuristic algorithms and their application areas such as intelligent control and robotics, time series prediction, pattern recognition and optimization of complex problems are presented in.[69] Das *et al.*[70-72] presented a Modified Genetic Algorithm (MfGA) based Fuzzy C-Means algorithm to overcome the shortcomings of the Fuzzy C-Means (FCM) algorithm. This algorithm efficiently segmented different types of multilevel and color images and this algorithms outperforms the conventional FCM and the GA based FCM algorithms in quantitatively and qualitatively. An unsupervised image segmentation approach is presented in combination of pyramidal image segmentation with the fuzzy *c*-means clustering algorithm.[73] Each layer of the pyramid is separated using root labeling approach into a number of regions. The cluster validity function is employed for grouping the minimum number of objects. Chauhan[74] presented some recent development of nature-inspired optimization techniques for fuzzy controller parameters. A comparative study of Type-2 Fuzzy Particle Swarm, Bee Colony and Bat Algorithms for optimizing the fuzzy controllers is presented by Olivas *et al.*[75]

6. Advanced Hybrid Metaheuristics

In the literature, a number of researchers targeted designing quantum-inspired evolutionary algorithms (QEA) by incorporating the features of quantum mechanics into the proper algorithmic framework.[76–79] These algorithms have been successfully applied for solving different combinatorial optimization problems. Han et al. introduced a quantum-inspired evolutionary algorithm on the basis of qubit probabilistic representation. The authors also applied the concept of superposition of states to build their algorithm. In addition to that, they used Q-gate to get an enhanced solution space.[77] Talbi et al.[80] proposed a novel quantum inspired genetic algorithm to solve the Travelling Salesman problem by applying the thoughts of quantum computing.[76]

The popularity of quantum computing was increased after the anticipation of quantum mechanical system after the early 1980s.[81] These quantum mechanical systems are intelligent enough to solve some specific computational problems efficiently.[82] Alfares et al. investigated that the idea of quantum algorithms can be effectively applied for solving few distinctive engineering optimization problems.[83] Hogg has developed a structure for structured quantum search where Grovers algorithm was used to relate the cost with the behavior of quantum gate.[84] Thereafter Hogg and Portnov extended this work and developed a novel quantum version of algorithm for combinatorial optimization.[85]

Later, Han and Kim developed an alternative version of QEA where the performance was assessed according to the angles of the rotation gates[77] and later, in Ref. 86, authors have presented a new improved form of this algorithm. Zhang et al. used a better approach to find best feasible solutions of the work done by Han et al. They presented another upgraded version in Ref. 87. Narayan et al. used a novel approach to modify the crossover operation. The authors have used the notions of quantum mechanics to develop a quantum behaved genetic algorithm.[88] Moreover, Li et al. introduced another modified genetic algorithm where the two genetic operators viz., crossover and mutation were adjusted using quantum probability representation.[89] Recently, Sunanda et al. introduced a efficient quantum behaved modified genetic algorithm based FCM method for true color image segmentation.[90] Later, another extended version, called quantum induced modified genetic algorithm based FCM was designed by Sunanda et al. The authors applied this method for color MRI image Segmentation.[91]

Some recent popular hybrid metaheuristics (quantum inspired metaheuristics) are presented in the subsequent subsections.

6.1. *Recent Hybrid Metaheuristic: Quantum Inspired Genetic Algorithm*

In the recent years, a large number of researchers targeted designing different quantum-inspired evolutionary algorithms, which basically incorporate the features of quantum mechanical system into the algorithmic framework.[76,77] Dey *et al.* proposed two variant of quantum inspired genetic algorithm for bi-level image thresholding.[92] After that, Dey *et al.* presented a paper to introduce a novel variant of quantum inspired genetic algorithm for bi-level image thresholding in 2014.[92] Another quantum version of quantum inspired particle swarm optimization has also been presented in that paper.[92] This quantum inspired genetic algorithm is presented here.

Algorithm 2. Steps of Quantum Inspired Genetic Algorithm
Input: Number of Generation: $\mathcal{G}$, Population size: $\mathcal{A}$
Output: Optimal threshold value: θ

1: Create population $\mathcal{P}$ with pixel intensity values at random.
2: Encode in pixel in $\mathcal{P}$ to (0,1).
3: **while** until termination condition is satisfied **do**
4:   Do Quantum Interference.
5:   Determine a threshold value on the basis of a given probability criteria.
6:   Evaluate fitness of each individual chromosome in $\mathcal{P}$.
7:   Save the best chromosome (r) (elitism).
8:   Based on a selection strategy, fill the pool of chromosomes for the subsequent generation.
9:   (r) is overwritten at the end of pool of chromosomes.
10:   Perform Quantum Crossover, Quantum Mutation and Quantum Shift operation one after another.
11:   Record the best chromosome and corresponding threshold value.
12: **end while**
13: Report the optimal threshold value.

In this proposed approach, it takes generation number($\mathcal{G}$) and population size($\mathcal{A}$) as input and produces optimal threshold value (θ) as output. At first, the population ($\mathcal{P}$) is randomly generated by choosing the image pixel intensity values. Thereafter, each member of ($\mathcal{P}$) is encoded to (0,1). The algorithm is executed until it reaches at the predefined termination condition. At each iteration, a special kind of quantum operation, called

quantum interference is encountered, which ensures the quantum computing (QC)'s property as given by

$$\sum_j c_j = 1 \tag{9}$$

where, $c_j \in \mathbb{C}$ (assuming j number of states). For a two-state qubit, $j = 2$
and a qubit is represented by

$$|\psi\rangle = c_1|0\rangle + c_2|1\rangle \tag{10}$$

Here, ϕ_j is the jth basis states of QC. Then, a threshold value is selected
based on a predefined probability criteria. The fitness of this threshold
is found out using a fitness function. After that, a selection strategy is
used to select best chromosomes to fill the chromosome pool for the next
generation. Three quantum operators, viz., quantum crossover, quantum
mutation and quantum shift are successive applied for population diversity.
After running the method for a predefined number of generations, it finds
the optimal threshold value.

6.2. *Recent Hybrid Metaheuristic: Quantum Inspired Ant Colony Optimization*

These works have been extended to multi-level domain by Dey *et al.* The
authors developed six different quantum version of metaheuristic algorithms
in Ref. 93. In this paper, a number of quantum inspired metaheuristics have
been introduced for multi-level image thresholding. Among them, quantum
inspired ant colony optimization and quantum inspired simulated annealing
are presented one by another in this subsection.[93]

Algorithm 3. Steps of Quantum Inspired Ant Colony Optimization for multi-level thresholding
Input: Number of Generation: $\mathcal{G}$, Population size: $\mathcal{V}$, Number of thresh-
olds: e, Persistence of trials: ρ and Priory defined number: q
Output: Optimal threshold value: θ

1: Create population (POP) with pixel's intensity values at random,
   which contains $\mathcal{V}$ initial strings. The string length is selected as
   $\mathcal{L} = \sqrt{L}$, where, L is the maximum pixel intensity value of the input
   gray scale image.
2: Encode pixels with (0,1) using the notion of qubits, which creates
   POP'.
3: POP' is updated using quantum rotation gate.

4: POP' is passed through a QC's property, called *quantum orthogonality* to generate POP''.

5: Based on a certain probability criteria ($POP'' > rand(0,1)$), e number of threshold values (pixel intensity values) are found from each string in POP. Let it produces POP^*.

6: Compute fitness of each element in POP^* using a fitness function and the best string is recorded.

7: Step 5 is repeated to produce POP^{**}.

8: Crete the pheromone matrix, τ.

9: $i = 1$.

10: **for** $(i \leq \mathcal{G})$ **do**

11:   **for** all $j \in POP''$ **do**

12:     **for** all k_{th} position in j **do**

13:       **if** $(rand(0,1) > q)$ **then**

14:         $POP''_{jk} = \arg\max \tau_{jk}$.

15:       **else**

16:         $POP''_{jk} = rand(0,1)$.

17:       **end if**

18:     **end for**

19:   **end for**

20:   Calculate the fitness value of POP''.

21:   Record and update the best string from POP^{**}.

22:   Using POP^{**}, the best string along with its threshold values is recorded.

23:   **for** all $j \in POP''$ **do**

24:     **for** all k_{th} position in j **do**

25:       $\tau_{jk} = \rho\tau_{jk} + (1-\rho)b$.

26:     **end for**

27:   **end for**

28:   $i = i + 1$

29: **end for**

30: The optimal threshold values is recorded in θ.

The authors have applied the features of quantum principles in the frameworks of popular metaheuristic, called Ant Colony Optimization to introduce a novel algorithm, known as Quantum Inspired Ant Colony Optimization. This algorithm has been designed to find optimal number of threshold values for multi-level image thresholding.

At initial, a starting population (POP) is being created using pixel intensity values at random. POP contains $\mathcal{V}$ strings, each one of them has a length $\mathcal{L} = \sqrt{L}$, where L denotes the maximum pixel intensity value (in the input image). After that, each pixels is encoded with (0,1) using the notion of qubits. It creates POP'. Thereafter, POP' goes through the popular feature of QC, called "quantum orthogonality", which produces POP''. Then, a predefined number of thresholds are chosen on the basis of a probability criterion. At the same time, a pheromone matrix, τ_j is created for each individual ant j. Thereafter, POP'' is updated using τ. Thereafter, τ is updated. The procedure is executed for $\mathcal{G}$ number of generations and finally, the optimal threshold values are reported, θ. ρ, popularly known as persistence of trials. The value of ρ has been selected between [0,1] for experimental purpose.

6.3. Recent Hybrid Metaheuristics: Quantum Inspired Simulated Annealing

Algorithm 4. Steps of Quantum Inspired Simulated Annealing for multi-level thresholding Input: Starting temperature: $\mathcal{T}_{mx}$, Final temperature: $\mathcal{T}_{mn}$, Reduction factor: ξ, Number of thresholds: e, Number of Iterations: $\mathcal{I}$

Output: Optimal threshold values: θ

1: Create initial configuration, P, with randomly selected pixel intensity value. The configuration's length is taken as $\mathcal{L} = \sqrt{L}$, where, L denotes the maximum pixel intensity value.

2: Encode pixels to (0,1) using the thought of qubits. Let it creates P'.

3: Applying quantum rotation gate, P' is updated.

4: The feature of QC, called *quantum orthogonality* is applied to generate P''.

5: Find e number of thresholds (pixel intensity values) from the element in P, satisfying the probability criteria given by $P'' > rand(0,1)$. Let it produces P^*.

6: Compute fitness value of the configuration (in P^*) using a fitness function. Let it be denoted by $\mathcal{F}(P^*)$.

7: $\mathcal{T} = \mathcal{T}_{mx}$.

8: **repeat**

9:     **for** $j = 1$ to $\mathcal{I}$ **do**

10:         Perturb P to produce V.

11:         Steps 2-4 are repeated to produce V^*.

12:         Compute fitness $E(V^*, T)$ of the configuration V^*.

13:     **if** $(\mathcal{F}(Z^*) - \mathcal{F}(Z^*) > 0)$ **then**

14:         Set $P = Z$, $P^* = Z^*$ and $\mathcal{F}(Z^*) = \mathcal{F}(Z^*)$.

15:     **else**

16:         Set $P = Z$, $P^* = Z^*$ and $\mathcal{F}(Z^*) = \mathcal{F}(Z^*)$ with probability $\exp(-(\mathcal{F}(P^*) - \mathcal{F}(Z^*)))/\mathcal{T}$.

17:     **end if**

18:     **end for**

19:     $\mathcal{T} = \mathcal{T} \times \xi$.

20: **until** $\mathcal{T} >= \mathcal{T}_{mn}$

21: The optimal threshold values are reported in $\theta = P^*$.

Like the above method, here, at initial, an configuration, P is generated by selecting a number of pixel intensity values at random. The length of it has been selected as $\mathcal{L} = \sqrt{L}$, where, L denotes the maximum pixel intensity value. Thereafter, each pixel is encoded to (0,1) using the theory of qubit in P, which creates P'. Then, P' undergoes though "quantum orthogonality", which produces P''. Again, a probability criterion is used to find predefined number pixels as threshold values. The proposed method starts working with a very high temperature, say $\mathcal{T}_{mx}$. For each assigned temperature, it executes for $\mathcal{I}$ number of iterations and then the temperature is reduced by a reduction factor, ξ. When the temperature reaches at $\mathcal{T}_{mn}$, the method stops execution. At each value of $\mathcal{I}$, it searches for a better configuration, (Z) as because the old configuration is perturbed at random at multiple points. By this way, a new configuration, Z^* is created from Z. The acceptance or rejection of Z and Z^* is done on the basis of the criterion given by $\mathcal{F}(Z^*) > \mathcal{F}(P^*)$; otherwise, the newly created configuration can also be accepted with a probability, given by $\exp(-(\mathcal{F}(P^*) - \mathcal{F}(Z^*)))/\mathcal{T}$. the authors have chosen the value of ξ within the range of $[0.5, 0.99]$.

6.4. *Recent Hybrid Metaheuristics: Quantum Inspired Particle Swarm Optimization*

The above mentioned algorithms were focused on developing procedures regarding binary and multi-level image thresholding.[92-95,95-99] Later, a functional change in the working features of these algorithms was brought to the multi-level and color domain by Dey *et al.*[100-103] The authors have developed six different quantum inspired metaheuristic algorithms to facilitate them to search optimum threshold values for real life true color images. In the subsection, a quantum inspired particle swarm optimization for multi-level color image thresholding, proposed by Dey *et al.*, is presented.

Algorithm 5. Steps of Quantum Inspired Particle Swarm Optimization for multi-level color image thresholding Input: Number of generation: $\mathcal{G}$, Population size: $\mathcal{S}$, Acceleration coefficients: ξ_a and ξ_b, Number of classes: e, Inertia weight: ω

Output: Optimal threshold values for three basic components: θ_R, θ_G and θ_B

1: The initial population (P) having $\mathcal{S}$ number of particles, is being created with image pixel intensity value at random. (P) contains 3 individual particles for the three basic color components. Each particle in P is selected as $\mathcal{L} = 3 \times \lfloor \sqrt{L} \rfloor$, where L is the maximum intensity value of each component.

2: Encode each pixel in (P) to $(0,1)$ (real value) using the notion of quantum bits. Let it generates P'.

3: Update P' using quantum rotation gate, and then P' goes through quantum orthogonality, which produces P''.

4: For each basic color component, three different classes (e classes for each one) are being created from P based on $(\beta_i)^2 < random(0, 1)$ in P'' where, i is the qubit's position in P''. Finally, it generates P^*.

5: Using P^*, the fitness of each particle is computed.

6: Record the best particle. Record the fitness values in X_R, X_G and X_B, respectively.

7: Set, $X = X_R + X_G + X_B$.

8: $j = 1$

9: **while** $j \leq \mathcal{G}$ **do**

10:     $j = j + 1$

11:     **for** all $k \in P''$ **do**

12:         Use equation (12) to compute particle's velocity.

13:         Using equation (12), update particle's position.

14:         Update P' and P^* by executing steps (3)-(5).

15:         Compute fitness of each particle in P^*.

16:         Update best particle, the threshold values and their fitness values.

17:     **end for**

18: **end while**

19: The optimal threshold values are documented in θ_R, θ_G and θ_B.

In this algorithm, the initial population (P) of $\mathcal{S}$ particles is created by choosing pixel intensity values at random. Since, it handles color image, it chooses the length of each particle in P as $\mathcal{L} = 3 \times \lfloor \sqrt{L} \rfloor$. It performs some similar stems as discussed in the above mentioned algorithm.

Generation wise, the velocity and position of each particle is changed by using the following formula.

$$v_k^{t+1} = \omega * v_k^t + \xi_a * rand(0,1) * (p_k^t(D) - y_k^t)$$
$$+ \xi_a * rand(0,1) * (p_g^t(D) - y_k^t) \tag{11}$$
$$y_k^{t+1} = y_k^t + v_k^{t+1} \tag{12}$$

The velocity and the position of kth particle at t^{th} generation are represented as v_k^t and y_k^t, respectively. p_k^t and p_g^t are the particle's best and global best location of kth particle. It is run for $\mathcal{G}$ number of generations and optimum threshold values are determined.

7. Comparison Among Some Popular Advanced Hybrid Metaheuristic Algorithms

A brief comparison of different features of some popular quantum inspired metaheuristics, introduced by Dey *et al.*,[93] is presented in this section. The proposed algorithms have been designed for gray-level image thresholding.[93] Different characteristics of these algorithms are presented here in a tabular form in Table 1, which include parameters settings (required for implementation of metaheuristics, generally done before execution), convergence rate, I&D component (I stands for Intensification and D stands for Diversification) and a sample CPU time(s) (for Lena image, level 3).[93,104]

Table 1.   Different characteristics of the algorithms proposed by Dey *et al.*[93]

Measures	QIACO	QIPSO	QIGA
Parameter	Population size, Number of generation, Priori defined number, Persistence of trials, No. of thresholds	Population size, Number of generation, Inertia weight, Acceleration coefficients, No. of thresholds	Population size, Number of generation, Crossover probability, Mutation probability, No. of thresholds
	QIDE	**QISA**	**QITS**
	Population size, Number of generation, Scaling factor, Crossover constant, No. of thresholds	Initial temperature, Final temperature, Number of Iterations, Reduction factor, No. of thresholds	Number of generation, No. of thresholds

(*Continued*)

Table 1.   (*Continued*)

Measures			
Convergence	QIACO	QIPSO	QIGA
	Generally slow, depends on pheromone evaporation	Generally rapid	Generally rapid
	QIDE	QISA	QITS
	Generally fast	It assigns probability to different deteriorating moves to avoid trapping	It avoid trapping in local searching
I&D component	QIACO	QIPSO	QIGA
	Update pheromone	Fitness, local search	Crossover, mutation and selection
	QIDE	QISA	QITS
	Mutation and crossover	Cooling schedule, acceptance strategy	Neighbor selection, aspiration criteria
CPU time	QIACO	QIPSO	QIGA
	13.07	2.13	10.47
	QIDE	QISA	QITS
	10.39	15.50	16.41

8. Conclusion

In this chapter, the details about hybridization of metaheuristic algorithms, is presented. The outline of the number of popular metaheuristics is provided in a separate section. Some renowned representative examples of recent metaheuristics are also described in more detail. The emergent research area of hybridization was divided here into two different categories to enrich the quality and worth of the paper. In addition, a detailed review is provided for each category of hybridization. Finally, the characteristics of a number of recent hybrid metaheuristics are provided in tabular format to compare their performances. This paper will gratify as an introductory idea for researchers targeting to design hybrid metaheuristics.

References

1. G. A. E.-N. A. Said, A. M. Mahmoud, and E. M. El-Horbaty, A Comparative Study of Meta-heuristic Algorithms for Solving Quadratic Assignment

Problem, *International Journal of Advanced Computer Science and Applications.* **5**(1), 1–6 (2014).

2. I. H. Osman and G. Laporte, Metaheuristics: a bibliography, *Annals of Operations research.* **63**(5), 513–623 (1996).

3. K. Sorensen, Metaheuristic - the metaphor exposed, *International Transactions in Operational Research.* **22**, 3–18 (2012).

4. J. Holland, *Adaptation in neural artificial systems.* Ann. Arbor, MI: University of Michigan (1975).

5. S. Kirkpatrik, C. D. Gelatt, and M. P. Vecchi, Optimization by simulated annealing, *Science.* **220**, 671–680 (1983).

6. F. Glover and M. Laguna, *Tabu Search.* Kluwer, Boston, MA (1997).

7. F. Glover, Tabu search, part I, *ORSA Journal on Computing.* **1**, 190–206 (1989).

8. F. Glover, Tabu search, part II, *ORSA Journal on Computing.* **2**, 4–32 (1990).

9. K. Kennedy and R. Eberhart, Particle swarm optimization, *In: Proceedings of the IEEE International Conferenceon Neural Networks (ICNN95), Perth, Australia.* **4**, 1942–1948 (1995).

10. M. Dorigo, V. Maniezzo, and A. Colorni, The ant system: Optimization by a colony of cooperating agents, *IEEE Transactions on Systems, Man, Cybernetics - Part B.* **26**(1), 29–41 (1996).

11. D. Karaboga, *An idea based on honey bee swarm for numerical optimization.* Technical Report TR06, Erciyes University, Engineering Faculty, Computer Engineering Department (2005).

12. R. Storn and K. Pricei, Differential evolution — a simple and efficient heuristic for global optimization over continuous spaces, *Journal of Global Optimization.* **11**(4), 341–359 (1997).

13. U. K. Chakraborty, *Advances in Differential Evolution.* Springer-Verlag, Heidelberg (2008).

14. X.-S. Yang and S. Deb, Cuckoo search via lévy flights, *World Congress on Nature & Biologically Inspired Computing (NaBIC 2009). IEEE Publications.* pp. 210–214 (2009).

15. C. Sur, S. Sharma, and A. Shukla, *Solving Travelling Salesman Problem Using Egyptian Vulture Optimization Algorithm A New Approach*, In eds. M. A. Klopotek, J. Koronacki, M. Marciniak, A. Mykowiecka, and S. T. Wierzchon, *Language Processing and Intelligent Information Systems*, vol. 7912, *Lecture Notes in Computer Science*, pp. 254–267. Springer, Berlin, Heidelberg (2013).

16. J. A. Ruiz-Vanoye, O. Daz-Parra, F. Cocòn, A. Soto, M. D. los À. B. Arias, G. Verduzco-Reyes, and R. Alberto-Lira, Meta-Heuristics Algorithms based on the Grouping of Animals by Social Behavior for the Traveling Salesman Problem, *International Journal of Combinatorial Optimization Problems and Informatics.* **3**(3), 104–123 (2012). ISSN 2007-1558.

17. X.-S. Yang. A new metaheuristic bat-inspired algorithm. In *Nature Inspired Cooperative Strategies for Optimization (NICSO 2010)*, vol. 284, *Studies in Computational Intelligence*, pp. 65–74 (2010).

18. A. Askarzadeh, A novel metaheuristic method for solving constrained engineering optimization problems: Crow search algorithm, *Computers & Structures.* **169**, 1–12 (2016).

19. K. Krishnanand and D. Ghose. Detection of Multiple Source Locations using a Glowworm Metaphor with Applications to Collective Robotics. In *Swarm Intelligence Symposium*, pp. 84–91 (2005).

20. C. Blum and A. Roli, *Metaheuristic in combinatorial optimization: overview and conceptual comparison.* Technical Report, IRIDIA (2001–2013).

21. F. Glover and G. A. Kochenberger, *Handbook on Metaheuristics.* Kluwer Academic Publishers (2003).

22. K. hammouche, M. Diaf, and P. Siarry, A comparative study of various meta-heuristic techniques applied to the multilevel thresholding problem, *Engineering Applications of Artificial Intelligence.* **23**, 678–688 (2010).

23. I. Rechenberg, *Evolutionsstrategie: Optimierung technischer Systeme nach Prinzipien der biologishen Evolution.* Stuttgart, Germany: Frommann-Holzbog (1973).

24. C. R. Reeves, Using genetic algorithms with small populations, *Proceedings of the Fifth International Conference on Genetic Algorithms, Morgan Kaufman, San Mateo, CA, USA.* pp. 92–99 (1993).

25. P. Hansen, N. Mladenovic, J. Perez, and J. Perez, Variable neighbourhood search: methods and applications, *Annals of Operations Research.* **175**, 367–407 (2010). doi: 10.1007/s10479-009-0657-6.

26. C. Sur, S. Sharma, and A. Shukla. Egyptian Vulture Optimization Algorithm- A New Nature Inspired Meta-heuristics for Knapsack Problem. In *9th International Conf. on Computing and Information Technology (IC2IT2013)*, pp. 227–237 (2013).

27. K. Kielkowicz and D. Grela, Modified bat algorithm for nonlinear optimization, *International Journal of Computer Science and Network Security.* **16** (10) (October, 2016).

28. M. S. Turgut and O. E. Turgut, Hybrid Artificial Cooperative Search Crow Search Algorithm for Optimization of a Counter Flow Wet Cooling Tower, *International Journal of Intelligent Systems and Applications in Engineering.* **5**(3), 105–116 (2017).

29. A. F. Sheta. Solving the economic load dispatch problem using crow search algorithm. In *8th International Multi-Conference on Complexity, Informatics and Cybernetics (IMCIC 2017)*, pp. 95–100 (2017).

30. K. N. Krishnanand, P. Amruth, M. H. Guruprasad, S. V. Bidargaddi, and D. Ghose. Glowworm-inspired Robot Swarm for Simultaneous Taxis towards Multiple Radiation Sources. In *IEEE International Conference on Robotics and Automation*, pp. 958–963 (May, 2006).

31. K. Krishnanand and D. Ghose, Glowworm Swarm Optimization for Simultaneous Capture of Multiple Local Optima of Multimodal Functions, *Swarm Intelligence.* **3**(2), 87–124 (2009).

32. A. G. Karegowda and M. Prasad. A survey of applications of glowworm swarm optimization algorithm. In *International Conference on Computing and information Technology (IC2IT-2013)*, pp. 38–42 (2013).

33. V. K. Ojha, A. Abraham, and V. Snásel, Metaheuristic design of feedforward neural networks: A review of two decades of research, *Engineering Applications of Artificial Intelligence*. **60**, 97–116 (April, 2017).

34. F. Yin, H. Mao, and L. Hua, A hybrid of back propagation neural network and genetic algorithm for optimization of injection molding process parameter, *Materials & Design*. **32**(6), 3457–3464 (June, 2011).

35. M. Yaghini, M. M. Khoshraftar, and M. Fallahi, A hybrid algorithm for arti cial neural network training, *Engineering Applications of Artificial Intelligence*. **26**(1), 293–301 (January, 2013).

36. C.-F. Juang, A hybrid of genetic algorithm and particle swarm optimization for recurrent network design, *IEEE Transactions on Systems, Man, and Cybernetics, Part B (Cybernetics)*. **34**(2), 997–1006 (Apr, 2004).

37. R. Irani and R. Nasimi, Evolving neural network using real coded genetic algorithm for permeability estimation of the reservoir, *Expert Systems with Applications*. **38**(8), 9862–9866 (Sep, 2011).

38. D. Kim, H. Kim, and D. Chung, *A modified genetic algorithm for fast training neural networks*, In eds. J. Wang, X. Liao, and Z. Yi, *Advances in Neural Networks*, vol. 3496, *Lecture Notes in Computer Science*, pp. 660–665. Springer, Berlin, Heidelberg (2005).

39. S. Ding, C. Su, and J. Yu, An optimizing BP neural network algorithm based on genetic algorithm, *Artificial Intelligence Review*. **36**(2), 153–162 (Aug, 2011).

40. S. De, S. Bhattacharyya, and P. Dutta. OptiMUSIG : An Optimized Gray Level Image Segmentor. In *Proceedings of 16th International Conference on Advanced Computing and Communications (ADCOM 2008)*, pp. 78–87 (2008).

41. S. De, S. Bhattacharyya, and P. Dutta. Multilevel Image Segmentation Using Variable Threshold based OptiMUSIG Activation Function. In *Proceedings of National Conference on Nanotechnology and its Application in Quantum Computing (NAQC 2008)*, pp. 44–51 (September, 2008).

42. S. De, S. Bhattacharyya, and P. Dutta. Optimized Multilevel Image Segmentation: A Comparative Study. In *Proceedings of IEEE National Conference on Computing and Communication Systems (CoCoSys-09)*, pp. 200–205 (2009).

43. S. De, S. Bhattacharyya, and P. Dutta. Multilevel Image Segmentation using OptiMUSIG Activation Function with Fixed and Variable Thresholding: A Comparative Study. In eds. J. Mehnen, M. Koppen, A. Saad, and A. Tiwari, *Applications of Soft Computing: From Theory to Praxis, Advances in Intelligent and Soft Computing*, pp. 53–62, Springer- Verlag, Berlin, Heidelberg (2009).

44. S. De, S. Bhattacharyya, and S. Chakraborty. Multilevel Image Segmentation by a Multiobjective Genetic Algorithm Based OptiMUSIG Activation Function. In eds. S. Bhattacharyya and P. Dutta, *Handbook of Research on Computational Intelligence for Engineering, Science and Business*, vol. 1, pp. 122–162, IGI Global, Hershey, PA, USA (2012).

45. S. De, S. Bhattacharyya, and S. Chakraborty. Multilevel & Color Image Segmentation by NSGA II based OptiMUSIG activation function. In eds.

S. Bhattacharyya, P. Banerjee, D. Majumdar, and P. Dutta, *Handbook of Research on Advanced Hybrid Intelligent Techniques and Applications*, pp. 321–348, IGI Global, Hershey, PA, USA (2015).

46. S. De, S. Bhattacharyya, and S. Chakraborty. True Color Image Segmentation by an Optimized Multilevel Activation Function. In *Proceedings of 2010 IEEE International Conference on Computational Intelligence and Computing Research (2010 IEEE ICCIC)*, pp. 545–548 (2010).

47. S. De, S. Bhattacharyya, and S. Chakraborty, Color image segmentation using parallel OptiMUSIG activation function, *Applied Soft Computing*. **12** (10), 3228–3236 (2012).

48. S. De, S. Bhattacharyya, and S. Chakraborty. Efficient Color Image Segmentation by a Parallel Optimized (ParaOptiMUSIG) Activation Function. In eds. B. K. Tripathy and D. P. Acharjya, *Global Trends in Intelligent Computing Research and Development*, pp. 19–50, IGI Global, Hershey, PA, USA (2013).

49. S. De, S. Bhattacharyya, and S. Chakraborty. Color Image Segmentation by NSGA-II based ParaOptiMUSIG Activation Function. In *2013 International Conference on Machine Intelligence Research and Advancement (ICMIRA-2013)*, pp. 105–109 (December, 2013).

50. S. De, S. Bhattacharyya, and S. Chakraborty. Application of Pixel Intensity Based Medical Image Segmentation Using NSGA II Based OptiMUSIG Activation Function. In *2014 International Conference on Computational Intelligence and Communication Networks (CICN2014)*, pp. 262–267 (2014).

51. D. Sarkar and J. M. Modak, ANNSA: a hybrid artificial neural network/simulated annealing algorithm for optimal control problems, *Chemical Engineering Science*. **58**(14), 3131–3142 (July, 2003).

52. J. Ilonen, J.-K. Kamarainen, and J. Lampinen, Differential evolution training algorithm for feed-forward neural networks, *Neural Processing Letters*. **17**(1), 93–105 (Feb, 2003).

53. A. Slowik, Application of an adaptive differential evolution algorithm with multiple trial vectors to artificial neural network training, *IEEE Transactions on Industrial Electronics*. **58**(8), 3160–3167 (Aug, 2011).

54. J.-R. Zhang, J. Zhang, T.-M. Lok, and M. R. Lyu, A hybrid particle swarm optimization and backpropagation algorithm for feedforward neural network training, *Applied Mathematics and Computation*. **185**(2), 10–37 (Feb, 2007).

55. A. Ismail and A. Engelbrecht. Global optimization algorithms for training product unit neural networks. In *IEEE-INNS-ENNS Int. Jt. Conf. Neural Netw.*, vol. 1, pp. 132–137 (2000).

56. J.-R. Zhang, J. Zhang, T.-M. Lok, and M. R. Lyu, A hybrid particle swarm optimization-back-propagation algorithm for feedforward neural network training, *Applied Mathematics and Computation*. **185**(2), 1026–1037 (Feb, 2007).

57. B. Al-kazemi and C. Mohan. Training feedforward neural networks using multi-phase particle swarm optimization. In *9th Int. Conf. Neural Inform. Process.*, vol. 5, pp. 2615–2619 (2002).

58. C.-J. Lin, C.-H. Chen, and C.-T. Lin, A hybrid of cooperative particle swarm optimization and cultural algorithm for neural fuzzy networks and its prediction applications, *IEEE Transactions on Systems, Man, and Cybernetics, Part C.* **39**(1), 55–68 (Dec, 2009).

59. H. Dhahri, A. Alimi, and A. Abraham, *Hierarchical particle swarm optimization for the design of beta basis function neural network*, In eds. A. Abraham and S. M. Thampi, *Intelligent Informatics*, vol. 182, *Advances in Intelligent Systems and Computing*, pp. 193–205. Springer, Berlin, Heidelberg (2013).

60. C. Ozturk and D. Karaboga. Hybrid artificial bee colony algorithm for neural network training. In *IEEE Congress on Evolutionary Computation*, pp. 84–88 (2011).

61. J. Ye, J. Qiao, M. ai Li, and X. Ruan, A tabu based neural network learning algorithm, *Neurocomputing.* **70**(4), 875–882 (Jan, 2007).

62. Q.-K. Pan, P. Suganthan, M. F. Tasgetiren, and J. Liang, A self-adaptive global best harmony search algorithm for continuous optimization problems, *Applied Mathematics and Computation.* **216**(3), 830–848 (Apr, 2010).

63. M.-H. Horng, M.-C. Lee, R.-J. Liou, and Y.-X. Lee, *Firefly meta-heuristic algorithm for training the radial basis function network for data classification and disease diagnosis*, In eds. R. Parpinelli and H. S. Lopes, *Theory and New Applications of Swarm Intelligence*, pp. 115–132. InTech (2012).

64. R. A. Vázquez. Training spiking neural models using cuckoo search algorithm. In *IEEE Congress on Evolutionary Computation (CEC)*, pp. 679–686 (2011).

65. M. Ghalambaz, A. Noghrehabadi, M. Behrang, E. Assareh, A. Ghanbarzadeh, and N. Hedayat, A hybrid neural network and gravitational search algorithm (hnngsa) method to solve well known Wessinger's equation, *World Academy of Science, Engineering and Technology.* **5**, 803–807 (Jan, 2011).

66. Y. Zhang, L. Wu, , and S. Wang, Bacterial foraging optimization based neural network for short-term load forecasting, *Journal of Computational Information Systems.* **6**(7), 2099–2105 (Jan, 2010).

67. A. A. Taleizadeh, F. Barzinpour, and H.-M. Wee, Meta-heuristic algorithms for solving a fuzzy single-period problem, *Mathematical and Computer Modelling.* **54**(5–6), 1273–1285 (Sep, 2011).

68. N. Yalaoui, Y. Ouazene, F. Yalaoui, L. Amodeo, and H. Mahdi, Fuzzy-metaheuristic methods to solve a hybrid flow shop scheduling problem with pre-assignment, *International Journal of Production Research.* pp. 3609–3624 (Mar, 2013).

69. O. Castillo and P. Melin, eds. Studies in Computational Intelligence, Springer Verlag, Berlin, Heidelberg (2016).

70. S. De, S. Das, S. Bhattacharyya, and P. Dutta, *Multilevel image segmentation using Modified Genetic Algorithm (MfGA) based Fuzzy C-means*, In eds. S. Bhattacharyya, I. Pan, A. Mukherjee, and P. Dutta, *Hybrid Intelligence for Image Analysis and Understanding.* Willy (2016).

71. S. Das and S. De. Multilevel color image segmentation using modified genetic algorithm (MfGA) inspired fuzzy c-means clustering. In *2016 Second*

IEEE International Conference on Research in Computational Intelligence and Communication Networks (ICRCICN 2016), pp. 78–83 (2016).

72. S. Das and S. De. A modified genetic algorithm based fcm clustering algorithm for magnetic resonance image segmentation. In *Proceedings of the 5th International Conference on Frontiers in Intelligent Computing: Theory and Applications (FICTA)*, pp. 435–443 (2016).

73. M. R. Rezaee, P. M. J. Zwet, B. P. F. Lelieveldt, R. J. Geest, and J. H. C. Reiber, A Multiresolution Image Segmentation Technique Based on Pyramidal Segmentation and Fuzzy Clustering, *IEEE Transactions on Image Processing.* **9**(7), 1238–1248 (2000).

74. S. Chauhan, Review of recent nature-inspired optimization techniques for fuzzy controller parameters, *International Journal of Engineering Studies and Technical Approach.* **2**(4), 49–64 (2016).

75. F. Olivas, L. A.-Angulo, J. Perez, C. Caraveo, F. Valdez, and O. Castillo, Comparative study of type-2 fuzzy particle swarm, bee colony and bat algorithms in optimization of fuzzy controllers, *Algorithms.* **10**(3), 1–27 (2017). doi: 10.3390/a10030101.

76. K. H. Han and J. H. Kim, Genetic quantum algorithm and its application to combinatorial optimization problem, *in Proceedings of 2000 Congress on Evolutionary Computation, Piscataway, NJ: IEEE Press.* **2**, 1354–1360 (2000).

77. K. H. Han and J. H. Kim, Quantum-inspired evolutionary algorithm for a class combinational optimization, *IEEE Transaction on Evolutionary Computation.* **6**(6), 580–593 (2002).

78. S. Dey, S. Bhattacharyya, and U. Maulik, Quantum inspired automatic clustering for multi-level image thresholding, *in Proceedings of International Conference On Computational Intelligence and Communication Networks (ICCICN 2014), RCCIIT, Kolkata, India.* pp. 247–251 (2014).

79. S. Dey, S. Bhattacharyya, and U. Maulik, Quantum behaved multi-objective pso and aco optimization for multi-level thresholding, *in Proceedings of International Conference On Computational Intelligence and Communication Networks (ICCICN 2014), RCCIIT, Kolkata, India.* pp. 242–246 (2014).

80. H. Talbi, A. Draa, and M. Batouche, A new quantum inspired genetic algorithm for solving the traveling salesman problem, *in Proceedings of IEEE International Conference on Industrial Technology (ICIT04).* pp. 1192–1197 (2004).

81. P. Benioff, Quantum mechanical models of turing machines that dissipate no energy, *Physical Review Letters.* **48**(23), 1581–1585 (1982).

82. L. K. Grover, Quantum computers can search rapidly by using almost any transformation, *Physical Review Letters.* **80**(19), 4329–4332 (1998).

83. F. Alfares and I. I. Esat, Quantum algorithms; how useful for engineering problems, *Proc. of the Seventh World Conference on Integrated Design and Process Technology, Austin, Texas, USA* (2003).

84. T. Hogg, Highly structured searches with quantum computers, *Physical Review Letters.* **80**, 2473–2476 (1998).

85. T. Hogg and D. A. Portnov, Quantum optimization, *Information Sciences.* **128**, 181–197 (2000).

86. K. H. Han and J. H. Kim, Quantum-inspired evolutionary algorithms with a new termination criterion, h-epsilon gate, and twophase scheme, *IEEE Transactions on Evolutionary Computation.* **8**, 156–169 (2004).

87. G. Zhang, W. Jin, and N. Li, An improved quantum genetic algorithm and its application, *Lecture Notes in Artificial Intelligence.* **2639**, 449–452 (2003).

88. A. Narayanan and M. Moore, Quantum inspired genetic algorithm, *Proc. of the 1996 IEEE Conference on Evolutionary Computation (ICEC '96), Nayoya University, Japan.* pp. 61–66 (1996).

89. B. Li and Z. Q. Zhuang, Genetic algorithm based-on the quantum probability representation, *Lecture Notes in Computer Science.* **2412**, 500–505 (2002).

90. S. Das, S. De, S. Bhattacharyya, and A. E. Hassanien, Color MRI image segmentation using QIMfGA based FCM, *First International Symposium on Signal and Image Processing (ISSIP 2017)* (Accepted) (2017).

91. S. Das, S. De, and S. Bhattacharyya, *True Color Image Segmentation using Quantum Induced Modified Genetic Algorithm based FCM Algorithm,* In ed. S. Bhattacharyya, *Quantum-Inspired Intelligent Systems for Multimedia Data Analysis).* IGI Global (Accepted) (2018).

92. S. Dey, S. Bhattacharyya, and U. Maulik, Quantum inspired genetic algorithm and particle swarm optimization using chaotic map model based interference for gray level image thresholding, *Swarm and Evolutionary Computation.* **15**, 38–57 (2014).

93. S. Dey, I. Saha, S. Bhattacharyya, and U. Maulik, Multi-level thresholding using quantum inspired meta-heuristics, *Knowledge-Based Systems.* **67**, 373–400 (2014).

94. S. Dey, S. Bhattacharyya, and U. Maullik, *Quantum Behaved Swarm Intelligent Techniques for Image Analysis: A Detailed Survey.* Handbook of Research on Swarm Intelligence in Engineering (2015).

95. S. Dey, S. Bhattacharyya, and U. Maullik, *Optimum Gray Level Image Thresholding using a Quantum Inspired Genetic Algorithm.* Advanced Research on Hybrid Intelligent Techniques and Applications (2015).

96. S. Bhattacharyya and S. Dey, An efficient quantum inspired genetic algorithm with chaotic map model based interference and fuzzy objective function for gray level image thresholding, *in Proceedings of 2011 IEEE International Conference on Computational Intelligence and Communication Networks (CICN), Gwalior, India.* pp. 121–125 (2011).

97. S. Bhattacharyya, P. Dutta, S. Chakraborty, R. Chakraborty, and S. Dey, Determination of optimal threshold of a gray-level image using a quantum inspired genetic algorithm with interference based on a random map model, *in Proceedings of 2010 IEEE International Conference on Computational Intelligence and Computing Research (ICCIC 2010), Coimbatore, India.* pp. 422–425 (2010).

98. S. Dey, S. Bhattacharyya, and U. Maulik, Chaotic map model based interference employed in quantum inspired genetic algorithm to determine the optimum gray level image thresholding, *Global Trends in Intelligent Computing Research and Development.* pp. 68–110 (2013).

99. S. Dey, I. Saha, U. Maulik, and S. Bhattacharyya, New quantum inspired meta-heuristic methods for multi-level thresholding, *International Conference on Advances in Computing, Communications and Informatics (ICACCI), Mysore, India.* pp. 373–400 (2013).

100. S. Dey, S. Bhattacharyya, and U. Maulik, Efficient quantum inspired meta-heuristics for multi-level true colour image thresholding, *Applied Soft Computing.* **56**, 472–513 (2017).

101. S. Dey, S. Bhattacharyya, and U. Maulik, New quantum inspired meta-heuristic techniques for multi-level colour image thresholding, *Applied Soft Computing.* **46**, 677–702 (2016).

102. S. Dey, S. Bhattacharyya, and U. Maulik, Quantum inspired meta-heuristic algorithms for multi-level thresholding for true colour images, *in Proceedings of IEEE Indicon 2013, Mumbai, India.* pp. 1–6 (2013).

103. S. Dey, S. Bhattacharyya, and U. Maulik, New quantum inspired tabu search for multi-level colour image thresholding, *in Proceedings of 8th International Conference On Computing for Sustainable Global Development (INDIACom-2014), BVICAM, New Delhi.* pp. 311–316 (2014).

104. T. Arora and Y. Gigras, A survey of comparison between various meta-heuristic techniques for path planning problem, *International Journal of Computer Engineering & Science.* **3**(2), 62–66 (2013).

Part I
Research

Chapter 2

Hybrid TLBO-GSA Strategy for Constrained and Unconstrained Engineering Optimization Functions

Alok Kumar Shukla*,†, Pradeep Singh and Manu Vardhan

*Department of Computer Science and Engineering,
NIT Raipur-492010, India*
† *akshukla.phd2015.cs@nitrr.ac.in*

In recent literature, hybridization of meta-heuristics is one of the vital approaches for solving the optimization problems that combine a homogeneous and heterogeneous meta-heuristics algorithm for refinement that can be deterministic or stochastic. It plays a conspicuous role, especially in the context of enhancing the search capability of algorithms and fascinating trade-off amongst the various conflicting tasks and also simultaneously tries to minimize any substantial demerits. This chapter introduces a new hybrid meta-heuristic Optimization algorithm (TLBO-GSA) with the incorporation of Teaching Learning based Optimization (TLBO) and Gravitational Search Algorithm (GSA) for solving the unconstrained or constrained Optimization problems. The main purpose of this chapter is to alleviate the convergence of hybrid meta-heuristic algorithm and reduce the computational over-head when we solve the benchmark Optimization problems. To avoid entrapping into local optima during the evolution process, we employ gravitational search operator (acceleration) in the teaching phase to resolve the premature convergence. The efficiency of the proposed method is simulated on twenty-three unconstrained and a real-world engineering (constrained) benchmark problems, and results demonstrate that TLBO-GSA is superior to other reported meta-heuristic algorithms in terms of convergence rate. The proposed methodology, resolves the premature convergence and tried to move from an exploitation-oriented point of view to an exploration-oriented point of view for worthy convergence.

Keywords: Meta-heuristics, stochastic, optimization, unconstrained.

---

*Corresponding author.

1. Introduction

In computational intelligence and operational research fields, Optimization technique plays a vital role to find the best solutions from possible feasible circumstances.[1] With the emergence development of computer science, some real-world problems can be transformed into Optimization problems. All aspects of economist and human-life, almost are covered by using the Optimization process. Most research has been accomplished in the computational intelligence and operational research fields, including a specific measure of the model, data discovery, computer recreations, and scientific improvement, respectively.[2] The goal of computer science branch is to find the specific approximations of related factors, which bring about either minimum or maximum with respect to the constraints of a hard and soft computing functions with a sensible time limit.[3]

In many scientific and engineering disciplines, a large number of constrained Optimization problems have been investigated like pressure vessel design and Coil Compression Spring etc. The aim of non-linear Optimization problem $x = (x_1, ..., x_r) \in R^r$ is to minimize the function value $f(x) \in R$. One common method to deal with complex optimization problems(for example, constrained) is to introduce a penalty term (α) in the objective function $f(x)$ to penalize constraint violations, expressed as $\phi(x) = f(x) + \alpha * \phi(g(x))$, where ϕ, real-valued function $\phi > 0$, ϕ refers to fitness function, and g refers to dynamic penalty function. To solve this problem, many meta-heuristics algorithms have attracted researchers interest from various domains over the last few years.[4]

The term meta-heuristic mentions as inexact algorithms for optimization that are not particularly connected for a specific problem. In the 1993s, the origins of meta-heuristics have found in the Artificial Intelligence (AI) and Operations Research (OR) communities,[5,6] respectively. Meta-heuristic has classified into two main categories, namely population based and single solution based. The established meta-heuristic algorithms have assessed the most notable performance metric, for example, high convergence and accuracy with respect to single or multi-objective optimization problems.[7] These meta-heuristics algorithm have few restrictions to solve the multi-objective problems(MOPs), because of structure limitation form in the algorithms. Each of these meta-heuristics has its own particular chronicled foundation over the latest decade, meta-heuristics have gained significant ground in estimated look strategies for taking care of complex optimization problems. Meta-heuristics based Optimization algorithms have mostly established by the family of Evolutionary Algorithms (EAs)[8] and Swarm Algorithms (SAs),[9] such as Teaching Learning Based Optimization (TLBO), Ant Colony Optimization (ACO), Genetic Algorithm (GA), Harmony Search (HS), Taboo Search (TS), Multi-objective PSO (MOPSO), and other Optimization techniques i.e. Fuzzy Logic, Game Theory.

Some meta-heuristics are motivated by common procedures such as evolution, others are extensions of less sophisticated algorithm i.e. local search based heuristic algorithms.[10] The key point of any meta-heuristic algorithms are solving the exploitation and exploration issues, respectively. A single objective based meta-heuristic algorithms are out of line and uncontingent in real life Optimization problems. To overcome problems, researchers have introduced the concept of hybrid meta-heuristics (HMs). It is a combination of at least two algorithms that run together and complement to each other and create a gainful cooperative vigor from their reconciliation.[11] However, a more realistic optimization is to simultaneously satisfy multiple objective such as minimum number of feature, accuracy, and trade-off between these objectives. In the most recent years, a critical

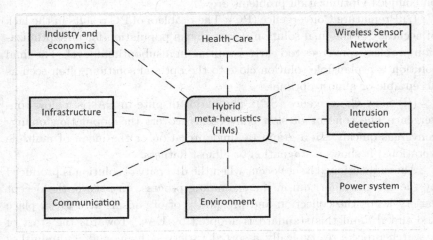

Fig. 1.   HMs algorithms used in different optimization applications

number has been accounted for that don't absolutely take after the worldview of a single traditional meta-heuristic. Despite what might be expected, they join different algorithmic methods, regularly beginning from single algorithms of other research domains for advancement. These methodologies are usually mentioned to as hybrid meta-heuristics as depicted in Fig. 1.

Several hybrid meta-heuristic algorithms related to constrained and unconstrained engineering Optimization functions have studied in section 2. By

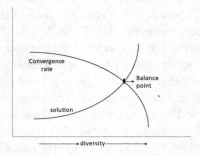

Fig. 2.   Compromising optimal solution and convergence rate of meta-heuristic algorithms

hybridizing of EAs, efficient to handling of vagueness, uncertainty, and impression[12] can be achieved performance. The most critical concerns of EAs on complex Optimization problems are:

(i) Premature Convergence (PC): The problem of PC results in the lack of accuracy of the final solution means that a population for an Optimization problem converges too early, resulting in a suboptimal level. The final solution is a plausible solution close to the optimal solution, often seen as acceptable or almost optimal.

(ii) Slow Convergence (SC): The major dispute in EAs is a slow convergence.The concept of slow convergence covers the population quality converges quickly. In a graph (a single iteration or the mean of multiple iterations) it shows a stagnation or almost flatness.

Above-mentioned issues occur when the diversity of solution is produced by the specific algorithm in the examining process. In nature, the decent variety keeps the collection and prosperity of organisms at a given place and time,[13] and this standard is adopted by EAs. Towards the start of a search procedure, typically assorted variety is high, and it diminishes as the populace is moving towards the global optimal solution. With the help of high diversity of convergence, (gives) it guarantees to find the best solution with highest fit solutions, but leads to slow convergence during this process, and thus there are some trade-off between convergence and accuracy. Besides this, fast convergence may lead to global optimality and neglected solution. This situation is shown in Fig. 2. In this figure, show the trade-off between convergence and accuracy for fittest solution.

Clearly, this is a perfect approach, and this present reality is much grayer and things are not vague.It merits work in search process as diversity, which is identified with the broader exploration and exploitation. Hybrid meta-heuristics algorithms find the optimal solution from local with global searching capabilities for Optimization applications. Indeed, even with adequate variety of diversity, there is no assurance to tackle the convergence issue since convergence is a much scrambled issue. To empower this, hybridization is a worthy procedure to advance an assorted variety along with search for the global optimum.[14] In Ref. 15, introduced the recent developments of hybrid meta-heuristics for unconstrained engineering Optimization which devoted to complex optimization problems. In this chapter, a taxonomy of hybrid meta-heuristics with a combination of homogeneous meta-heuristic algorithms such as Teaching- learning-Based-Optimization (TLBO) and Gravitational Search (GS) method is presented attempting to provide a good convergence and accuracy. The organization of this chapter describes as follows. Section 2, provide the literature reviews. In Section 3, we summarize the state-of-art of meta-heuristic for the Optimization problems and discuss the proposed methodology. In Section 4, present the experiments and testing results of different algorithm to solve global Optimization problems followed by our discussion and conclusions in Section 5.

2. Literature Survey

We generally characterize optimization issues as problems that can not be comprehended to optimal, or to any ensured bound, by any correct strategy inside a sensible time limit. During the first two decades of meta-heuristics, variety of literature have been dedicated on optimization problems, such as suite of single and multi-objective global optimization functions,[16,17] feature selection,[18] combinatorial Optimization,[19] image segmentation,[18] bio-informatics,[21] wireless sensor networks,[22] privacy and security,[23] and capacitate p-median problem.[24] All of these Optimization problems work on the principal of diverse phenomena. In recent years, several research advocate on Optimization approaches for optimizing the incompatible enactment objectives of real-life applications. Specifically, In 2015, Nasir and Tokhi[25] is delivered a hybrid meta-heuristics known as spiral-dynamic bacteria-chemotaxis algorithms for global unconstrained optimization problems. Using this algorithm, author control the flexible manipulator system. S. R. K. S and S. Murugan[26] presented a comprehensive survey and tutorial for global numerical problems. This investigation pbest and gbest idea of PSO is added to ordinary DA to manage the search procedure for potential agent solutions and PSO is then instated with pbest of DA to additionally exploit the search domain. M. M. Mafarja and S. Mirjalili[18] provided a review of recent studies on feature selection approaches. It is also discussed the future research trends in the fields of data mining. Li *et al.*[27] has integrated the Optimization methods such as PSO and ABC known as PS-ABC for global numerical problems. By hybrid meta-heuristic, author tried to reduce the stagnation behavior of the ants and computational complexity for global search to initial solutions generated by the employed bees. Vega-alvarado *et al.*[28] investigated the improved version of artificial bee colony called as MABC. It was used for global optimal solution and a version of the random walk as resident explorer, adapted to handle design constraints with some constraint scheme. Mahdavi *et al.*[29] provided a survey state-of-the-art meta-heuristic algorithms for large-scale global continues Optimization problems. In Ref. 19, integrate the evolutionary algorithms (EAs) and simulated annealing (SA) approaches for hard computing Optimization problems. By using quantum inspired GA, Quantum Inspired SA, Quantum Inspired DE and Quantum Inspired PSO, evaluate the performance trade-off mechanisms on the image segmentation based algorithms.[30] Here, various evolutionary methods and the related mechanical features of the segmentation mechanism has been discussed by K. Ting *et al.* and R. Raidl[31] and surveyed the most representative HMs and their major applications from a historical perspective. Zesong *et al.*[32] provided a review of recent studies on wireless sensor approaches and discussed its future research trends. Clearly, it is not conceivable to cover everything in this chapter, and along these lines we concentrates on some key focuses concerning the most recent improvements. As given in Refs. 12,33–35, researchers have studied different variants of hybrid meta-heuristics algorithms for solving complex optimization problems.

3. The Standard TLBO and Standard GSA

In this section, we elaborate the standard TLBO and GSA method which is used in this chapter.

3.1. *Teaching Learning Based Optimization (TLBO)*

TLBO is a efficient meta-heuristic Optimization algorithm that has pragmatic to a variety of real-world engineering problems. TLBO algorithm has been introduced by Rao *et al.*[36] based on teaching-learning phenomena. In TLBO, the best potential solutions to Optimization problem are considered as learners known as a population. Nowadays, TLBO algorithm is more superfluous to deal with in the real-world engineering problems. It has characteristics of simple computation and less memory requirement for computation of algorithms. The TLBO algorithm is the most popular approach in the evolutionary techniques because of the rapid convergence rate and less adjusting parameters. The primary determination of this algorithm is to find the best learner through cooperation and sharing information between the students. The working behaviour of TLBO algorithm depends on the extremely sophisticated learners so that they can produce better results marks or grades. The group of the learners also called as a class. They learn through neighbor learning phenomena. The position of the ith learner is presented as: $X_{i,k} = [X_{i,1}, X_{i,2}, ..., X_{i,D}]$ see Eq.(1), where L_k represent the lower value, and L_k represent the upper value of the D dimension in the search space $X_{i,D} \in [L_k, U_k]$.

$$X_{i,k} = L_k + r_1 * (U_k - L_k) \tag{1}$$

where $i = 1, 2, ..., nPop$, $k = 1, 2, 3, ..., D$, r_1 as signifies random variable, L_k signifies the lower bound, and U_k signifies the upper bound value, respectively. The simulation of a classical learning process to all learners are categories into two significant phases of TLBO algorithm: a) Teacher phase; b) Learner Phase. The best learner is obtained from the teacher phase through the knowledge learning from the neighbors and the learner phase find the best learner through the interaction between different learner groups.

3.1.1. *Teacher phase*

In this phase, learners acquire knowledge by the teacher. The teacher upgrade knowledge and emanate messages via the class thereby improve the grade mean of the whole class. The teacher is a measurement of gaining optimum result obtained so far from the Optimization problems. As a good teacher update knowledge through the learner's knowledge. A teacher can increase the mean result of class to a certain value which depends on the capability of the whole class. Let $M_{i,k} = 1/(nPop)\Sigma X_{i,k}$ be the mean value of the particular subject where $k = 1, 2, 3, ..., D$. The updating equation of process as described in Eq. (2):

$$X_{i,k}^{new} = X_{i,k}^{old} + r_2 * (X_{teacher,k} - T_f * M_{i,k}) \tag{2}$$

where, $T_f = round(1 + r(0,1))$, $X_{teacher,k}$ is the best learner of adopted population at current iteration of algorithm, r_2 is the random numbers lies between 0 and 1, respectively; T_f is a teaching factor that decides the value of the mean to be changed. In every iteration, $X_{i,k}^{new}$ is the updated from the value of $X_{i,k}^{old}$. $X_{i,k}^{new}$ and $X_{i,k}^{old}$ denotes the kth learners select after or before learning from the teacher, respectively. To the balance between exploration and exploitation search ability whole the course of a run is critical for an optimization algorithm.[37]

3.1.2. *Learner phase*

The second part of this process is learner phase, to increases the knowledge of learners by the two dissimilar ways: one way is through input from the teacher, and the next way is through mutual interaction between themselves. The goal of each learner is randomly interacted to peer learners and enhance communication grade. To select the ith learner as as X_p and another random learner is X_q $(p \neq q)$ through the mutual interaction with learners. The updating equation of the ith learner X_p in the learning phase can be described as follow[36]:

For $i = 1$: nPop
Randomly choose two learners X_p and X_q
if $f(X_p) < f(X_q)$
$newX_i = oldX_i + r * (X_p - X_q)$
else
$newX_i = oldX_i + r * (X_q - X_p)$
End For

where r is a uniformly distributed random number between 0 and 1, $f(X_p)$ and $f(X_q)$ are the best solution of the learners X_p and X_q, respectively. Considering the size of learner group is nPop, where learner communicates from a good learner to acquire knowledge.

3.2. *Gravitational Search Algorithm (GSA)*

Gravitational Search Algorithm (GSA) is a noticeable evolutionary algorithm by proposed E. Rashedi *et al.* in 2009, which imitates the Newton's gravitation law.[38] In GSA population, each outcome is presented as an agent that has volume, position, and speed. In the summation, the volume of each agent denotes the quality of the corresponding solution. Further, each agent is attracted by all the other agents. The gravitational force acting on each factor is ascertained by the Newton's widespread law of gravity and the speed of each factor is calculated according to Newton's law of movement. After applying gravitational force, the agents can investigate the search space to search for the ideal outcomes. GSA has numerous attractive features, such as easy to implement, reliable performance, and less number of tuning constraints similar to other EAs. The GSA has been a mathematical representation in the following way. Suppose that a model with N agents. The model starts with the random positioning of all agents in the search space for better solution. During all periods, the representation of gravitational forces (F) in the agent j with respect to the agent i at a precise time bound as t are defined as Eq. (3).

$$F_{i,j}^k = G_t * \frac{M_{p,i}^t * M_{a,j}^t}{R_{p,i}^t + e} * (x_j^k(t) + x_i^k(t)) \tag{3}$$

where $M_{a,j}^t$ presents the dynamic (active) gravitational mass, $M_{p,i}^t$ presents the passive gravitational mass, G(t) represent the gravitational constant at time (t), and e is a small constant. $R_{i,j}^t$ represent the Euclidean Distance(ED) between two agents i and j, respectively. The G(t) is estimated as following in Eq. (4):

$$G_t = G_0 * exp\frac{alpha * iter}{max_{iter}} \tag{4}$$

Here, the value of alpha generally used as 20,[38] G_0 set to 100 are descending coefficient and beginning worth individually, *iter* is the present cycle, and max_{iter} represent the maximum number of iterations for evolutions. In a problem space with the measurement k, the total force that follows up on specialist/agent i is figured as the accompanying Eq. (5)

$$F_i^d(t) = \sum_{j=1, j \neq i}^{N} rand_j F_{i,j}^k(t) \tag{5}$$

Here, $rand_j$ represent a random number which lies between as interval [0, 1]. As indicated by the law of motion, the speeding up of a specialist/agent is corresponding to the outcome force and converse of its mass, so the increasing speed of all operators ought to be figured as Eq. (6):

$$acc_i^k(t) = \frac{f_i^k(t)}{M_{i,i}^t} \tag{6}$$

As shown in above-mentioned equation (6), t represent a specific or sensible time and $M_{i,i}^t$ represent the mass of object i and $rand_j$ represent a random number which lies between as interval [0, 1]. In the GSA algorithm, at initial entirely masses are appointed with arbitrary values. Each mass is a candidate solution. The gravitational constant (GC), total forces, and accelerations are figured as (4), (5), and (6) individually.

3.3. *The Hybrid TLBO-GSA Algorithm*

Recently, each meta-heuristic algorithms necessities to address the exploration and exploitation of a search space. The term exploration determines the alleviated learners in the new search space and term exploitation exploits the promising solutions in the search space by self-experience. As explained in Refs. 20 and 31, we can hybridized two algorithms as homogeneous or heterogeneous, respectively. We introduced an innovative framework of hybridization called as TLBO-GSA to integrate the deterministic Optimization as GSA method into TLBO algorithms. The basic concept of TLBO-GSA is to combine the ability of agents in teacher phase with the local search capability of GSA. The main objectives of this proposed work are to alleviate the premature convergence of TLBO, and improve its convergence rate. The overall framework of proposed method is depicted in Fig. 3. The mathematical formulation of teacher and learner phase is described in below sub-sections.

3.3.1. *Teacher phase*

In this phase, the teacher upgrade knowledge and emanate messages through the class thereby improve the grade mean of the whole class. The teacher is a measurement of gaining optimum result obtained so far from the optimization problems. As a good teacher update knowledge through the learner's knowledge. A teacher can increase the mean result of class to a certain value which depends on the capability of the whole class. Let $M_{i,k} = 1/(nPop)\Sigma X_{i,k}$ be the mean value of the particular subject where $k = 1, 2, 3, ..., D$. The updating equation of process with incorporated of GSA local search capability is described in Eq. (7):

$$X_{i,k}^{new} = X_{i,k}^{old} + r_3 * (X_{teacher,k} - T_f * M_{i,k}) + r_4 * (acc_{i,k}^t - T_f * M_{i,k}) \quad (7)$$

where, $T_f = round(1 + r(0, 1))$, $X_{teacher,k}$ is the best learner of adopted population at current iteration of algorithm, r_3 and r_4 is the random numbers lies between 0 and 1, respectively; T_f is a teaching factor that decides the value of the mean to be changed, and $acc_{i,k}^t$ is the acceleration of each learners. In every iteration, $X_{i,k}^{new}$ is the updated from the value of $X_{i,k}^{old}$.

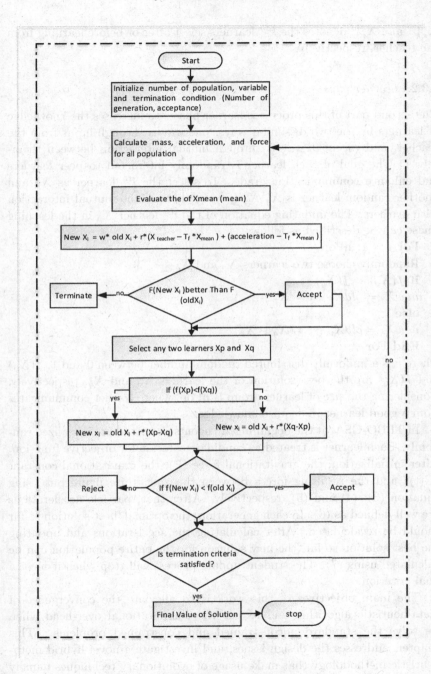

Fig. 3. Overall structure of TLBO-GSA

$X_{i,k}^{new}$ and $X_{i,k}^{old}$ denotes the kth learners select after or before learning from the teacher, respectively.

3.3.2. Learner phase

The second part of this process is learner phase, to increases the knowledge of learners by the two dissimilar ways: one way is through input from the teacher, and the next way is through mutual interaction between themselves. The goal of each learner is randomly interacted to peer learners and enhance communication grade. To select the ith learner as X_p and another random learner is X_q X_q $(p \neq q)$ through the mutual interaction with learners. The updating equation of the ith learner X_p in the learning phase can be described as follows:

For $i = 1$: nPop
Randomly choose two learners X_p and X_q
if $f(X_p) < f(X_q)$
$newX_i = oldX_i + r * (X_p - X_q)$
else
$newX_i = oldX_i + r * (X_q - X_p)$
End For

where r is a uniformly distributed random number between 0 and 1, $f(X_p)$ and $f(X_q)$ are the best solution of the learners X_p and X_q, respectively. Considering the size of learner group is nPop, where learner communicates from a good learner to acquire knowledge.

In TLBO-GSA, at the beginning, all agents (learners) are initialized randomly. Each learner is treated as candidate solution for objective function. After initialization, the gravitational force (F), the gravitational constant (G(t)) and the resulting forces between the agents are figure out using equation (3), (4) and (5), respectively. After that, particle accelerations are well-defined as (6). In each generation, the optimal/best solution so far should be recalculated. After calculating the accelerations and updating the best solution so far, the new solution for the entire population can be calculated using (7). The student update process will stop when it meet a final criterion.

The main objectives of this work is to alleviate the convergence of meta-heuristic algorithm and reduce the computational over-head when we solve the standard unconstrained and constrained problems. This chapter, addresses the design issues, and investigate a novel hybrid meta-heuristic methodology that make usage of evolutionary techniques namely gravitational search algorithm (GSA) and TLBO method to improve the convergence rate.

4. Experimental Results

To demonstrate the presentation of proposed (TLBO-GSA) strategy with other conventional strategies on the twenty-three benchmark problem is carried out in Tables 1–3, respectively. The behaviour of these standards benchmark problems are continuous, uni-modality/multi-modality and have dissimilar degrees of freedom. TLBO-GSA is also applied to a real-world Optimization problem. The experiments have conducted based on evaluation parameters like population size (nPop), maximum allowed iterations (max_{iter}), and experiments results are mean over 30 independent runs as shown in Tables 4–6. An experimental comparative study is performed with benchmark evolutionary algorithm(PSO,PSOGSA,and RSA) and hybrid meta heuristic. The performance evaluation criteria to EAs on benchmark problems are the best solution and average of best solution to each independent run. In the subsection, Tables 4–6 allowed the maximum number of iteration (max_{iter}) set as 1000, the number of population set as 50 except PSOGSA population as 30.

4.1. *Parameter Setting*

All experiments are simulated on the machine with Intel core i7 2.67 GHz processor, 6 GB RAM, Windows 8 O.S, and MATLAB environment. For a fair comparison, all EAs were tested with the same tuning features and same computing platform. To overcome the premature convergence, each EAs were runs 30 time with random initial population. The stopping condition of algorithms were the maximum number of iterations and independent

Table 1.   Seven Uni-modal Test Functions.

Fun.No.	Name of function	Formula	Range
F1	Sphere	$F_{Min} = \sum_{j=1}^{D} X_j^2$	[-100, 100]
F2	Schwefel 2.22	$F_{Min} = \sum_{j=1}^{D} \mid X_j \mid + \prod_{j=1}^{D} \mid X_j \mid$	[-10, 10]
F3	Schwefel 1.2	$F_{Min} = \sum_{j=1}^{D} (\sum_{i=1}^{j} X_j)^2$	[-100, 100]
F4	Schwefel 2.21	$F_{Min} = max_j \mid X_j \mid, 1 <= i <= n$	[-100, 100]
F5	Rosenbrock	$F_{Min} = \sum_{j=1}^{n-1} [100(X_{j+1} - X_j^2)^2 + (X_j - 1)^2]$	[-30, 30]
F6	Step	$F_{Min} = \sum_{j=1}^{D} (\mid X_j + 0.5 \mid)^2$	[-100, 100]
F7	Quartic	$F_{Min} = \sum_{j=1}^{D} j X_j^4 + rand(0, 1)$	[-1.28, 1.28]

Table 2.   Six Multi-modal Test Functions.

No.	Function	Formula	Range
F8	Schwefel	$F_{Min} = \sum_{j=1}^{D} X_j \sin(\sqrt{\mid X_j \mid})$	[-500, 500]
F9	Rastrigin	$F_{Min} = \sum_{j=1}^{D} [X_j^2 - 10\cos(2\Pi X_j) + 10]$	[-5.12, 5.12]
F10	Ackley	$F_{Min} = -20exp(-0.2\sqrt{1/n \sum_{j=1}^{D} X_j^2})$ $+ exp(1/n \sum_{j=1}^{D} \cos(2\Pi X_j)) + 20 + e$	[-32, 32]
F11	Griewank	$F_{Min} = 1/4000 \sum_{j=1}^{D} X_j^2 - \prod_{j=1}^{D} \cos(x_j/\sqrt{(j)})$	[-600, 600]
F15	Penalized	$Fmin = \frac{\pi}{n}\{10\sin^2(\pi y_i) + \sum_{i=1}^{n-1}(y_i - 1)^2$ $[1 + 10\sin^2(\pi y_{i+1})]+$ $(y_n - 1)^2\}$ $+ \sum_{i=1}^{n} u(x_i, 10, 100, 4), y_i = 1 + \frac{1}{4}(x_i + 1)$ $u(x_i, a, k, m) = \begin{cases} k(x_i - a)^m, x_i > a, \\ 0, -a \le x_i \le a, \\ k(-x_i - a)^m, x_i < -a, \end{cases}$	[-50, 50]
F13	Penalized 2	$F min = 0.1\{\sin^2(3\pi x_1)$ $+ \sum_{i=1}^{n-1} (x_i - 1)^2 [1 + \sin^2(3\pi x_{i+1})]$ $+ (x_n - 1)$ $[1 + \sin^2(2\pi x_n)]\} + \sum_{i=1}^{n} u(x_i, 5, 100, 4)$	[-50, 50]

runs for a better solution. The EAs run on benchmark problem until corresponding stopping criteria would meet.

4.2. *Benchmark Optimization Problems*

To testify the performance of existing EAs strategies and proposed TLBO-GSA strategy on diverse twenty-three benchmark problems in which seven uni-modal test function in Table 1, six multi-modal in Table 2, and ten multi-modal with low dimensional are shown in Table 3.

4.3. *A Comparison with other Meta-heuristic Algorithm*

We evaluated TLBO-GSA algorithm in standard test functions for minimization and also compared the results with other meta-heuristic such as RGA, PSO, GSA, and PSOGSA. For every algorithm evaluation, population size set as 50 and dimension set as 30, and maximum iteration is 1000 for functions of uni-modal and multi-modal functions.

Results of experiments in Table 4 shows that, TLBO-GSA provides better solution than other reported algorithms for all functions except $F5$.

Table 3. Ten Multi-modal test functions with low dimension benchmark functions used in our experimental study.

No.	Function	Formula	Range
F14	Foxholes	$F_{Min} = \frac{1}{1/500 + \sum_{j=1}^{25} \frac{1}{j + \sum_{i=1}^{2}(X_i - a_{i,j})}}$	[-65.536, 65.536]
F15	Kowalik	$F_{Min} = \sum_{j=1}^{11} \left(a_j - \frac{x_1 * (b_1^2 + b_i x_2)}{b_1^2 + b_i x_3 + x_4} \right)^2$	[-5, 5]
F16	6 Hump Camelback	$F_{Min} = 4x_1^2 - 2.1x_1^4 + 1/3x_1^6 + x_1 x_2 - x_2^2 + 4x_2^4$	[-5, 5]
F17	Branin	$F_{Min} = (x_2 - \frac{5.1}{4\Pi}x_1^2 + \frac{5}{\Pi}x_1)^2$ $+ 10(1 - \frac{1}{8\Pi})cos x_1 + 10$	[-5, 10] [0, 15]
F18	GoldStein-Price	$F_{Min} = [1 + (x_2 + x_1^2 + 1)^2(19 - 14x_1 + 3x_1^2$ $- 14x_2 + 6x_1 x_2 + 3x_2^2)[30 + (2x_1 - 3x_2)^2]$ $(18 - 32x_1 + 12x_1^2 + 48x_2 - 36x_2 x_1 + 27x_2^2)$	[-2, 2]
F19	Hartman 3	$F_{Min} = \sum_{j=1}^{4}(c_1 exp - [\sum_{i=1}^{3} a_{i,j}(x_j - p_{i,j})^2])$	[0, 1]
F20	Hartman 6	$F_{Min} = \sum_{j=1}^{4}(c_1 exp - [\sum_{i=1}^{6} a_{i,j}(x_j - p_{i,j})^2])$	[0, 1]
F21	Shekel 5	$F_{Min} = \frac{1}{-\sum_{j=1}^{5}[(x - a_i)(x - a_i)^T] + c_i}$	[0, 10]
F22	Shekel 7	$F_{Min} = \frac{1}{-\sum_{j=1}^{7}[(x - a_i)(x - a_i)^T] + c_i}$	[0, 10]
F23	Shekel 10	$F_{Min} = \frac{1}{-\sum_{j=1}^{10}[(x - a_i)(x - a_i)^T] + c_i}$	[0, 10]

The largest difference in performance between them occurs when applied in uni-modal functions.

As shown in Table 5, TLBO-GSA provides better solution than other reported algorithms for all functions except $F11$ and $F12$. The difference in performance is relatively lesser as compare to uni-modal functions.

The behaviour of all benchmark problems as shown in Table 6 is minimization of the corresponding problem and find-out the global optimal solution. In this Table, the first 7 problems notation as ($F14$ and $F20$) are multi-modal with fix size of dimension with good converge eve shown by proposed method. While the remaining on multi-modal Optimization problems, PSOGSA gives the better solution. Our objective is moving towards symmetric search space by using the gravitational operator (accelerator) on the benchmark problems.

4.4. *Engineering Optimization Problem*

In an earlier section, learner capability and accelerator operator have been used by TLBO-GSA algorithm in well-known functions. As the efficacy of

Table 4. Minimization result of standard benchmark functions in Table 1 with pop as 50 except PSOGSA[40]($pop = 30$) and number of maximum iterations set as 1000.

Function	Performance	RGA[38]	PSO[38]	GSA[38]	PSOGSA[40]	TLBO-GSA
F1	Best Solution	23.13	1.8* 10-03	7.3* 10-11	4.91E-19	1.71E-20
	Average Solution	23.87	1.2* 10-03	7.1* 10-11	6.66E-19	4.51E-20
F2	Best Solution	1.07	2	4.03 *10-5	3.18E-09	3.80E-12
	Average Solution	1.13	1.9 *10-3	4.07*10-5	3.79E-09	1.48E-11
F3	Best Solution	5.6 * 10+3	4.1*10+3	0.16 *10+3	43.2038	40.3806
	Average Solution	5.6*10+3	2.2*10+3	0.15*10+3	409.936	308.06
F4	Best Solution	11.78	8.1	3.7 * 10-6	2.96E-10	1.69E-10
	Average Solution	11.94	7.4	3.7*10-6	3.37E-10	2.6e8-10
F5	Best Solution	1.1*10+3	3.6*10+4	25.16	22.4221	29.8958
	Average Solution	1.0 * 10+3	1.7 *10+3	25.16	56.2952	67.3597
F6	Best Solution	24.01	1.0 *10-3	8.3 *10-11	5.76E-19	3.76E-20
	Average Solution	24.55	6.6 * 10-3	7.7 * 10-11	7.40E-19	9.76E-20
F7	Best Solution	0.06	0.04	0.018	2.77E-02	2.09E-02
	Average Solution	0.06	0.04	0.015	5.09E-02	4.89E-02

Table 5. Minimization result of benchmark functions in Table 2 with pop as 50 except PSOGSA (pop =30) and number of maximum iterations set as 1000.

Function	Performance	RGA[38]	PSO[38]	GSA[38]	PSOGSA[40]	TLBO-GSA
F8	Best Solution	-8	-95	-25	-12569	-15
	Average Solution	-8	-95	-23	-12213.7	-8
F9	Best Solution	5.9	55.1	15.32	19.1371	14.2867
	Average Solution	5.71	56.6	14.42	22.6777	21.2987
F10	Best Solution	2.13	9.0*10-3	6.9 *10-6	5.97E-12	7.01E-13
	Average Solution	2.16	6.0*10-3	6.9*10-6	6.68E-12	8.41E-13
F11	Best Solution	1.16	0.01	0.29	1.11E-16	1.11E-11
	Average Solution	1.14	0.0081	0.04	1.48E-03	6.48E-08
F12	Best Solution	0.051	0.29	0.01	6.43E+00	0.58
	Average Solution	0.039	0.11	4.2 *10-13	2.34E+01	3.44E+01
F13	Best Solution	0.081	3.1 *10-18	3.2 * 10-32	7.87E-19	5.87E-20
	Average Solution	0.032	2.2*10-23	2.3 *10-32	7.78E-19	6.91E-20

the proposed (TLBO-GSA) method is also explored on the real-life engineering problem. The main aim is to minimize the total production cost of Pressure Vessel Design (PVD) problem including the cost of material, forming, and welding parts. It has four design variables:

- Thickness of Shell (x_1),
- Thickness of Head (x_2),
- Inner radius of Shell (x_3),
- Length of Shell (x_4),

Table 6. Minimization result of benchmark functions in Table 3 with pop as 50 except PSOGSA (pop =30) and number of maximum iterations set as 1000.

Function	Performance	RGA[38]	PSO[38]	GSA[38]	PSOGSA[40]	TLBO-GSA
F14	Best Solution	0.998	0.998	3.7	0.998	0.996
	Average Solution	0.998	0.998	3.7	1.49	1.81
F15	Best Solution	4.0 * 10-3	2.8*10-3	8.0*10-3	3.07E-04	1.87E-04
	Average Solution	1.7*10-3	7.1 * 10-4	7.4 *10-4	8.56E-04	7.46E-04
F16	Best Solution	-1.0313	-1.0316	-1.0316	-1.0316	-1.0317
	Average Solution	-1.0315	-1.0316	-1.0316	-1.0316	-1.0316
F17	Best Solution	0.3996	0.3979	0.3979	0.3979	0.3979
	Average Solution	0.398	0.3979	0.3979	0.3979	0.3979
F18	Best Solution	5.7	3	3	3	3
	Average Solution	3	3	3	3	3
F19	Best Solution	-3.8627	-3.8628	-3.8628	-3.8628	-3.8628
	Average Solution	-3.8628	-3.8628	-3.8628	-3.8628	-3.8628
F20	Best Solution	-3.3099	-3.2369	-2.0569	-2.6375	-3.4063
	Average Solution	-3.3217	-3.2031	-1.9946	-8.92E-01	-8.96E-01
F21	Best Solution	-5.6605	-6.629	-6.0748	-10.1532	-5.0819
	Average Solution	-2.6824	-5.1008	-5.0552	-7.25959	-7.8648
F22	Best Solution	-7.3421	-9.1118	-9.3399	-10.4029	-9.4029
	Average Solution	-10.3932	-10.402	-10.402	-7.53978	-7.2698
F23	Best Solution	-6.2541	-9.7634	-9.4548	-10.5364	-10.1697
	Average Solution	-4.5054	-10.536	-10.536	-7.52233	-7.41033

Here, variable x_1 and x_2, are integer multipliers of 0.0625. The variable x_3 and x_4, are representing the continuous variables values which ranges as $40 \leqslant x_3 \leqslant 80$ and $20 \leqslant x_4 \leqslant 60$. One of the most popular real-life nonlinear constrained problem such as pressure vessel design, is introduced by Sandgren. It is expressed as follows: $\vec{X} = [x_1, x_2, x_3, x_4]$ min $f(\vec{X}) = 0.6224x_1x_3x_4 + 1.7781x_2x_3x_3 + 3.1611x_1'x_1x_4 + 19.84x_1x_1x_4$.

When the pressure vessel design constraints problem is solved by using TLBOGSA method, the optimal value of x_1, x_2, x_3, and x_4 are 1.141, 0.619, 58.08 and 49.89 achieved, respectively. Also get the cost of the objective problem is 7263.16. The experimental performance criteria are minimum fitness evaluations as 50,000 and ten independents run. The reported result of TLBOGSA is better than sandgen.[41]

5. Conclusion

To solve the complex optimization problems, hybrid meta-heuristic are widely used. In this chapter, a new hybrid algorithm has been investigated utilizes merits of TLBO and GSA to improve exploration capacity of learners. The main idea is to integrate the abilities of TLBO and GSA in exploration and exploitation, respectively. Our proposed approach not only improved the performance of TLBO and GSA but also manage the exploration and the exploitation trade-off in the algorithms. It is easy to implement and requires relatively less number of adjusting constraints. The experiment results are validated by using the proposed (TLBO-GSA) method with the aid of twenty-three unconstrained and constrained benchmark functions and also compared to existing RGA, PSO, GSA and PSOGSA algorithm. The performance criteria are the best solution and average solution and the proposed method acquired the outstanding results. The results have also proved that the performance of TLBO-GSA is better than RGA, PSO, GSA, and PSOGSA in terms of best solution and average solution.

References

1. L. Bianchi, M. Dorigo, L. Maria, and W. J. Gutjahr, A survey on metaheuristics for stochastic combinatorial optimization, *Natural Computing.* **8** (2), 239–287 (2009). doi: 10.1007/s11047-008-9098-4.
2. I. Boussaïd, J. Lepagnot, and P. Siarry, A survey on optimization metaheuristics, *Information Sciences.* **237**, 82–117 (2013). doi: 10.1016/j.ins.2013.02.041.
3. L. Wang and X.-l. Zheng, A knowledge-guided multi-objective fruit fly optimization algorithm for the multi-skill resource constrained project scheduling problem, *Swarm and Evolutionary Computation.* (June), 1–10 (2017). ISSN 2210-6502. doi: 10.1016/j.swevo.2017.06.001. URL http://dx.doi.org/10.1016/j.swevo.2017.06.001.
4. K. Srikanth, L. K. Panwar, B. Panigrahi, E. Herrera-Viedma, A. K. Sangaiah, and G.-G. Wang, Meta-heuristic framework: quantum inspired binary grey wolf optimizer for unit commitment problem, *Computers & Electrical Engineering* (2017).
5. C. R. Reeves, *Modern Heuristic Techniques for Combinatorial Problems.* John Wiley & Sons, Inc. (1993).
6. S. Tuo, L. Yong, F. Deng, Y. Li, Y. Lin, and Q. Lu, HSTLBO: A hybrid algorithm based on Harmony Search and Teaching-Learning-Based Optimization for complex high-dimensional optimization problems, *PLoS ONE.* **12**(4), 1–23 (2017).
7. O. Cord, S. Cagnoni, P. Mesejo, and O. Ib, A survey on image segmentation using metaheuristic-based deformable models: State of the art and critical analysis, *Applied Soft Computing.* **44**, 1–29 (2016).
8. W.-y. Wang and Y.-h. Li, Evolutionary learning of BMF Fuzzy-neural networks using a reduced-form genetic algorithm, *IEEE Transactions on Systems, Man, and Cybernetics Part B: Cybernetics.* **33**(6), 966–976 (2003).

9. S. Das, A. Abraham, and A. Konar, Particle Swarm Optimization and Differential Evolution Algorithms: Technical Analysis, Applications and Hybridization Perspectives, *Advances of computational intelligence in industrial systems.* **38**, 1–38 (2008).

10. X. F. Xie and J. Liu, Multiagent optimization system for solving the traveling salesman problem (TSP), *IEEE Transactions on Systems, Man, and Cybernetics, Part B: Cybernetics.* **39**(2), 489–502 (2009). ISSN 10834419. doi: 10.1109/TSMCB.2008.2006910.

11. W. Shao, D. Pi, and Z. Shao, A hybrid discrete optimization algorithm based on teaching probabilistic learning mechanism for no-wait flow shop scheduling, *Knowledge-Based Systems.* **107**, 219–234 (2016). ISSN 0950-7051. doi: 10.1016/j.knosys.2016.06.011. URL http://dx.doi.org/10.1016/j.knosys.2016.06.011.

12. C. Blum, J. Puchinger, G. R. Raidl, and A. Roli, Hybrid metaheuristics in combinatorial optimization: A survey, *Applied Soft Computing Journal.* **11**(6), 4135–4151 (2011). ISSN 1568-4946. doi: 10.1016/j.asoc.2011.02.032. URL http://dx.doi.org/10.1016/j.asoc.2011.02.032.

13. Y. Wang and F. Wan, A Hybrid Particle Swarm Optimizer with Sine Cosine Acceleration Coefficients, *Information Sciences* (2017). ISSN 0020-0255. doi: 10.1016/j.ins.2017.09.015. URL http://dx.doi.org/10.1016/j.ins.2017.09.015.

14. S. M. A. Salehizadeh, P. Yadmellat, and M. B. Menhaj, Local optima avoidable particle swarm optimization, *2009 IEEE Swarm Intelligence Symposium, SIS 2009 - Proceedings.* pp. 16–21 (2009). doi: 10.1109/SIS.2009.4937839.

15. T. Cheng, M. Chen, P. J. Fleming, Z. Yang, and S. Gan, A novel hybrid teaching learning based multi-objective particle swarm optimization, *Neurocomputing.* **22**, 11–25 (2016). ISSN 0925-2312. doi: 10.1016/j.neucom.2016.10.001. URL http://dx.doi.org/10.1016/j.neucom.2016.10.001.

16. R. Cheng, M. Li, Y. Tian, X. Zhang, and S. Yang. Benchmark Functions for CEC ' 2017 Competition on Evolutionary Many-Objective Optimization. Technical Report (2017).

17. K. Ting, T. O., Yang, X. S., Cheng, S., and Huang. Hybrid Metaheuristic Algorithms : Past , Present , and Future Hybrid Metaheuristic Algorithms: In *Recent Advances in Swarm Intelligence and Evolutionary Computation.* Springer International Publishing, pp. 71–83 (2015). ISBN 9783319138268. doi: 10.1007/978-3-319-13826-8.

18. M. M. Mafarja and S. Mirjalili, Hybrid Whale Optimization Algorithm with simulated annealing for feature selection, *Neurocomputing.* pp. 1–11 (2017). doi: 10.1016/j.neucom.2017.04.053.

19. F. J. Rodriguez, C. García-martínez, and M. Lozano, Hybrid Metaheuristics Based on Evolutionary Algorithms and Simulated Annealing: Taxonomy, Comparison, and Synergy Test, *IEEE Transactions on Evolutionary Computation.* **16**(6), 787–800 (2012).

20. D.-h. Chen and Y.-n. Sun, A self-learning segmentation frameworkthe Taguchi approach, *Computerized Medical Imaging and Graphics.* **24**(5), 283–296 (2000).

21. P. Lopez-garcia, E. Onieva, E. Osaba, A. D. Masegosa, and A. Perallos, A meta-heuristic based in the hybridization of Genetic Algorithms and Cross Entropy methods for continuous optimization, *Expert Systems With Applications*. **55**, 508–519 (2016). ISSN 0957-4174. doi: 10.1016/j.eswa.2016.02.034. URL http://dx.doi.org/10.1016/j.eswa.2016.02.034.

22. M. Pereyra, P. Schniter, É. Chouzenoux, J.-c. Pesquet, J.-y. Tourneret, S. Member, A. O. Hero, and S. Mclaughlin, A Survey of Stochastic Simulation and Optimization Methods in Signal Processing, *IEEE Journal of Selected Topics in Signal Processing*. **10**(2), 224–241 (2016).

23. C.-w. Tsai, M.-c. Chiang, A. Ksentini, and M. Chen, Metaheuristic Algorithms for Healthcare: Open Issues and Challenges, *Computers and Electrical Engineering*. **53**, 421–434 (2016). ISSN 0045-7906. doi: 10.1016/j.compeleceng.2016.03.005. URL http://dx.doi.org/10.1016/j.compeleceng.2016.03.005.

24. Y. Chen, J.-k. Hao, and F. Glover, A Hybrid Metaheuristic Approach for the Capacitated Arc Routing Problem, *European Journal of Operational Research*. **253**(1), 25–39 (2016). doi: 10.1016/j.ejor.2016.02.015.

25. A. N. K. Nasir and M. O. Tokhi, Novel metaheuristic hybrid spiral-dynamic bacteria-chemotaxis algorithms for global optimisation, *Applied Soft Computing Journal*. **27**, 357–375 (2015). ISSN 1568-4946. doi: 10.1016/j.asoc.2014.11.030. URL http://dx.doi.org/10.1016/j.asoc.2014.11.030.

26. S. R. K. S and S. Murugan, Memory based Hybrid Dragonfly Algorithm for numerical optimization problems, *Expert Systems With Applications*. **83**, 63–78 (2017). doi: 10.1016/j.eswa.2017.04.033.

27. Z. Li, W. Wang, Y. Yan, and Z. Li, PS ABC: A hybrid algorithm based on particle swarm and artificial bee colony for high-dimensional optimization problems, *Expert Systems With Applications*. **42**(22), 8881–8895 (2015). ISSN 0957-4174. doi: 10.1016/j.eswa.2015.07.043. URL http://dx.doi.org/10.1016/j.eswa.2015.07.043.

28. E. Vega-alvarado, E. A. Portilla-flores, M. B. Calva-yáñez, G. Sepúlveda-cervantes, J. A. Aponte-rodríguez, E. Santiago-valentín, and J. M. A. Rueda-meléndez, Hybrid Metaheuristic for Designing an End Effector as a Constrained Optimization Problem, *IEEE Access*. **5**, 6002–6014 (2017).

29. S. Mahdavi, M. Ebrahim, and S. Rahnamayan, Metaheuristics in large-scale global continues optimization: A survey, *Information Sciences*. **295**, 407–428 (2015). ISSN 0020-0255. doi: 10.1016/j.ins.2014.10.042. URL http://dx.doi.org/10.1016/j.ins.2014.10.042.

30. S. Dey, S. Bhattacharyya, and U. Maulik, Efficient quantum inspired metaheuristics for multi-level true colour image thresholding, *Applied Soft Computing Journal*. **56**, 472–513 (2017). ISSN 1568-4946. doi: 10.1016/j.asoc.2016.04.024. URL http://dx.doi.org/10.1016/j.asoc.2016.04.024.

31. R. Raidl, A Unified View on Hybrid Metaheuristics, *Hybrid metaheuristics*. pp. 1–12 (2006).

32. Z. Fei, S. Member, B. Li, S. Yang, C. Xing, H. Chen, and L. Hanzo, A Survey of Multi-Objective Optimization in Wireless Sensor Networks: Metrics , Algorithms, and Open Problems, *IEEE Communications Surveys & Tutorials*. **19**(1), 550–586 (2017).

33. F. Javidrad and M. Nazari, A new hybrid particle swarm and simulated annealing stochastic optimization method, *Applied Soft Computing Journal.* **60**, 634–654 (2017). ISSN 1568-4946. doi: 10.1016/j.asoc.2017.07.023. URL http://dx.doi.org/10.1016/j.asoc.2017.07.023.

34. R. Baños, J. Ortega, C. Gil, A. L. Márquez, and F. D. Toro, A hybrid meta-heuristic for multi-objective vehicle routing problems with time windows, *Computers & Industrial Engineering.* **65**(2), 286–296 (2013). doi: 10.1016/j. cie.2013.01.007.

35. F. Ramadhani, M. A. Hussain, H. Mokhlis, and S. Hajimolana, Optimization strategies for Solid Oxide Fuel Cell (SOFC) application: A literature survey, *Renewable and Sustainable Energy Reviews.* **76**(February 2016), 460–484 (2017). ISSN 1364-0321. doi: 10.1016/j.rser.2017.03.052. URL http://dx.doi.org/10.1016/j.rser.2017.03.052.

36. R. V. Rao, V. J. Savsani, and D. P. Vakharia, Computer-Aided Design Teaching learning-based optimization: A novel method for constrained mechanical design optimization problems, *Computer-Aided Design.* **43**(3), 303–315 (2011). ISSN 0010-4485. doi: 10.1016/j.cad.2010.12.015. URL http://dx.doi.org/10.1016/j.cad.2010.12.015.

37. A. Nickabadi, M. M. Ebadzadeh, and R. Safabakhsh, A novel particle swarm optimization algorithm with adaptive inertia weight, *Applied Soft Computing Journal.* **11**(4), 3658–3670 (2011). ISSN 15684946. doi: 10.1016/j.asoc.2011.01.037.

38. E. Rashedi, H. Nezamabadi-pour, and S. Saryazdi, GSA: A Gravitational Search Algorithm, *Information Sciences.* **179**(13), 2232–2248 (2009). ISSN 0020-0255. doi: 10.1016/j.ins.2009.03.004. URL http://dx.doi.org/10.1016/j.ins.2009.03.004.

39. K. A. Publishers and G. Talbi, A Taxonomy of Hybrid Metaheuristics, *Journal of Heuristics.* **8**(5), 541–564 (2002).

40. S. Mirjalili and S. Z. M. Hashim, A new hybrid PSOGSA algorithm for function optimization. In *International Conference on Computer and Information Application (ICCIA)*, IEEE, pp. 374–377 (2010, December).

41. E. Sandgren, Nonlinear integer and discrete programming in mechanical design optimization, *Journal of Mechanisms, Transmissions, and Automation in Design.* **112**(2), 223–229 (1990). ISSN 07380666. doi: 10.1115/1.2912596. URL http://www.scopus.com/inward/record.url?eid=2-s2.0-0025448058&partnerID=tZOtx3y1.

Chapter 3

Review on Hybrid Metaheuristic Approaches for Optimization in Multibiometric Authentication System

Aarohi Vora*, Chirag Paunwala[†] and Mita Paunwala[‡]

*Electronics and Communication Department,
Gujarat Technological University, Ahmedabad,
Gujarat 382424, India
vaarohi@gmail.com

[†] Electronics and Communication Department,
Sarvajanik College of Engineering and Technology, Surat,
Gujarat 395007, India
cpaunwala@gmail.com

[‡] Electronics and Communication Department,
C K Pithawala College of Engineering and Technology, Surat,
Gujarat 395007, India
mpaunwala@yahoo.co.in

In recent scenario, major areas of application such as forensics, government and commercial domain demands higher accuracy and reliability to identify individuals in real-time. Biometrics is the automated measurement of ubiquitous and unique characteristic of an individual which can distinguish an individual from the mass. The design of a multi-biometrics system in real-time applications is an exciting research due to the limitations of unimodal biometric systems. The risk of attack to Multibiometric framework keeps on varying from time to time and hence adaptive systems are needed which can adapt to these varying security levels. Metaheuristic is an advanced level technique designed to choose a heuristic which results into a promising solution for the optimization issue with inadequate data. Hybrid metaheuristic is essentially a technique that results from the combination of a metaheuristic with other techniques of optimization. Hybrid metaheuristic approaches have progressed significantly in managing the real life optimization issues effectively. The application of metaheuristics techniques like Ant Colony Optimization (ACO), Particle Swarm Optimization

(PSO), Genetic Algorithms (GA), Hybrid GA-PSO and Quadrature Programming (QP) Optimization for Support Vector Machines in developing real time multi-biometric authentication systems are discussed in this chapter.

Keywords: ACO, GA, Hybrid PSO-GA, LWSR, Multibiometric System, Metaheuristics, PSO, Score Level Fusion, SVM.

1. Introduction

Unibiometric system utilize an individual's anatomical and behavioral characteristics viz. face, finger vein, iris, handprints, fingerprints, signature, speech, typing rhythm, gait, etc. to distinguish and identify him/her for accessing the system.[1,2] Biometric qualities show a strong association of an individual dependent upon their identity which are less liable to be forged.[1,2] These frameworks prevent false claims as they involve genuine individual traits for accessing the system.[1,2] Every biometric trait needs to be first enrolled in the system and save as a template in the database during enrollment stage.[1,3,4] Biometric recognition involves either verifying or identifying an individual.[1,3,4]

Unimodal frameworks experience the ill effects of a few issues such as obstreperous sensor information, lacking distinction, unaccessible invariant representations, and so forth.[3-6] These issues result in increasing error rates and reduce system reliability.[3-6] Multimodal frameworks conquer a portion of the issues related to unimodal frameworks utilizing an efficient combinational fusion rule and hence accomplish higher recognition accuracy and better performance.[3-6] Sensor, Feature, Score and Decision are the four noteworthy fusion levels in multimodal frameworks.[1,3,4] Sensor and Feature level Fusion are conducted prior to matching while Score and Decision Level Fusion are conducted after matching.[1,3,5]

Sensor Level Fusion includes uniting different sensors' crude information, e.g. from the fingerprint sensor, iris sensor, camera, and so forth.[1,3,7,8] Raw data is separated from the numerous sensors and combined to deliver crude amalgamated data.[1,3] There are three possible categories in which sensor level fusion can occur to secure the data in trustworthy and descriptive mode.[1,3] Firstly, when different representations of the same biometric trait are obtained from the solitary sensor are fused using either an averaging or mosaic techniques. A case is the introduction of pictures containing different fingerprints to mosaic plainly a full unique finger impression picture. In second case, numerous occurrences acquired from different sensors are assembled to fuse the data fluctuation from various sensors.[1] Lastly manifold biometric traits from different modalities obtained from different sensors are consolidated together.[1] But this last combination is very less studied in research field. One of the implementation of this case is observed in paper[8] where palm prints and palm vein images are fused at sensor level with 95% recognition accuracy.[8]

In Feature level fusion, features obtained from various biometrics are consolidated into a single vector.[1,3] A composite template is formed by utilizing a specific combination technique which is then utilized for recognition.[1,3] Feature level contains data that helps to process crude biometric information and therefore it is accepted as more effective level as compared to the score and decision level.[1,3] Feature level combination is carried out in two phases; one is normalization of features and other is selection of features element.[9] Normalization is required to make features rotation invariant. This level of fusion suffers from curse of dimensionality and hence this issue is addressed by feature selection technique.[1,9] This fusion is often difficult to accomplish because the feature sets originating from different biometric traits may not be compatible for consolidation.[1,10,11] If the feature vectors are derived from the same trait then resultant feature vector is obtained by calculating the weighted mean of all features.[1,12,13] But if they are derived from different traits then the resultant feature vector is obtained by concatenation.[1,12,13]

Score Level Fusion integrates proximity value outputted from a matching module.[1,3,14–16] These proximity values provide ample amount of information that can help categorizing genuine and impostor users.[1,3,15–17] Match score level fusion is carried out via Combinational approach and Classification Approach.[3,5] In classification approach scores from different matchers are treated as vectors to be fed as an input to the classifier.[17,18] These input patterns train the classifier and after that fused scores are calculated by the proximity of patterns from the separating hyperplane.[17] In the combinational approach, end decision is reached out by linking the scores of individual matchers into a scalar score.[1,3,17] The scores are normalized for functional integration from various modalities.[1,3,17]

Decision Level Fusion integrates the verdicts from each modality.[1,3,19] This verdicts are obtained at almost last stages so they provide very vague information.[1,3,19] Hence, it reduces recognition performance of this level.[1,3,19] The verdicts outputted from various modalities are integrated using algorithms like "AND" or "OR" rules, majority voting rule, Dempster-Shafer Theory of Evidence, Bayesian decision fusion, etc.[1,3,19–23]

Metaheuristic algorithms are intended to solve approximately an extensive variety of hard optimization issues without having to profoundly adjust to every issue.[24,25] These algorithms address the issues which do not have satisfactory problem-specific solutions.[24,25] Hard optimization issuess cannot be solved optimally with exact bound or by any deterministic technique within a given time constrain.[24] With a specific end goal to discover satisfactory answers for these issues, metaheuristics can be utilized.[24] These algorithms find their applications in varied areas viz. Engineering, Finance, etc.[24,25] Generally, these algorithms are inspired from nature.[24,25] Instead of using gradient or Hessian matrix as objective function they utilize stochastic methods to optimize parameters that should be fitted to the current issue.[24,25] There has been impressive advancement of metaheuristics in todays scenario and it can very well be appreciated by significant increment in the processing capabilities of computing platforms due to advancement of parallel architectures.[24,25] This hardware Upgradation has optimized the CPU timing cost of these algorithms.[24,25]

Metaheuristics addresses an optimization issue effectively by balancing properly between the **Expansion** and **Escalation** characteristics of the search space.[24,25] **Escalation** distinguishes pursuit space with high solutions whereas **Expansion** strengthens the hunt in some encouraging zones of the collected search experience.[24,25]

There are several Metaheuristic algorithms namely Ant colony optimization, Bat algorithm, Genetic Algorithm, Particle Swarm Optimization, iterated local search, Simulated annealing, Cuckoo Search Algorithm, Bacteria Foraging, Tabu search, etc.[24,25] Some of these algorithms are motivated from natural process of evolution while others some of them are expansions of greedy heuristics and local search algorithms.[24,25] In recent times, instead of following traditional metaheuristics, different algorithms of other research areas on optimization are consolidated giving direction to development of hybrid metaheuristics.[24,25] Hybrid Metaheuristics lead to exploration of new research directions.[24,25]

The primary inspiration driving the hybridization of various Metaheuristics is to correlate the characteristics of various optimization methodologies as hybrids are believed to profit by cooperative energy.[24,25] Indeed, picking up a satisfactory blend of complementary algorithms can be the key for accomplishing top execution in tackling numerous hard optimization issues.[24,25] The most important issue is to build up an effective hybrid approach by utilizing expertise from various areas of optimization.[24,25] Moreover, the literature shows that these hybrid metaheuristics cannot be generalized i.e. a certain hybrid might work well for specific problems, but it might perform poorly for others.[24,25] Nevertheless, there are hybridization types that have appeared to be effective for many applications.[25] They may fill in as a direction for new advancements.

In most of the researches taking place in the domain of multimodal framework; score level fusion is widely accepted as the information can easily be fused while increasing the recognition performance of the system.[1,3,4,6] Thus in this chapter, techniques used for fusion at score level as well as techniques used for the optimization of algorithms using Metaheuristic will be discussed.

The chapter contains four sections described as follows: Section 2 reviews about the advances done in the Score fusion and Metaheuristic Optimization. Section 3 explains Metaheuristics for optimization of fusion parameters in rule based method and classifier based method at score level. Section 4 whirls around the discussion and summary of Application of Metaheuristics in developing multimodal framework adaptable to varying security levels.

2. Review on Score Level Fusion and Metaheuristic Optimization Techniques

Recent advances in the area of multimodal framework has led to the development of several score fusion algorithms in the literature.[1,3–6,14–18] In Ref. 6, authors proposed sum rule for fusing face, fingerprint, and hand geometry modalities. Authors in Ref. 15 fused iris and face modalities by assigning weights based on their false accept rate (FAR) and false reject rate (FRR) to achieve greater recognition accuracy than sum rule.[1,15] Several strategies have been devised to appoint said weights with changing levels of precision and performance.[1,16] Another aspect of multimodal framework based on dynamic selection of matching scores is designed by authors in Ref. 26. This framework selects a score based upon maximum likelihood criteria but the performance achieved by this approach is not consistent and hence it is not used.[26] Frischholz *et al.*[7] proposed a BioID system model which generates several confidence levels by utilizing diverse decision methodologies on face, voice and lip movement.[1,7] For higher security level, all three of the modals must agree while for lower security any two of the modals must agree in order to make a decision. Although this system provides adaptive levels of security but it does not provide systematic procedure to vary security levels.

This section elaborates about the classifier based methods utilized for score fusion. In this type of algorithms, scores from various modalities are treated as feature vectors.[17,18,27] The fusion approach in such application is therefore viewed as a classification problem.[17,18,27] A classifier constructs a separation hyperplane for genuine and impostor scores distribution in an authentication system.[17,18,27] This category of fusion involves various classifier techniques viz. Support vector machines (SVM), Bayesian classifier, Artificial Neural Network (ANN), Decision Tree, Linear Discriminant analysis (LDA) etc. for fusion of scores.[3,5,17,18,27]

Decision Tree algorithm[6] designs a predictive class tree based on specific attribute of data. Information gain at each node of the tree is maximized to find out a tested attribute. Although the algorithm provides a clear view of data structure but it is very much sensitive to change in dataset.[6] ANN consists of layers of artificial neurons interlinked by synaptic connections along with weights associated with each links.[5] ANN is trained by adjusting the weights centered on the error generated by back-propagation algorithm.[5] Output is generated by transforming weights and scores of each link using either Multilayer Perceptron (MLP) and Radial Basis Function (RBF) transform.[5,14] RBF is preferred widely as it results into higher recognition accuracy and learning capability as compared to MLP.[5,14] Bayesian classifier converts scores into probabilistic densities and fuses them by product rule.[5,14] Bayesian algorithms provide optimal fusion if densities are known.[5,14] The authors of Ref. 14 utilize the joint density modelling conditioned on the identity and biometrics quality as an input to in Bayesian Belief Network (BBN) and it outperforms the sum rule.[5,14]

Decision Tree and ANN generate a class label instead of score hence their thresholds cannot be adjusted.[5] Bayesian networks get confused when mutually exclusive hypothesis are used for fusion.[5] As for example Bayesian networks cannot distinguish between fuzzy fast walking and slow running.[5] Bayesian networks cannot handle both events with same probabilities and hence it gets confused. The disadvantage of Bayesian networks over Support vector machine is that if the underlying probabilities of the scores are not known or not properly estimated then the classifier may be inefficient to provide the proper classification of individuals.[5] For effective multimodal fusion, SVM algorithm generates a score instead of class label.[5,17,18,27] Hence, ROC can be constructed in order to identify the recognition rate of the system. In Bayesian classifiers such score values cannot be calculated and hence it can be used as a classifier and not a fuser.[5]

Linear SVM constructs a separation boundary between the training samples so as to maximize the separation from it to the support vectors.[3,17,27] A non-linear SVM is developed by transforming feature space using kernels.[3,17,27] In order to generate fused scores the signed distance from the test sample to the hyperplane is computed.[3,17,27] In classification based fusion technique, SVM cost function is optimized using Quadrature Programming (QP) solver.[3] SVM outperforms all other methods in terms of recognition accuracy.[3,17,27]

Recent advances in the area of multibiometric framework involve metaheuristic techniques in fusion process in order to obtain optimum performance. An adaptive multimodal management algorithm (AMBM) was proposed by Veeramachaneni *et al.* which utilized the combination of PSO and Bayesian decision fusion.[28] AMBM fuses decisions from several modalities using Bayesian rule and PSO is used to arrive at final decision.[28] Srinivas *et al.* designed a score level multibiometric framework consisting of combination of LWSR and PSO.[29] This paper computes weights to be assigned for all modalities using PSO.[29] Raghavendra *et al.*[30] fused facial images using PSO for better authentication.[30] This paper utilizes PSO to compute the optimum weight for LWSR and select optimal fused feature.[30] L. Mezai and F. Hachouf[31] integrated scores of face and voice using PSO and belief functions.[31] PSO estimates confidence factor and fusion is carried out using Dempster-Shafer (DS) algorithm. Kumar *et al.* proposed an adaptive multibiometric framework using Hybrid PSO in order to obtain optimal fusion strategy and parameter.[32] The authors experimented various score fusion strategies viz. sum rule, LWSR, product and exponential sum on iris and palmprint; face and speech; fingerprint and hand geometry.[32] Amioy Kumar and Ajay Kumar[33] proposed a multibiometric framework using ant colony optimization (ACO) for fusing (1) face and fingerprint (2) palmprint and iris. Kumar *et al.* obtained fusion parameters for varying security levels by applying ACO to bimodal hand knuckle framework.[34] Romain Giot *et al.* selected fusion parameters by using fast EER computing based fitness function for GA.[35] Cherifi Dalila and Hafnaoui Imane[36] developed a multibiometric framework by combining GA and PSO to find optimum weights for LWSR.[36] Aniesha *et al.* optimized weights in LWSR using Genetic and Evolutionary computation (GEC)-based algorithm for face and periocular biometrics.[37] Their work showed that the concept of GEC score fusion enhances recognition accuracy of the system.[37]

PSO algorithm leads to premature convergence and hence it gets stuck in local minima.[36] Bacterial foraging algorithm has the ability to decide directions for obtaining optimal result.[24,25,34,36] This technique is not applicable in designing online biometric framework as it undergoes intensive computation to arrive at an optimal result.[24,25,34,36] GA suffers from convergence and costly fitness function issues.[34,36] ACO involves probabilistic tactic and hence it does not stuck into local minima as compared to PSO.[34,38] Ants follow the path where high concentration of pheromone is deposited.[34,38] Unlike PSO, ACO does not provide solutions in terms of local/global best positions.[33] Thus the need arises to develop formulas that provide local and global position updates. Authors in Ref. 39 updates probabilities selection of each path followed by ants bounded between upper and lower values via local and global position updates in PSO.[33,39]

2.1. *Score Level Fusion Techniques*

The score combination is performed by consolidating the proximity values of various matchers by either using rule based fusion viz. sum, product, LWSR, etc. and classifier based fusion such as SVM.[3,14–18] In this section, majorly two techniques LWSR and SVM are discussed and then the meta-heuristics used for optimization of parameters in these two techniques are reviewed.

Normalization techniques are used on scores from individual biometric models before applying rule based fusion technique in order to convert them in common range.[3,40–42] Normalization scales the score set and transforms them to common domain for compatibility of individual biometric models. Several normalization techniques are provided in literature viz. min-max, decimal scaling, z-score, tanh, double sigmoid and MAD Median rule.[5,40–42] Literature review shows that min max method is the only method which retains its original distribution before and after the normalization and also maps the scores from different models to a common range.[40–42] Hence for the fusion of multimodal systems in most of the applications of multimodal framework, min-max normalization method is utilized.[40–42] After normalization of scores, the unimodal systems now become compatible with each other and hence they can be integrated at score level.[3,6] There are two types of scores one is a similarity score and other is distance score. If the scores are already normalized, then in order to convert similarity score to distance score equation Eq. (1) is utilized.

$$Distance = 1 - Similarity. \tag{1}$$

2.2. *Linear Weighted Sum Rule (LWSR)*

In simple sum rule for fusion, the scores obtained from various biometric modalities are directly summed up.[3,6] It means that each of the modality is given equal importance.[3,6] But practically, each modality does not provide the same recognition accuracy every time.[3-5,16] As for example if face and fingerprint system is considered then fingerprint system is more robust as compared to face which means that face is more erroneous as compared to fingerprint.[3] Thus it is required to weigh different modalities depending upon the error levels of all.[3-5,16]

Almost all biometric models involved in fusion process have different error values and hence they are weighed depending upon their error values.[3,15,16] A stronger biometric model must be assigned higher weight as compared to weaker biometric model.[3,15,16] Hence the effect of more erroneous modality is lowered down so as to enhance the recognition rate of fused framework.[3,15,16] Several weight assignment strategies are proposed in literature for effective fusion in a multimodal system.[3,15,16]

In the literature of rule based fusion techniques at score level, LWSR has been proved to produce higher recognition performance as compared to other methods without having any training session involved in it.[3,15,16] If there are N number of modalities involved in fusion, each modality generates normalized score S_i and each modality is assigned weight w_i, then the fused score S_f is represented as equation Eq. (2).

$$S_f = \sum_{i=1}^{N} S_i * w_i \qquad (2)$$

LWSR does not require any training session for its implementation. Hence it is less time consuming and computationally efficient. LWSR is easy to implement and computationally effective and hence it is widely used in rule based fusion.[4,5,16]

The selection of the fusion parameters i.e. weight parameters for LWSR in development of multimodal framework is subjected to the desired security level stated in terms of FAR and FRR.[33,34] FAR is the percentage of impostors accepted and FRR is the percentage of genuine users rejected.[1,4,5,16] These error rates are complementary to each other and hence practically it is not possible to minimize both of them simultaneously.[3,4,15,16] Multibiometric frameworks are evaluated based upon their error rates such as FAR, FRR/GAR and EER.[43] But, however the wavering requirements of security levels of a system urge the development of an adaptive framework designed on basis of error rates utilized as the performance evaluation indices.[34,43] Different cost parameters are assigned to error rates so as to obtain diverse security levels.[34,43] In an application where false acceptance is not tolerable, cost parameter to be assigned to FAR is greater as compared to cost parameter to be assigned to FRR i.e. high security applications have $CFA > CFR$.[34,43] While in low security application where false rejection is not tolerable cost of false rejection is higher as compared to cost of false acceptance i.e. $CFR > CFA$.[34,43] Hence, adaptive multimodal framework is designed by utilizing CFA and CFR.[33,43] CFA and CFR range in the interval [0 2] and hence they can be varied in step of 0.1 which provides total 20 discrete security levels.[33,43] The fusion parameters i.e. weights at score level are calculated by utilizing error rates of individual modalities and the suitable fusion rules.[34,43] Hence in order to optimize the fusion parameters, metaheuristic algorithms such as PSO, GA, Hybrid GA-PSO and ACO are widely used for the score level fusion.[33–37,39,43] This review emphasizes the usage of these Metaheuristic Techniques that will be used for the optimization of the weight parameters to be assigned to all the modalities involved in the fusion.

3. Metaheuristic Algorithms in Score Level Fusion

Block diagram for metaheuristic optimization at score level is shown in Fig. 1. The multimodal framework comprises of two biometric sensors. Each biometric sensor processes individually and extracts features from both the biometric modalities. Then the feature templates are compared with the stored templates to compute the matching scores.[33–37,39,43] Thereafter the fusion is done using score level fusion methods viz. rule based methods and classifier based methods.[33–37,39,43] While doing fusion, the weight to be applied to each of the matcher is optimized by metaheuristic algorithm based upon the values of FAR, FRR and EER of the system. After that decision is made whether person is granted access to the system or not.[33–37,39,43]

The administration of the multimodal sensors must be flexible according to the coveted level of security.[33–37,39,43] The level of risk on a biometric framework can shift and hence, it is essential for it to provide different security levels.[33–37,39,43] The adaptive security requirement is sufficed by designing a Bayesian cost E quantified in terms of CFA, CFR, FAR and FRR as depicted in equation Eq. (3)[33–37,39,43]

$$E = CFA * FAR(\alpha) + CFR * FRR(\alpha) \tag{3}$$

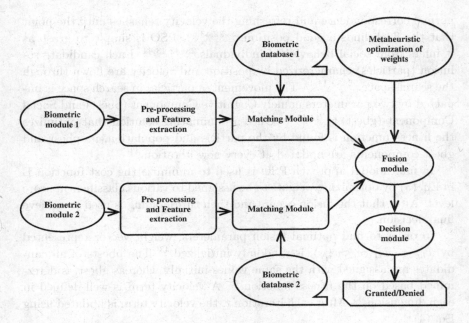

Fig. 1.   Score Fusion using Metaheuristic Optimization

where, $FAR(\alpha)$ = global FAR and $FRR(\alpha)$ = global FRR at decision threshold α and CFA+CFR=2.[28] The cost function E is optimized by selecting suitable amalgamation rule, parameters and decision threshold.[43] Metaheuristic Algorithms viz. PSO, GA, Hybrid PSO-GA and ACO are used to optimize cost function.[33–37,39,43] In rest of the chapter, all above stated four Metaheuristic Algorithms are discussed with their application to search for optimize weight parameters at score level for multimodal framework.

3.1. *Score Level Fusion using PSO*

Kennedy and Eberhart in 1995[44] introduced PSO portraying the social conduct of birds flock endeavoring to travel to a good environs.[28–32,43,44] Each bird inside the flock examines its updated position with respect to the best position achieved by it so far i.e. pbest position.[28–32,43,44] In addition to this, they also recognize the candidate which has achieved best position i.e. gbest position.[28–32,43,44] Now every bird of the flock update their velocity and move towards global best position.[28–32,43,44] The procedure of normal correspondence and refreshing the velocity rehashes until the point that the flock finds a good position.[28–32,43,44] PSO is simple to grasp as it infers from social behavior of individuals.[28–32,43,44] Each candidate solution (particles) characterized by position and velocity are flown through the search space.[28–32,43,44] The movement of particles in search space is impacted by two parameters namely Cognitive Component (pbest) and Social Component (gbest).[28–32,43,44] Once a dominating solution that optimizes the fitness function is found by the particle and population, its pbest and gbest components are updated at every new iteration.[43]

In multimodal approach PSO is used to minimize the cost function E in Eq. (3) by optimizing weights to be assigned to various classifiers at score level. After that the fusion occurs and then thresholding is used to achieve final decision.

In order to find optimal fusion parameters, weight vector represented by $w_{iq} = (w_{i1}, w_{i2}, w_{iN})$, is randomly initialized.[43] The pbests of all candidates are assigned with the same values initially whereas gbest, is determined based on the fitness function.[43] A velocity term is well defined in each dimension.[43] After each iteration t, the velocity term is updated using Eq. (4)[43]

$$V_{iq}^{(t+1)} = \omega * V_{iq}^{(t)} + U[0,1] * \psi_1 * (w_{pq}^{(t)} - w_{iq}^{(t)}) + U[0,1] * \psi_1 * (w_{gq}^{(t)} - w_{iq}^{(t)}) \tag{4}$$

where $U[0,1]$= random variable with uniform distribution, ω= inertia weight.[43] Inertia weight lies between 0 and 1 and it maintains a balance between global and local search abilities of the algorithm.[43] $\psi 1$ and $\psi 2$ = accelerator coefficients, wpq=pbest of particle, w_{gq}=gbest position of population and w_{iq}= position vector/weights of fusion.[43] Updated particle position represents updates in weights of fusion parameters and it is expressed in Eq. (5).[43]

$$w_{iq}^{(t+1)} = w_{iq}^{(t)} + V_{iq}^{(t+1)} \tag{5}$$

PSO is applied to a training dataset in order to compute optimal weights to carry out fusion.[43] After this, test dataset is evaluated based upon system designed by PSO weights.[43] The particle velocity and position are updated using Eqs. (4) and (5).[43] The particles at the new position are evaluated for the Bayesian error.[43] Subsequently, the pbest and gbest is updated.[43] This is repeated for a preset number of iterations.[43]

3.2. *Score Level Fusion using Genetic Algorithms (GA)*

John Holland *et al.*[45] introduced GA motivated by the genetic evolution phenomena and hence it mimics the reproduction process observed in biological populations.[35,43,45,46] GA widely used evolutionary optimization technique for engineering problems.[35,45,46] GA consists of chromosomes i.e. each candidate solution of a specific problem.[35,45,46] The space search in GA is initiated from a randomly generated population that evolve over successive generations.[35,45,46] GA optimizer employs three operators namely selection, Crossover and Mutation to spread its populace from one generation to another.[35,45,46] Selection operator picks up suitable individual chromosomes depending on survival of fittest phenomena in order to generate varying generations.[35,45,46] Crossover operator disseminates features of good surviving designs from the current population into the future population, which will have a better fitness value on average.[35,45,46] Mutation aids in global search of search space and hence avoids the algorithm from getting trapped in local minima.[35,45,46]

For a multibiometric framework, the score fusion is carried out by parameterizing fusion function by GA with the fitness function defined as EER.[35] Equation of GA is same as Eq. (2). Every weight parameter w represents chromosomes of GA while the fitness function is given by its EER.[35,45,46]

Hence the task is to minimize EER while optimizing weights of the scores in the fusion system.[35,45,46] This function is evaluated on the score set and EER is calculated for all prefix number of iterations.[35,45,46] The weights at which convergence is obtained are said to be optimal.[35,45,46]

3.3. *Score Level Fusion using Hybrid GA-PSO*

Although GA has wide range of applications but utilizing it for large scale optimization could be extremely time and computational costly as it necessitates extensive functional evaluations for convergence.[36,43] Unlike GA, PSO constructively communicates between particles and hence information passage is effectively carried out.[36] The only disadvantage of PSO is it converges prematurely because of the high rate of information flow between particles, bringing about the generation of comparable particles with a loss in diversity that builds the likelihood of being trapped in local optima.[36] Hence a Hybrid GA-PSO system is developed that deals with these apprehensions.[36] Hybrid GA-PSO combines the evolutionary natures and social interactions of both algorithms.[36]

Hybrid GA-PSO picks up N randomly generated initial population which are sorted by fitness.[36] Population in case of multibiometric framework is the weight vector of different matchers.[36] Thereafter the whole set is divided into two sub-sets ψG and ψP according to a user defined probability.[36] Set ψP adjusts the particles using the PSO algorithm while set ψG creates new generations using GA algorithm.[36] The entire dataset splits into two parts out of which one part is processed by the selection, crossover and mutation processes in case of GA while the other part is processed by velocity and position update in case of PSO.[36] Both generated populaces are joined into one single populace of N people, which are then arranged in planning for rehashing the whole run.[36] The fitness function to be minimized is characterized by EER and hence the task is to minimize the value of EER.[36] For each set of individuals, EER of the fused scores is computed.[36] The solution with lowest EER will be best fit solution. Once again population will be rearranged and sorted.[36] Evaluation of the fitness costs of the offspring is once again run and the weights to produce the minimum EER value is picked as optima.[36]

3.4. Score Level Fusion using Ant Colony Optimization (ACO)

Marco Dorigo[38] introduced ACO based upon probabilistic technique consisting a part of metaheuristic optimization in it based on the behaviour of ants.[33,34,39] Every ant leaves equal amount of pheromone level in order to guide other ants towards the food while recording their position to acquire better solution in next iteration.[33,34,39] It consists of two important parameters viz. Q which is a pheromone constant and ρ which is an evaporation factor and its value is less than 1.[33,34,39] Each ant selects its suitable solution from the set of all possible solutions.[33,34,39] Thereafter, for every ant, the objective function E given in Eq. (3) is computed and pheromone level of all solution is updated utilizing the initial pheromone level, cost function E as described in Eq. (3), pheromone constant Q and ρ evaporation factor as portrayed in Eq. (6)[33,34,39]

$$\tau_{(i)}(t+1) = \begin{cases} \rho * \tau_{(i)}(t) + \frac{Q}{E} & if\ i^{th}\ ant\ is\ selected\ in\ t^{th}\ iteration \\ \rho * \tau_{(i)}(t) & if\ i^{th}\ ant\ is\ not\ selected \end{cases} \qquad (6)$$

where Q = pheromone constant = [0.005,0.01], E = Objective function, ρ = evaporation constant and $\tau_i(t)$ = pheromone level at t^{th} iteration.[33,34,39]

The Bayesian error E in Eq. (3) is computed by incorporating CFA and CFR as the weights to the FAR and FRR.[33,34,39] CFA, match scores and the fusion rules are given as inputs to the ACO.[33,34,39] ACO minimizes E by selecting the input parameters and outputs the optimal once corresponding to the each security level.[33,34,39] ACO algorithm is run for each values of CFA as the optimized fusion parameters to be obtained highly depends upon the values of CFA.[33,34,39] Each ant in the search space is represented by $X_{md} = (X_{m1}, X_{m2}, ..X_{mD})$, where the first subscript denotes mth solution and D denote the dimension which is equal to "N+1" where N denotes the number of modality.[33,34,39] Each ant with equal amount of pheromone initially is represented by X_{md} =(w1, w2, F), where first two parameters are the weights assigned and last parameter is the fusion rule.[33,34,39] Weights computed by ACO will be used in LWSR fusion in order to obtain consolidated scores.[33,34,39] For each ant, cost function E is computed and the fusion parameter which minimizes the value of E is selected as optimum and the update on the pheromone level at $(t + 1)^{th}$ iteration where i denote the ith ant as described in Eq. (6).[33,34,39] The major drawback of ACO technique is that for smaller values of ρ i.e. approximately tending to 0 pheromone levels of ant saturates.[33,34,39] Thus an ant get stuck on a particular path and hence to address this issue the value of ρ is initially set to 1 due to which all paths have the same probability but no scope of optimization and then gradually decrease the value in steps of 0.005 to get the global optimal value.[33,34,39] This strategy not only prevents the ants from being dragged on any non-optimal path but also allows them to navigate to an optimal path.[33,34,39] Selection of number of ants and the number of iterations required for convergence of algorithm depends upon the application and the researcher.[33,34,39]

If any of the ants minimizes the objective function (E), the value of the pheromone level increases by Q/E; where Q is a constant in the range [0.005, 0.01].[33,34,39] Along with the update of the pheromone levels, the probability of the ith ant is computed for the next iterations as given in Eq. (7).[33,34,39]

$$P_i = \frac{\tau_i(t)}{\sum_{k=1}^{D} \tau_k(t)}. \tag{7}$$

Equation (6) improves the probability of selecting ants having more pheromone level and minimizing E in the next iteration.[33,34,39] The search space in current versions of ACO are bounded by upper and lower levels i.e. L and U.[33,34,39] The local best, the global best and the current position (denoted by A_{lb}, A_{gb} and A_{cp}, respectively) are calculated for all ants at every iteration.[33,34,39] From A_{lb}, A_{gb} and A_{cp}, L and U are derived as the limiting values.[33,34,39] At the first iteration, an equal amount of pheromone is assigned to all the paths and the probabilities are calculated accordingly.[33,34,39] From the next iteration onwards, the probabilities are calculated using the modified version of Eq. (7) as given in Eq. (8).[33,34,39]

$$P_i = \frac{\tau_i(t)}{\sum_{k=L}^{U} \tau_k(t)}. \tag{8}$$

3.5. Metaheuristic Optimization of Classifier Based Fusion

This section of the chapter focuses on Quadrature Optimization Programming (QOP) of Support Vector machine Algorithm for multimodal fusion at score level. SVM as a classifier is considered a very efficient as it has high generalization capability.[3,17,18,47–49] Therefore, SVM separates training patterns into two classes with a hyperplane which maximizes margin between classes of patterns and hence minimizes the misclassification error.[3,17,18,47–49]

Let (X_i, y_i), where $i = 1, 2, ...N$ be the set of training samples and $X_i \in R^d$; where d is the dimension of the input space and each sample belongs to a class labeled by $y_i \in (-1, +1)$.[3,17,18,47–49] For a genuine score vector the value y_i is set to 1, and for an impostor score vector its value is set to 1.[3,17,18,47–49] After training phase, testing sample X_T is inputted in order to classify it to one of the classes.[3,17,18,47–49]

SVM consists of two important terms: (i) W which is a weight vector associated with the training patterns and other term is b which is a bias term. Tupple (W,b) controls the decision function of the SVM classifier.[3,17,18,47–49] The main idea is to learn these parameters form the training patterns. W represents the vector direction perpendicular to hyperplane and b is the distance measure of moving the hyperplane parallel to itself for optimization.[3,17,18,47–49]

SVM used for two class classification works mainly for three different cases[3,17,18,47–49]: (i) Linearly separable dataset; (ii) Linearly non separable dataset; (iii) Nonlinear dataset.

When the training samples are linearly separable, SVM constructs an optimal hyperplane maximizing the separation between two classes.[17,18,48,49] The maximum margin separation between two classes is $\frac{2}{\|W\|}$.[17,18,48,49] When the hyperplane is optimal then there exist no training patterns between the two parallel hyperplane.[17,18,48,49] Thus it is a constrained Quadrature Optimization problem (QOP) and its solution is obtained by solving KT conditions.[17,18,48,49] KT condition searches for the convergence point of an optimal hyperplane where every local minimum becomes a global minimum.[17,18,48,49] QOP is solved using Lagrangian function.[17,18,48,49] Lagrange multipliers λ associated with training samples can either be zero or positive.[17,18,48,49] When λ^* is greater than 0, the associated patterns will be support vectors.[17,18,48,49] QOP provides with a primal-dual relationship.[17,18,48,49] Primal problem is subjected to more number of constraints as compared to dual problem.[17,18,48,49] Primal problem requires 3 parameters namely W, b and λ to be searched for optimal hyperplane.[17,18,48,49] On the contrary, dual formulation is used to find out only optimal values of λ by maximising the Lagrangian function.[17,18,48,49] Thus dual problem is solved to find out the optimal value of λ and plug its value to obtain optimum values of W and b for optimal hyperplane.[17,18,48,49]

Practically, in most of the real world applications, datasets are always nonlinear in nature and hence it is essential to understand the concept of SVM classification using QP solver.[17,18,48,49] In case of nonlinearly separable dataset, slack variable ζ is introduced in order to define the extent of violation for optimal separation.[17,18,48,49]

SVM maximizes the margin by keeping the number of points with ζ greater than 0 as small as possible.[17,18,48,49] Thus the ll optimization problem turns out to be minimizing the cost function given in Eq. (9) subject to the constraint given in Eq. (10).[17,18,48,49]

$$J(W,\zeta) = [\frac{1}{2}(W^T W) + C\sum_{i=1}^{N} *\zeta_i]|\zeta_i \geq 0 \qquad (9)$$

$$y_i(W^T X_i + b) \geq 1 - \zeta_i \qquad (10)$$

The new constraint C permits a functional margin that is less than 1, and contains a penalty of cost $C\zeta_i$ for any data point that falls within the margin on the correct side of the separating hyperplane (i.e., when $0 < \zeta_i \leq 1$), or on the wrong side of the separating hyperplane (i.e., when $\zeta_i > 1$).[17,18,48,49] Thus it classifies the training data correctly and softens the constraints to allow for non-separable data with a penalty proportional to the amount by which the training pattern is misclassified.[17,18,48,49] Here the term $\Sigma\zeta_i$ is an upper bound on the number of training errors.[17,18,48,49] Lagrangian function for linearly non-separable case is given by Eq. (11)[17,18,48,49]

$$L(W,b,\zeta,\lambda,\mu) = \frac{1}{2}(W^T W) + C\sum_{i=1}^{N}\zeta_i + \sum_{i=1}^{N}\lambda_i[1-\zeta_i-y_i(W^T X_i+b)] - \sum_{i=1}^{N}\mu_i\zeta_i$$
$$(11)$$

where, μ is the Lagrange multiplier for the slack variables.[17,18,48,49] Apply KT conditions on Eq. (11) to obtain optimal values of W and b produces Eqs. (12)–(16).[17,18,48,49]

$$\lambda_i^* + \mu_i^* = C|\frac{\partial L}{\partial \zeta_i}. \tag{12}$$

$$1 - \zeta_i - y_i(W^T X_i + b) \leq 0 \tag{13}$$

$$\zeta_i, \lambda_i, \mu_i \geq 0 \tag{14}$$

$$\lambda_i[1 - \zeta_i - y_i(W^T X_i + b)] = 0 \tag{15}$$

$$\zeta_i \mu_i = 0 \tag{16}$$

Primal problem for linearly non separable dataset involves problem of finding out four parameters viz. W, b, λ and μ. The solution of such a formulation may converge to an optimal solution but the convergence time is very large and hence dual formulation of such problems also exists.[48,49] The dual formulation for linearly non separable dataset is expressed in Eq. (17) with constraints on value of λ expressed in Eqs. (18) and (19).

$$L(W, b, \zeta, \lambda, \mu) = \sum_{i=1}^{N} \lambda_i - \sum_{i,j=1}^{N} \lambda_i \lambda_j y_i y_j X_i^T X_j \tag{17}$$

$$0 \leq \lambda_i \leq C \tag{18}$$

$$\sum_{i=1}^{N} \lambda_i^* y_i = 0 \tag{19}$$

Support vectors include data on the margin as well as those on the wrong side of the margin contains nonzero λ_i.[17,18,48,49] The decision function for linearly non separable dataset is given in Eq. (20).[17,18,48,49]

$$f(X_T) = sgn(\sum_{i \in S} \lambda_i y_i (X_i X_T) + b^*) \tag{20}$$

Most of the datasets cannot be separated using a simple hyperplane.[17,18,48,49] The input data is represented into a high-dimensional feature space through some nonlinear mapping.[17,18,48,49] In this feature space, the optimal hyperplane is constructed.[17,18,48,49] This type of nonlinear mapping retains nearly all the simplicity of an SVM separating hyperplane.[17,18,48,49] Thus the Lagrangian function for nonlinear SVM changes to Eq. (21) subject to the constraint given in Eqs. (18) and (19).[17,18,48,49]

$$L(W, b, \zeta, \lambda, \mu) = \sum_{i=1}^{N} \lambda_i - \sum_{i,j=1}^{N} \lambda_i \lambda_j y_i y_j K(X_i, X_j) \qquad (21)$$

Where, $K(X_i, X_j) = \phi(X_i)^T \phi(X_j)$ is the kernel function.[17,18,48,49] In nonlinear mapping, kernel functions are sufficient enough to train SVM without explicitly using the mapping function.[17,18,27,48,49] The kernel defines a similarity measure between two data points and thus allows one to incorporate prior knowledge of the problem domain.[17,18,27,48,49] Thus solving the dual of Eq. (21) and applying KT conditions optimal value of W and b for optimal hyperplane is obtained as in Eqs. (22) and (23).[17,18,27,48,49]

$$W^* = \sum_{i=1}^{N} \lambda_i^* y_i \phi(X_i) \qquad (22)$$

$$b^* = y_j - \phi(X_j^T) W^* \qquad (23)$$

Initially, training and testing data are cross validated as in case of linear SVM.[17,18,27,48,49] Thereafter parameters of kernel functions are obtained using grid search method. Thereafter, SVM is trained linearly in higher dimensional feature space. The decision function for hyperplane is given by Eq. (24).[17,18,27,48,49]

$$f(X_T) = sgn(\sum_{i \in S} \lambda_i y_i K(X_i, X_T) + b^*) \qquad (24)$$

The concept of SVM and its optimization using QP solver is clear till now. Hence now optimization of SVM as a fuser in multimodal framework will be explained. Unlike traditional SVM that is used as a classifier a slight modification is done in order to make it work as a fuser.[17,18,27] It integrates score based on the proximity of the test pattern to the separating surface.[17,18,27] Initially SVM is trained in the same way as the nonlinear SVM case. After training is carried out the decision function in Eq. (24) is modified to get the fused score $S_T \epsilon R$ as given in Eq. (25).[17,18,27,48,49]

$$S_T = \sum_{i \in S} \lambda_i y_i K(X_i, X_T) + b^* \qquad (25)$$

The decision threshold parameter to obtain ROC curves for comparison of different fusion methods.[17,18,27] This modification allows the comparison of different fusion methods in terms of their ROC plots along with their performance curves.[17,18,27] Generally three kernel functions namely polynomial, RBF and MLP kernel are used.[17,18,27] But the research review shows that SVM using RBF kernel provides better recognition performance as compared to other methods.[18,27] RBF is expressed as Eq. (26).[17,18,27,48,49]

$$K(X_i, X_T) = exp\left(\frac{-\|X_i - X_T\|^2}{2\sigma^2}\right) \tag{26}$$

SVM trained using RBF kernel requires only one parameter i.e. sigma σ to be taken into consideration.[17,18,27,48,49] The optimum value of sigma σ i.e. standard deviation for the radial basis function and the parameter C which is penalty parameter is chosen through cross validation process using grid search method given in Refs. 17, 18, 27 and 48–50. In n-fold cross-validation, the training set is first divided into n subsets.[17,18,27,48–50] In the ith (i = 1,2, . . . , n) iteration, the ith set (validation set) is used to estimate the performance of the classifier trained on the remaining (n-1) sets (training set).[17,18,27,48–50] The performance is generally evaluated by cost, e.g. classification accuracy or mean square error (MSE).[17,18,27,48–50] The final performance of classifier is evaluated by mean costs of n folds subsets.[17,18,27,48–50] In grid-search process, pairs of (C, σ) are inputted and the one with the best cross-validation accuracy is picked up.[17,18,27,48–50] In most of the research literature, a grid-search on (C, σ) using 10-fold cross-validation is carried out as the cross-validation procedure prevents the overfitting problem as well as the computational time to find optimal parameters by grid-search is less.[17,18,27,48–50] Furthermore, the grid-search can be easily parallelized because each (C, σ) is independent.[17,18,27,48–50]

4. Summary of Metaheuristic Optimization Algorithm at Score Level Fusion

This chapter intended to review critically about which Metaheuristics will be better suited in application to development of Multibiometric framework. As the security level of Multibiometric system varies from time to time, an arrangement is needed for adaptation of these systems to this varying security levels. Thus the metaheuristic optimization of fusion parameters is required which minimizes the cost function defined by the error rates of the system. As can be observed from wide research survey, score fusion is the widely used level of fusion due to its ease of availability and higher recognition performance. Thus this chapter reviewed about the techniques used for fusion at score level i.e. mainly LWSR and SVM. Metaheuristics that were used to optimize fusion weights of LWSR were GA, PSO, GA-PSO and ACO while the Quadrature Optimization Programming (QOP) solver was used to optimize cost function of SVM.

Table 1. Comparative Analysis of Metaheuristic Algorithms in Score Level Fusion

Author	Database and Modalities fused	Metaheuristic algorithm	EER
Cherifi Dalia et al.[36]	Face+Fingerprint (NIST BSSR1)	PSO	0.62
		GA	0.44
		Hybrid GA-PSO	0.43
	Face+Speech (BANCA)	PSO	1.07
		GA	1.07
		Hybrid GA-PSO	0.91
Giot et al.[35]	Face+Fingerprint (NIST BSSR1)	GA	0.48
	Face+Speech (BANCA)		1.05
Amjoy Kumar et al.[34]	Left Index+ Right Index (PolyU knuckle Database)	ACO	0.006
	Left Middle+Right Middle (PolyU knuckle Database)		0.012
	Left Middle+Left Index (PolyU knuckle Database)		0.004
	Right Middle + Right Index (PolyU knuckle Database)		0.006
Sandip Kumar et al.[39]	Face+Left Iris (CASIA Iris and Face locally generated)	ACO	0.025
	Face+Right Iris (CASIA Iris and Face locally generated)		0.024
	Left Iris + Right Iris (CASIA Iris and Face locally generated)		0.023
	Face+Left Iris+Right Iris (CASIA Iris and Face locally generated)		0.025

With regards to comparing the optimization methods with each other there are several focuses to consider. Comparison of Metaheuristics is shown in Table 1 for LWSR score level fusion. It is clear from the results compared in Table 1 that GA, PSO, and GA-PSO generally result in similar best accuracies but they differ in terms of time utilization. GA covers large search space and hence requires high computational time while PSO because of its fast operation requires less time. But on the other hand PSO gets quickly stuck to local minima. Hybrid GA-PSO gains the advantage of both algorithms by including the benefit of fast searching of PSO and covering of large search space by GA. But as hybrid GA-PSO computes cost function thrice in a given iteration, it consumes more time but it reaches to global optima in less number of iterations. Thus hybrid GA-PSO practically is faster as compared to GA and PSO alone. Despite of the fact that GA and PSO generally provide good results, they would once in a while get stuck in local minima after large number of iterations of these programs. On the contrary hybrid GA-PSO almost always converge to a global point in the shortest time. As can be observed from results of author,[36] GA takes almost 105 sec, PSO takes 220 sec and GA-PSO takes about 315 sec to run 50 iterations but on the contrary GA takes 76 sec, PSO takes 38 sec and GA-PSO takes about 12 sec to reach global minima.

As can be observed PSO needs sigmoid function for the discrete values of velocity and position updates while ACO uses the pheromone based probabilities to decide the direction of the search on the optimal path. Further, the local and the global updates of these probabilities from the previous search paths are incorporated for the optimal selection of fusion parameters in the system. The different security levels are quantified in terms of CFA and ACO is employed for optimally select the fusion parameters corresponding to each of them. If the results of Refs. 29 and 34 are observed, it can be seen that as the value of CFA increases its error rates starts decreasing.

In case of fusion using SVM, QP solver is used to optimize the cost function and hence obtain weights, bias and Lagrange multiplier values of the training patterns. If the cross validation is performed well and optimized values of C and for RBF kernel are obtained then SVM fusion gives almost 93% of genuine acceptance at FAR of 0.005 in Ref. 17 and genuine acceptance of 90% at the same FAR in Ref. 27.

Thus it seems that classifier based fusion gives better result as compared to rule based methods. But classifier based methods cannot make the multibiometric system adaptable with the varying requirements of the security level. In this scenario, rule based methods can be used whose fusion parameters can be optimized using Metaheuristic Algorithms based upon the security requirement of the system. Hence Metaheuristic Algorithms are applied to the score level fusion of Multimodal framework in order to make this system adaptable to the varying security levels of the system.

Acknowledgment

This review is being published under the minor research project titled "New era of securing Manifold biometrics: Research on forensic and cyber security Augmentation", supported by the grant from GUJCOST, Government of India. (Grant No. GUJCOST/MRP/2015-16/2640).

References

1. M. O. Oloyede and G. P. Hancke, *Unimodal and Multimodal Biometric Sensing Systems: A Review,* IEEE Access, vol. 4, pp. 7532-7555, IEEE, 2016.
2. A.K.Jain, A.Ross and S.Prabhakar, *An Introduction to biometric recognition,* IEEE Transaction on Circuits and Systems for Video Technology, Special Issue on Image and Video-Based Biometrics, vol.14, no. 1,pp. 4-20, IEEE, 2004.
3. Anil Jain, Arun A. Ross and Karthik Nandakumar, *Handbook of Multibiometrics,* edition 1, Springer US, 2006.
4. Anil K. Jain, Karthik Nandakumar and Arun Ross, *50 Years of Biometric Research: Accomplishments, Challenges, and Opportunities,* Pattern Recognition Letters, vol. 69, pp. 1-40, Elsevier, 2016.
5. Pradeep K. Atrey, M. Anwar Hossain, Abdulmotaleb EI Saddik and Mohan S. Kankanhalli, *Multimodal Fusion for multimedia analysis: A survey,* Multimedia systems, vol. 16, no. 6, pp. 345-379, Springer, 2010.
6. Arun Ross and Anil Jain, *Information fusion in biometrics,* Pattern Recognition Letters, vol. 24, no. 13, pp. 2115-2125, Elsevier, 2003.
7. R. W. Frischholz and U. Dieckmann, *BiolD: a multimodal biometric identification system,* IEEE Computer Society, vol. 33, no. 2, pp. 64-68, IEEE, 2000.
8. F. R. Al-Osaimi, M. Bennamoun and A. Mian, *Spatially Optimized Data-Level Fusion of Texture and Shape for Face Recognition,* IEEE Transactions on Image Processing, vol. 21, no. 2, pp. 859-872, IEEE, 2012.
9. Yongsheng Gao and M. Maggs, *Feature-level fusion in personal identification,* Computer Society Conference on Computer Vision and Pattern Recognition (CVPR'05), pp. 468-473, IEEE, 2005.
10. X. Yang and D. Sun, *Feature-level fusion of palmprint and palm vein base on canonical correlation analysis,* 13th International Conference on Signal Processing (ICSP), pp. 1353-1356, IEEE, 2016.
11. Y. H. Dandawate and S. R. Inamdar, *Fusion based Multimodal Biometric cryptosystem,* International Conference on Industrial Instrumentation and Control (ICIC), pp. 1484-1489, IEEE, 2015.
12. S. C. Joshi and A. Kumar, *Design of multimodal biometrics system based on feature level fusion,* International Conference on Intelligent Systems and Control (ISCO), pp. 1-6, IEEE, 2016.

13. A. Rattani, D. R. Kisku, M. Bicego and M. Tistarelli, *Feature Level Fusion of Face and Fingerprint Biometrics*, International Conference on Biometrics: Theory, Applications, and Systems, pp. 1-6, IEEE, 2007.

14. K. Nandakumar, Y. Chen, S. C. Dass and A. Jain, *Likelihood Ratio-Based Biometric Score Fusion*, IEEE Transactions on Pattern Analysis and Machine Intelligence, vol. 30, no. 2, pp. 342-347, IEEE, 2008.

15. G. Gao, L. Zhang, J. Yang, L. Zhang and D. Zhang, *Reconstruction Based Finger-Knuckle-Print Verification With Score Level Adaptive Binary Fusion*, Transactions on Image Processing, vol. 22, no. 12, pp. 5050-5062, IEEE, 2013.

16. Aarohi Vora, Chirag Paunwala and Mita Paunwala, *Improved weight assignment approach for multimodal fusion*, International Conference on Circuits, Systems, Communication and Information Technology Applications (CSCITA), pp. 70-74, IEEE, 2014.

17. Aarohi Vora, Chirag Paunwala and Mita Paunwala, *Nonlinear SVM Fusion of Multimodal Biometric System*, International Conference on Communication and Computing track (ICCC), pp. 204-210, Elsevier, 2014.

18. Aarohi Vora, Chirag Paunwala and Mita Paunwala, *Statistical analysis of various kernel parameters on SVM based multimodal fusion*, Annual IEEE India Conference (INDICON), pp. 1-5, IEEE, 2014.

19. C. Li, J. Hu, J. Pieprzyk and W. Susilo, *A New Biocryptosystem-Oriented Security Analysis Framework and Implementation of Multibiometric Cryptosystems Based on Decision Level Fusion*, Transactions on Information Forensics and Security, vol. 10, no. 6, pp. 1193-1206, IEEE, 2015.

20. Sudhamani M. J., M. K. Venkatesha and Radhika K. R., *Fusion at decision level in multimodal biometric authentication system using Iris and Finger Vein with novel feature extraction*, Annual IEEE India Conference (INDICON), pp. 1-6, IEEE, 2014.

21. M. Hanmandlu, J. Grover and V. Madasu, *Decision Level Fusion Using t-Norms*, International Conference on Digital Image Computing: Techniques and Applications, pp. 33-38, IEEE, 2010.

22. S. Acharya, A. Fridman, P. Brennan, P. Juola, R. Greenstadt and M. Kam, *User authentication through biometric sensors and decision fusion*, 47th Annual Conference on Information Sciences and Systems (CISS), pp. 1-6, IEEE, 2013.

23. A. Kumar, M. Hanmandlu, H. Sanghvi and H. M. Gupta, *Decision level biometric fusion using Ant Colony Optimization*, International Conference on Image Processing, pp. 3105-3108, IEEE, 2010.

24. Ilhem Boussad, Julien Lepagnot and Patrick Siarry, *A survey on optimization metaheuristics*, Information Sciences, vol. 237, 2013, pp. 82-117, 2013.

25. Ning Xiong, Daniel Molina, Miguel Leon Ortiz and Francisco Herrera, *A Walk into Metaheuristics for Engineering Optimization: Principles, Methods and Recent Trends*, International Journal of Computational Intelligence Systems, vol. 8, no. 4, pp. 606-636, Taylor and Francis, 2015.

26. Tronci, Roberto, Giorgio Giacinto, and Fabio Roli, *Dynamic score selection for fusion of multiple biometric matchers*, 14th International Conference on Image Analysis and Processing (ICIAP), pp. 15-22, IEEE, 2007.

27. Wang, F. and Han, *Multimodal biometric authentication based on score level fusion using support vector machine*, Journal Opto-Electronics Review, vol. 17, no. 1, pp 5964, Springer, 2009.

28. Veeramachaneni, Kalyan, Lisa Ann Osadciw, and Pramod K. Varshney. *An adaptive multimodal biometric management algorithm*, IEEE Transactions on Systems, Man, and Cybernetics, Part C (Applications and Reviews), vol. 35, no. 3, pp. 344-356, IEEE, 2005.

29. N. Srinivas, K. Veeramachaneni and L. A. Osadciw, *Fusing correlated data from multiple classifiers for improved biometric verification*, 12th International Conference on Information Fusion, pp. 1504-1511, IEEE, 2009.

30. R. Raghavendra, Bernadette Dorizzi, Ashok Rao and G. Hemantha Kumar, *Particle swarm optimization based fusion of near infrared and visible images for improved face verification*, Pattern Recognition, vol. 44, no. 2, pp. 401-411, Elsevier, 2011.

31. Mezai, Lamia and Fella Hachouf, *Score-level fusion of face and voice using particle swarm optimization and belief functions*, IEEE Transactions on Human-Machine Systems, vol. 45, no. 6, pp. 761-772, IEEE, 2015.

32. A. Kumar, M. Hanmandlu, H. Sanghvi and H. M. Gupta, *Decision level biometric fusion using Ant Colony Optimization*, International Conference on Image Processing (ICIP), pp. 3105-3108, IEEE, 2010.

33. Kumar Amioy, and Ajay Kumar, *Adaptive management of multimodal biometrics fusion using ant colony optimization*, Information Fusion, vol. 32, pp. 49-63, Elsevier, 2016.

34. Amioy Kumar, Madasu Hanmandlu and H.M. Gupta, *Ant colony optimization based fuzzy binary decision tree for bimodal hand knuckle verification system*, Expert Systems with Applications, vol. 40, no. 2, pp. 439-449, Elsevier, 2013.

35. R. Giot, M. El-Abed and C. Rosenberger, *Fast learning for multibiometrics systems using genetic algorithms*, International Conference on High Performance Computing and Simulation, pp. 266-273, IEEE, 2010.

36. Cherifi Dalila and Hafnaoui Imane and Nait-Ali Amine, *Multimodal Score-Level Fusion Using Hybrid GA-PSO for Multibiometric System*, vol. 39, no. 2, pp. 209-216, Informatica, 2015.

37. Aniesha Alford, Caresse Hansen and Caresse Hansen, *GEC-based multibiometric fusion*, IEEE Congress on Evolutionary Computation (CEC), pp. 2071-2074, IEEE, 2011.

38. Dorigo, Marco and Luca Maria Gambardella, *Ant colony system: a cooperative learning approach to the traveling salesman problem*, IEEE Transactions on evolutionary computation, vol. 1, no. 1, pp. 53-66, IEEE, 1997.

39. Sandip Kumar, Singh Modak and Vijay Kumar Jha, *Enhancing Performance of Multibiometric System using Ant Colony Optimization based on Score Level Fusion*, International Journal of Computer Applications vol. 170, no. 6, pp. 33-38, 2017.

40. Anil Jain, Karthik Nandakumar and Arun Ross, *Score Normalization in Multimodal Biometric System*, Journal of Pattern Recognition, vol. 38, pp. 2270-2285, Elsevier, 2005.

41. Mingxing He, Shi-Jinn Horng, Pingzhi Fan, Ray-Shine Run, Rong-Jian Chen, Jui-Lin Lai, Muhammad Khurram Khan and Kevin Octavius Sentosa, *Performance evaluation of score level fusion in multimodal biometric systems*, Pattern Recognition, vol. 43, no. 5, pp. 1789-1800, Elsevier, 2010.

42. Madasu Hanmandlu, Jyotsana Grover, Ankit Gureja and H.M. Gupta, *Score level fusion of multimodal biometrics using triangular norms*, Pattern recognition letters, vol. 32, no. 14, pp. 1843-1850, Elsevier, 2011.

43. A. Kumar, V. Kanhangad and D. Zhang, *A New Framework for Adaptive Multimodal Biometrics Management*, IEEE Transactions on Information Forensics and Security, vol. 5, no. 1, pp. 92-102, IEEE, 2010.

44. James Kennedy, Russell Eberhart and Shi Y.H., *Swarm Intelligence*, Morgan Kaufmann Publishers, 2001.

45. J. H. Holland, *Adaptation in natural and artificial systems: an introductory analysis with applications to biology, control, and artificial intelligence*, Michigan Press, 1975.

46. R. Giot and C. Rosenberger, *Genetic programming for multibiometrics*, Expert Systems with Applications, vol. 39, no. 2, pp. 18371847, Elsevier, 2012.

47. Corinna Cortes and Vladimir Vapnik, *Support vector networks*, Machine Learning, vol. 20, no. 3, pp. 273297, Springer, 1995.

48. Sergios Theodoridis, Konstantinos and Koutroumbas, *Pattern Recognition*, Second Edition, Academic Press, Elsevier, 2003.

49. Christopher Bishop, *Pattern Recognition and Machine Learning*, 1st edition, Springer-Verlag, 2006.

50. Yongsheng Ding, Xinping Song and Yueming Zen, *Forecasting financial condition of Chinese listed companies based on support vector machine*, Expert Systems with Applications, vol. 34, no. 4, pp. 3081-3089, Elsevier, 2008.

Chapter 4

A Novel Membrane Computing Inspired Jaya Algorithm Based Automatic Generation Control of Multi-area Interconnected Power System

Tapan Prakash*,† and Vinay Pratap Singh‡

Department of Electrical Engineering,
National Institute of Technology, Raipur 492010, India
† tapanprakashsinha@gmail.com
‡ vinaymnnit@gmail.com

Automatic generation control (AGC) is a tool which helps the system to maintain the frequency within its targeted value by balancing the active power in the system. In this work, a novel membrane computing inspired Jaya algorithm (MCJA) is proposed and applied to tune the controller parameters for AGC of multi-area interconnected system. The proposed algorithm is designed by incorporating the concept of membrane computing in basic Jaya algorithm (JA). A two area non-reheat thermal plant is considered for AGC in this study. The objective function is designed by considering the integral errors of the frequency deviations of two areas and tie-line power deviation. Several cases with different sets of disturbances are considered to test the efficacy of the proposed controller. To validate the superior performance of the proposed controller, it is compared to particle swarm optimization (PSO), Jaya algorithm (JA) and membrane computing (MC) based controllers. Time-domain simulations are presented to depict better performance of the proposed controller. Additionally, a comparative statistical analysis is carried out to examine the robust and stable nature of the proposed algorithm.

Keywords: Automatic generation control; frequency deviations; integral errors; interconnected systems; Jaya algorithm; membrane computing; PID controller; tie-line power deviations; time-domain simulations.

1. Introduction

Presently, the power demand is increasing at an unprecedented rate. This increasing demand is resulting in restructuring of power system networks.[1]

---

*Corresponding Author.

The existing power system networks are either getting interconnected or are subjected to expansion of generation capacity. With the increasing demand, the load patterns are highly unpredictable and fluctuating. These fluctuations pose direct impact on the system frequency of the interconnected systems.[2] The system frequency observes a deviation with any load change. For networks which are interconnected, any load change in one area affects the frequencies of each area and the tie-line power. However, the deviations in frequencies and tie-line power should remain within targeted values.[3] To achieve this target, the active power balance in the system is required to be maintained. Automatic generation control (AGC) is a tool which takes care of active power balance in the system and thus, maintains the frequencies and the tie-line power deviations within their targeted values.[4]

The prime component of AGC is the controller which responds to increasing deviations in the frequencies and tie-line power and issues control signal so as to maintain them within acceptable range. Most preferred controllers found in the literature are the conventional controllers like proportional-integral (PI),[5] integral-derivative (ID)[6] and proportional-integral-derivative (PID) controllers.[6] The controller design is an important aspect of an AGC. As power system is vulnerable to different contingent scenarios, an efficient controller is always required. For effective performance of the controllers, their parameters should be properly tuned. In literature, traditional technique i.e. Zeigler-Nichols tuning method is reported to tune the parameters of the controllers.[7] However, this technique is not computationally efficient and ceases to yield optimal controller parameters with increase in size of plant.

The problems associated with the traditional techniques were eliminated with the introduction of meta-heuristics methods as controller tuning methods. In last two decades, several optimization techniques are reported to solve the problem of AGC. Some of the relevant techniques reported in the literature are particle swarm optimization (PSO),[8] non-dominated sorting genetic algorithm (GA),[9] artificial bee colony (ABC),[10] bat algorithm (BA),[11] bacteria foraging optimization algorithm (BFOA),[12] gray wolf optimization (GWO),[13] differential evolution (DE),[14] firefly algorithm (FA),[15] teacher-learner based optimization (TLBO),[16] Jaya algorithm (JA)[17] etc. Several meta-heuristics techniques mentioned above are efficient in solving AGC than the conventional techniques. However, some of them still suffers with low convergence rate, some of them are having weak exploration and exploitation capability, and some are prone to local minima trappings. This instigated the development of hybrid algorithms. A hybrid algorithm is the fusion of different algorithms to form an optimization framework where the advantages of each algorithms are exploited. Thus, the resultant hybrid algorithm works more efficiently in solving any optimization problem. Since, AGC is a complex problem, so it is required to develop a new hybrid meta-heuristic algorithm which can perform better than other algorithms. This motivated the present work to develop a new hybrid algorithm.

The tuning process of controller parameters affects the performance of AGC and so its importance can never be ignored. Another important aspect which dominantly affects the performance of AGC is the design of the objective function for tuning process. The reports in the literature suggest various design objectives such as settling times of frequency and tie-line power deviations, dominant eigenvalues and damping ratios, integral errors etc. Out of these, the most reported design objectives are the integral errors. Several integral errors such as integral absolute error (IAE), integral square error (ISE), integral time-squared error (ITSE) and integral time absolute error (ITAE) are reported in the literature. However, for an AGC ITAE is found to be more efficient among the integral errors.[17] These integral errors consider frequency deviations of different areas and the tie-line power deviations. The minimization of these errors is considered as the design objective.

In this work, a novel membrane computing inspired Jaya algorithm (MCJA) is proposed which is based on incorporation of concept of membrane computing (MC) in basic JA. JA is structurally simple and efficient algorithm. The performance of JA is enhanced with inclusion of concept of MC. The proposed algorithm is applied to tune controller parameters for AGC of two-area interconnected non-reheat thermal power plants. The design objective considered for the problem is minimization of ITAE of deviations in frequencies and tie-line power. A conventional PID controller with derivative filter is used for AGC. The proposed controller for AGC is tested under different scenarios of load disturbances. The test results of proposed controller are compared to PSO, JA and MC based controllers. Time-domain simulations are presented to further visualize the performance of the proposed controller for AGC. Additionally, a comparative analysis of statistical measures is performed to establish the robust and stable nature of the proposed algorithm.

Section 2 of the chapter describes the system model used in the study. The problem formulation for AGC is discussed in Section 3. The proposed algorithm i.e. MCJA is discussed in Section 4. Next section presents the simulation tests and results of AGC problem. The chapter is concluded in Section 6 with future research directions.

2. System Modelling and Description

The model used in this work is a two-area interconnected non-reheat thermal power plants.[12] Figure 1 presents the transfer function model of the studied system. In Fig. 1, controller 1 and controller 2 represent the conventional PID controller with a derivative filter. Area control errors (ACEs) represented as ACE_1 and ACE_2, respectively are inputs to the controllers. The control signals issued by these controllers are u_1 and u_2. R_1 and R_2 are speed regulation constants of the governors. B_1 and B_2 are frequency bias factors. The governor time constants are represented as T_{G1} and T_{G2}. The changes in governor positions are represented by ΔP_{G1} and ΔP_{G2}. T_{T1} and T_{T2} represents the turbine time constants. Turbine output powers are denoted as ΔP_{T1} and ΔP_{T2}. K_{PS1} and K_{PS2} denote gains of power system of area 1 and area 2, respectively. The time constants of the power systems for two-area are represented by T_{PS1} and T_{PS2}. The change in tie-line power is denoted by ΔP_{tie}. T_{12} and a_{12} are synchronization constant and a constant, respectively. The step load disturbances in the two area are represented by ΔP_{D1} and ΔP_{D2}. Δf_1 and Δf_2 are the frequency deviations of the two areas in Hz.

A conventional PID controller with a derivative filter is utilized in this work. Figure 2 shows the block diagram representation of controller structure. The input to the controller is ACE and the output control signal is u. K_p, K_i and K_d are gains of the controller. N is the derivative gain term for the filter and is used to reduce the effect of the noise in the signal. The transfer function of the controller is expressed as

$$TF_{\text{controller}} = K_p + K_i \left(\frac{1}{s}\right) + K_d \left(\frac{N}{1 + \left(\frac{N}{s}\right)}\right) \tag{1}$$

The input to the controller ACE for the two areas are given as

$$ACE_1 = B_1 \Delta f_1 + \Delta P_{\text{tie}} \tag{2}$$

$$ACE_2 = B_2 \Delta f_2 + a_{12} \Delta P_{\text{tie}} \tag{3}$$

3. Problem Formulation

Controller design techniques are very much dependent on the formulation of desired objective function. Thus, it is an utmost requirement of better

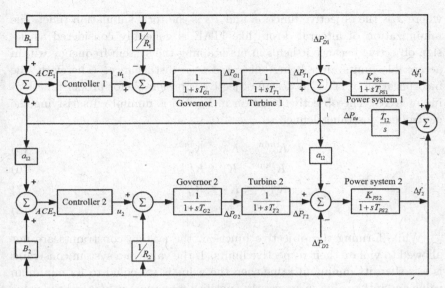

Fig. 1.   Transfer function model of two-area interconnected non-reheat thermal power plants

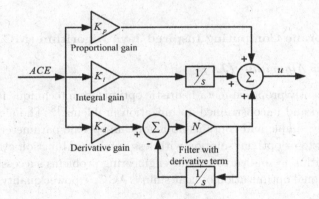

Fig. 2.   Controller structure

designed objective function so as to obtain desired controller performance. In this work, ITAE of the deviations in frequencies of the two areas with tie-line power deviations is considered for minimization. The designed objective function is expressed as

$$J = \int_{t=0}^{Ts} (|\Delta f_1| + |\Delta f_2| + |\Delta P_{\text{tie}}|) \cdot t \cdot dt \qquad (4)$$

where J is the objective function and Ts is the total simulation time. The minimization of integral errors like ITAE is generally considered as design objective because it helps in maintaining the system frequency within acceptable limits after being subjected to a disturbance. Therefore, the incorporation of ITAE as design objective is preferable for proper functioning of AGC. The objective function in Eq. (4) is minimized satisfying the controller constraint defined as

$$K_p^{\min} \leq K_p \leq K_p^{\max} \tag{5}$$
$$K_i^{\min} \leq K_i \leq K_i^{\max} \tag{6}$$
$$K_d^{\min} \leq K_d \leq K_d^{\max} \tag{7}$$
$$N^{\min} \leq N \leq N^{\max} \tag{8}$$

While forming the objective function, the system constraints are not allowed to violate their respective limits. If the value of a system constraint is less than its minimum value then the value is set equal to its minimum value and if the value surpasses the specified maximum value then the value is set equal to its maximum value. In such a way, the system constraints are taken care of.

4. Membrane Computing Inspired Jaya Algorithm (MCJA)

4.1. *Jaya Algorithm (JA)*

JA is a recently proposed meta-heuristic optimization technique for solving constrained and unconstrained optimization problems.[18] The algorithm is structurally simple and contains no algorithm-specific parameters. It produces near to or optimal solution with less number of function evaluations. This algorithm is applied to various engineering problems successfully such as dimensional optimization of heat sink,[19] AGC,[17] power quality improvement,[20] etc.

Let the population size be $(m \times n)$ where, m represents the number of candidate solutions and n represents the number of decision variables. The best and worst solutions for the qth decision variable at any rth iteration are denoted as $x_{q,\text{best}}^r$ and $x_{q,\text{worst}}^r$, respectively. Let $x_{p,q}^r$ is the current value for qth decision variable of pth solution at rth iteration and $X_{p,q}^r$ is the updated value of $x_{p,q}^r$. $x_{p,q}^r$ is updated according to

$$X_{p,q}^r = x_{p,q}^r + \alpha_{1,q}^r(x_{q,\text{best}}^r - |x_{p,q}^r|) - \alpha_{2,q}^r(x_{q,\text{worst}}^r - |x_{p,q}^r|) \tag{9}$$

where, $p = 1, 2, \ldots, m$ and $q = 1, 2, \ldots, n$. $\alpha_{1,q}^r$ and $\alpha_{2,q}^r$ are two evenly distributed random numbers in between 0 and 1 for qth decision variable at rth iteration, respectively. The better solutions are selected on the basis of fitness function evaluation. The process continues until any termination criterion is met.

4.2. *Proposed Algorithm*

The inspiration for the proposed algorithm is the architecture of membrane computing (MC) introduced by Peng *et al.*[21] Figure 3 represents the typical structure of membrane computing proposed by Peng *et al.*[21] In this structure, there are three layers: global store membrane; evolution membrane; and local store membrane. The principle task of these membranes is to evolve objects present within the system. The aim of local membrane is to store best object out of respective evolution membrane. The global membrane stores the best object obtained so far from the system.

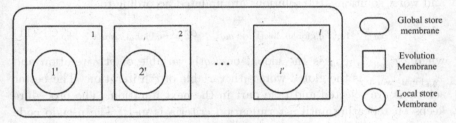

Fig. 3.   Structure of membrane computing proposed by Peng *et al.*[21]

The structure of proposed MCJA is depicted in Fig. 4. In this proposed structure, the initial solution sets are divided into several local classes (analogous to local store membrane of MC) of equal sizes. The evolution membrane is considered to be local best and worst solutions which are evolving out of local classes. The global best and worst solutions found out of whole population after combining whole local classes are considered to be the global store membrane.

Let us consider that initial population is divided in l local classes and from each class one best and one worst solution are evolved out. There will be l best and worst solutions regarded as local best and worst solutions, respectively. For each solution set within a local class, the update phase at the rth iteration is carried out using

$$X_{p,q}^r = x_{p,q}^r + \alpha_{1,q}^r(x_{q,\text{local-best}}^r - |x_{p,q}^r|) - \alpha_{2,q}^r(x_{q,\text{local-worst}}^r - |x_{p,q}^r|) \quad (10)$$

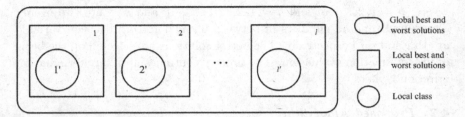

Fig. 4.   Structure of MCJA

where, $x^r_{q,\text{local−best}}$ is the local best qth variable of rth iteration and $x_{q,\text{local−worst}}$ is the local worst qth variable of rth iteration representing each local class. After updating all solutions within a class, the better solutions are selected on the basis of fitness function evaluation. Using the concept of MC, global best and worst solutions are identified after combining population of all classes. Succeeding to the identification of global best and worst solutions, the solutions are updated according to

$$X^r_{p,q} = x^r_{p,q} + \alpha^r_{1,q}(x^r_{q,\text{global−best}} − |x^r_{p,q}|) − \alpha^r_{2,q}(x^r_{q,\text{global−worst}} − |x^r_{p,q}|) \quad (11)$$

where, $x^r_{q,\text{global−best}}$ is the global best qth variable of rth iteration and $x^r_{q,\text{global−worst}}$ is the global worst qth variable of rth iteration. The better solutions are selected and take part in the next iteration. The procedure keeps on repeating until a termination criteria is met. The pseudo code is presented in Table 1 to list the steps of the proposed algorithm. The flowchart of MCJA is illustrated in Fig. 5.

4.3. Implementation of MCJA to AGC Problem

The desired objective function defined in Eq. (4) is minimized using proposed algorithm satisfying the constraint associated with the controller parameters. The boundary conditions of the controller parameters used in this work are defined as follows

$$0 \leq K_p \leq 2 \tag{12}$$
$$0 \leq K_i \leq 2 \tag{13}$$
$$0 \leq K_d \leq 2 \tag{14}$$
$$100 \leq N \leq 500 \tag{15}$$

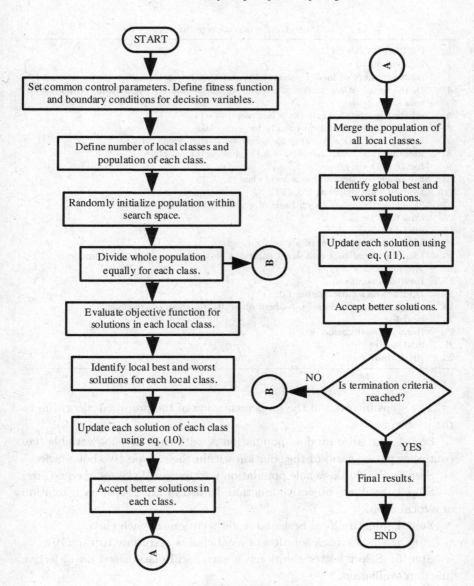

Fig. 5.   Flowchart of MCJA

Table 1.   Pseudo code of MCJA.

1.	INITIALIZATION
2.	Generation=0
3.	Define number of local classes and population for each class.
4.	Define termination criteria and generate initial random population within search space.
5.	**while** (termination criteria is not met)
6.	Divide whole population equally for each class.
7.	Evaluate objective function for solutions in each local class.
8.	Identify local best and worst solutions of each local class.
9.	**for** (each local class)
10.	**for** (each solution within a local class)
11.	Update solution using Eq. (10)
12.	Select better solutions on basis of objective function evaluations.
13.	**end for**
14.	**end for**
15.	Merge the population of all local classes.
16.	Identify global best and worst solutions on the basis of objective function evaluations.
17.	**for** (each solution)
18.	Update the solution using Eq. (11)
19.	Select better solutions on basis of objective function evaluations.
20.	**end for**
21.	Iteration = Iteration + 1
22.	**end while**
23.	Print results.

The steps involved in the implementation of the proposed algorithm to the problem are

Step 1: Initialize random population X with each decision variable (i.e. controller parameters) of the solution within their respective boundaries.

Step 2: Divide the whole population into five local classes of equal size.

Step 3: Evaluate objective function defined in Eq. (4) for each solution of a local class.

Step 4: Identify local best and worst solutions of each class.

Step 5: Update each solution of local classes according to Eq. (10).

Step 6: Select better solutions in each local class based on objective function evaluation.

Step 7: Combine all solutions of each classes to form X.

Step 8: Evaluate objective function to identify global best and worst solution.

Step 9: Update each solution according to Eq. (11).

Step 10: Select better solutions and form X.

Step 11: Stop if termination criteria is met or otherwise go to step 2.

5. Simulation Results and Discussion

All simulations for the studied system are carried out on MATLAB platform on Intel i5processor of 2.4 GHz. A two-area interconnected power system with two non-reheat thermal power plants is considered for the simulation study. Nominal parameters of the studied system are listed in Appendix A.[12] The controller design in this study is carried out with MCJA. To demonstrate the efficacy and superiority of MCJA, the proposed controller is compared with PSO, MC and Jaya based controllers. During all simulations, the initial size of the population is taken as 20 and 100 iterations. Four different test cases with varied set of disturbances (i.e. step load perturbations) are chosen for time domain simulations. A statistical tabulation is presented to establish the robust and stable nature of the proposed algorithm. Following test cases are considered:

Case 1: A load change with step increase of 5 % at $t = 0\,s$ in Area 1 with no change in Area 2.

Case 2: A load change with step increase of 5 % at $t = 0\,s$ in Area 2 with no change in Area 1.

Case 3: A load change with step increase of 5 % at $t = 0\,s$ in Area 1 with a load change with step decrease of 5 % at $t = 0\,s$ in Area 2.

Case 4: A load change with step increase of 5 % at $t = 0\,s$ in Area 2 with a load change with step decrease of 5 % at $t = 0\,s$ in Area 1.

Tables 2–5 presents the simulation results of the studied system. In all tables, the tuned numerical values of the controller parameters (i.e. K_p, K_i, K_d, and N) along with settling times of frequencies and tie-line power deviations and minimum ITAE are presented. In Table 2, the results of the system studied under Case 1 are listed. From the table, it is found the minimum value of ITAE (i.e. objective function) equal to 0.0658 is obtained from MCJA based controller. Additionally, the settling times of frequency deviations of area 1 and area 2 with tie-line power deviations are found to be 2.7553, 2,7630, and 3.1617, respectively with the proposed controller which is minimum in comparison to others. The time-domain simulations of frequency and tie-line power deviations are shown in Figs. 6–8. The figure illustration agrees with the tabulated results of Table 2. The figures suggest that a step load increase in area 1 is affecting the frequency of area 2 and tie-line power which is as per our expectations. From the figures, it can easily be identified that proposed controller is the best performer among all in terms of settling times. From the above discussion, it can be concluded that MCJA based controllers are outperforming others in solving AGC problem.

Table 2. Simulation results for case 1.

		PSO	JA	MC	MCJA
Controller parameters	K_p	1.3877	1.5534	2.0000	0.9901
	K_i	2.0000	1.9983	2.0000	2.0000
	K_d	0.7360	0.4162	1.2569	0.4024
	N	341.3211	487.6998	251.8398	346.7899
Settling times (s)	Δf_1	3.4443	2.7870	2.8628	2.7553
	Δf_2	3.4742	3.8118	4.5669	2.7630
	ΔP_{tie}	3.7014	4.3617	4.6870	3.1617
ITAE		0.0781	0.0724	0.0952	0.0658

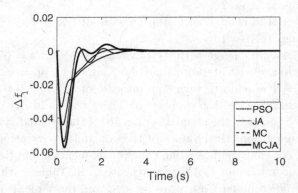

Fig. 6. Frequency deviation of area 1 for case 1

Table 3 presents the simulation results for case 2 in which a step load change of 5 % is provided to area 2 with no load change in area 1. The minimum value of objective function (i.e. ITAE) equal to 0.0664 is obtained for the proposed controller. The settling times of frequency deviations and tie-line power are less with the proposed controller. It is evident from the table that the performance of proposed controller is better in comparison

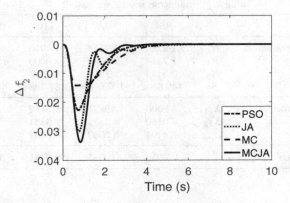

Fig. 7.   Frequency deviation of area 2 for case 1

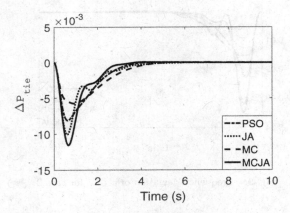

Fig. 8.   Tie-line power deviation for case 1

to other controllers. The time-domain simulations regarding this case are shown in Figs. 9–11. Figure 9 shows the deviation in frequency of area 1. From the figure, it can be observed that the settling time of the deviation in the frequency is minimum for the system with the proposed controller. The deviation in frequency of area 2 is illustrated in Fig. 10. A closer look of the figure reveals that the the system with proposed controller is performing better than others. The tie-line power deviation is shown in Fig. 11. From this figure, the superior performance of the proposed controller is ascertained.

Table 3.   Simulation results for case 2.

		PSO	JA	MC	MCJA
Controller parameters	K_p	1.2286	1.7113	1.4910	1.0806
	K_i	1.7548	2.0000	2.0000	2.0000
	K_d	0.3423	1.1969	0.7007	0.4333
	N	446.6502	100.0000	187.5981	451.6377
Settling times (s)	Δf_1	3.9000	3.9827	3.7772	2.8695
	Δf_2	3.0180	4.3857	1.9831	2.7045
	ΔP_{tie}	4.4194	5.5562	3.9462	3.3404
ITAE		0.0859	0.0983	0.0751	0.0664

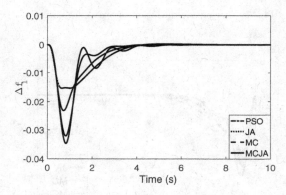

Fig. 9.   Frequency deviation of area 1 for case 2

The simulation results for case 3 in which there is a step load increase of 5 % in area 1 with a step load decrease of 5 % in area 2 are listed in Table 4. The tuned controller parameters for all controllers are presented in this table. It can be observed easily that the minimum value of ITAE equal to 0.1270 is obtained for the system with the proposed controller. Further observation of the table reveals that the settling times of frequency deviations and tie-line power are less for the system with the proposed controller. It can be concluded from the table that the performance of proposed controller is better in comparison to other controllers. The time-domain simulations for this case are shown in Figs. 12–14. From the figure, it is easily seen that the system with proposed controller is settling fast to steady-state in comparison to others when there are step load changes

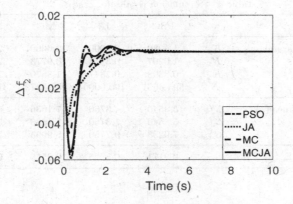

Fig. 10.   Frequency deviation of area 2 for case 2

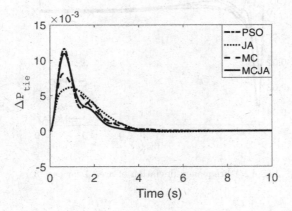

Fig. 11.   Tie-line power deviation for case 2

in both areas. This implies that the performance of proposed controller is better than others.

Table 5 depicts the simulation result for case 4 in which a step load increase of 5 % is provided to area 2 with a step load decrease of 5 % in area 1. From the table, it can be seen that the minimum value of objective function (i.e. ITAE) equal to 0.1452 is obtained for the system with the proposed controller. The settling times of frequency deviations and tie-line power deviation are lesser with the proposed controller in comparison to others. As a result, it can be ascertained from the table that the performance of the system with the proposed controller is better than others. The

Table 4. Simulation results for case 3.

		PSO	JA	MC	MCJA
Controller parameters	K_p	1.4080	2.0000	2.0000	2.0000
	K_i	1.0207	0.3473	0.9773	2.0000
	K_d	0.8398	0.7347	1.8870	2.0000
	N	394.3661	100.0000	282.3579	312.8771
Settling times (s)	Δf_1	5.8540	1.3760	7.1636	5.1969
	Δf_2	5.8540	1.3760	7.1636	5.1969
	ΔP_{tie}	7.9238	9.7150	8.9995	7.8208
ITAE		0.2171	0.5225	0.2556	0.1270

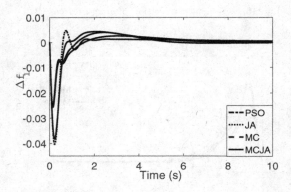

Fig. 12. Frequency deviation of area 1 for case 3

time-domain simulations for this case are shown in Figs. 15–17. Figure 15 shows the deviation in frequency of area 1. From the figure, it can be observed that the deviation settles down to zero quickly for the system with proposed controller. The deviation in frequency of area 2 is illustrated in Fig. 16. This figure reveals that the deviation is settling down fast for the system with proposed controller. The tie-line power deviation is shown in Fig. 17. From this figure, the better performance of the proposed controller is ascertained.

To test the robustness and stability of the proposed algorithm (i.e. MCJA), a comparative statistical analysis is carried out and the obtained results are listed in Table 6. A total of 20 independent runs are taken into account. The statistical measures included in this analysis are best, worst,

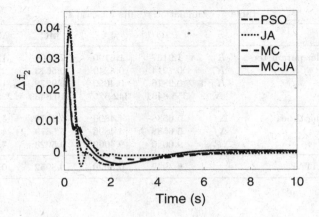

Fig. 13.   Frequency deviation of area 2 for case 3

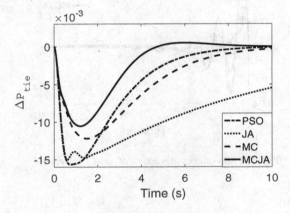

Fig. 14.   Tie-line power deviation for case 3

mean and standard deviation. The analysis is done for all four cases stated above. From the table, it can be observed that the minimum value for best, worst, mean and standard deviation for all the cases are obtained for the proposed method. This suggests that the proposed algorithm is stable and robust in nature. The probable reason behind such performance of the algorithm is the improvement in exploration capability of JA due to inclusion of MC concept.

Table 5.   Simulation results for case 4.

		PSO	JA	MC	MCJA
Controller parameters	K_p	1.9167	1.6190	2.0000	1.4410
	K_i	0.7214	0.4249	0.5613	2.0000
	K_d	0.2876	0.4050	0.9272	1.6688
	N	355.8431	342.6257	210.8439	223.2438
Settling times (s)	Δf_1	5.6538	4.4896	5.5679	4.6818
	Δf_2	5.6538	4.4896	5.5679	4.6818
	ΔP_{tie}	9.0040	9.4999	9.5923	7.3477
ITAE		0.3947	0.5090	0.3952	0.1452

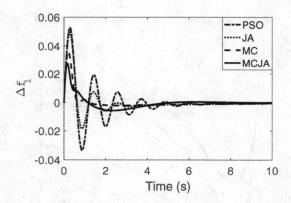

Fig. 15.   Frequency deviation of area 1 for case 4

6. Conclusion

In this study, a novel MCJA algorithm is proposed which is based on the inspiration and incorporation of MC into existing JA. The proposed algorithm
is implemented to design controller for AGC of two-area interconnected
non-reheat thermal power plants. The design objective considered for tuning the controller parameters is the integral error of frequency and tie-line
power deviations. To test the efficacy of the proposed controller, diverse
cases of step load changes are considered for both areas. The superiority of
the proposed controller is established by comparing it with PSO, JA and
MC based controllers. The simulations results ascertain the superior performance of the proposed controller. Further, time-domain simulations are

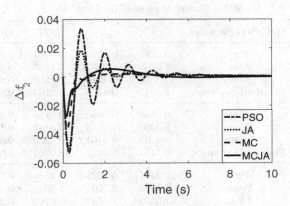

Fig. 16.   Frequency deviation of area 2 for case 4

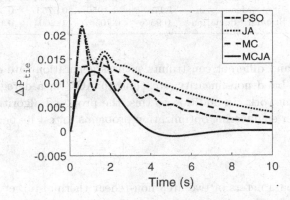

Fig. 17.   Tie-line power deviation for case 4

carried out for all cases illustrating the deviations in the frequencies of two areas and tie-line power. These simulations affirm the better performance of the controller designed with MCJA. Additionally, to test the robustness and the stability of the proposed algorithm, a comparative statistical analysis is conducted. The obtained results reveal the robust and stable performance of proposed algorithm. The present work is limited to the application of MCJA for controller design for AGC of simple two-area thermal system. However, the system can be more complex practically. The scope for future work lies in exploring the performance of controllers tuned by MCJA when applied to a more complex AGC problem including several

Table 6. Comparative statistical analysis.

Cases	Statistical measures	PSO	JA	MC	MCJA
Case 1	Best	0.0781	0.0724	0.0952	0.0658
	Worst	6.0399	1.5217	0.1495	0.0963
	Mean	1.3057	0.3645	0.1208	0.0799
	Standard deviation	2.3343	0.4424	0.0163	0.0096
Case 2	Best	0.0859	0.0983	0.0751	0.0664
	Worst	2.3290	1.0403	0.3482	0.1088
	Mean	0.4762	0.3304	0.1390	0.0894
	Standard deviation	0.7154	0.3117	0.0765	0.0132
Case 3	Best	0.2171	0.5225	0.2556	0.1270
	Worst	2.7905	2.7905	1.3604	0.4762
	Mean	1.0222	1.0784	0.6762	0.2726
	Standard deviation	0.9703	0.7511	0.29567	0.1283
Case 4	Best	0.3947	0.5090	0.39527	0.1452
	Worst	3.4068	2.7644	1.3514	0.4922
	Mean	1.17677	1.1950	0.67537	0.3206
	Standard deviation	0.9578	0.70567	0.2604	0.1192

types of fuels and different constraints such as generation rate constraint, governor dead-band non-linearity, etc. and to AGC in a deregulated environment framework. In addition to this, the proposed algorithm can be applied to other engineering optimization problems to test its performance.

Appendix A

The nominal parameters of two-area non-reheat thermal power plants are given below.[12] Power rating of the system $P_R = 2000$ MW; Nominal loading $P_L = 1000$ MW; System frequency $f_1 = f_2 = 60$ Hz; $B_1 = B_2 = 0.045$ p.u. MW/Hz; $R_1 = R_2 = 2.4$ Hz/p.u.; $T_{G1} = T_{G2} = 0.08$ s; $T_{T1} = T_{T2} = 0.3$ s; $K_{PS1} = K_{PS2} = 120$ Hz/p.u. MW; $T_{PS1} = T_{PS2} = 20$ s; $T_{12} = 0.545$ p.u.; $a_{12} = 1$.

References

1. K. Bhattacharya, M. Bollen, and J. E. Daalder, *Operation of restructured power systems.* Springer Science & Business Media (2012).
2. P. Kundur, N. J. Balu, and M. G. Lauby, *Power system stability and control.* vol. 7, McGraw-hill New York (1994).
3. K. Padiyar, *Power system dynamics.* BS publications (2008).

4. D. P. Kothari, I. Nagrath, *et al.*, *Modern power system analysis*. Tata McGraw-Hill Education (2011).
5. C. Chang and W. Fu, Area load frequency control using fuzzy gain scheduling of pi controllers, *Electric Power Systems Research*. **42**(2), 145–152 (1997).
6. L. C. Saikia, J. Nanda, and S. Mishra, Performance comparison of several classical controllers in agc for multi-area interconnected thermal system, *International Journal of Electrical Power & Energy Systems*. **33**(3), 394–401 (2011).
7. K. J. Åström, C. C. Hang, P. Persson, and W. K. Ho, Towards intelligent pid control, *Automatica*. **28**(1), 1–9 (1992).
8. S. P. Ghoshal, Optimizations of pid gains by particle swarm optimizations in fuzzy based automatic generation control, *Electric Power Systems Research*. **72**(3), 203–212 (2004).
9. S. Panda and N. K. Yegireddy, Automatic generation control of multi-area power system using multi-objective non-dominated sorting genetic algorithm-ii, *International Journal of Electrical Power & Energy Systems*. **53**, 54–63 (2013).
10. H. Gozde, M. C. Taplamacioglu, and I. Kocaarslan, Comparative performance analysis of artificial bee colony algorithm in automatic generation control for interconnected reheat thermal power system, *International Journal of Electrical Power & Energy Systems*. **42**(1), 167–178 (2012).
11. P. Dash, L. C. Saikia, and N. Sinha, Automatic generation control of multi area thermal system using bat algorithm optimized pd–pid cascade controller, *International Journal of Electrical Power & Energy Systems*. **68**, 364–372 (2015).
12. E. Ali and S. Abd-Elazim, Bacteria foraging optimization algorithm based load frequency controller for interconnected power system, *International Journal of Electrical Power & Energy Systems*. **33**(3), 633–638 (2011).
13. E. Gupta and A. Saxena, Grey wolf optimizer based regulator design for automatic generation control of interconnected power system, *Cogent Engineering*. **3**(1), 1151612 (2016).
14. B. Mohanty, S. Panda, and P. Hota, Differential evolution algorithm based automatic generation control for interconnected power systems with nonlinearity, *Alexandria Engineering Journal*. **53**(3), 537–552 (2014).
15. K. Naidu, H. Mokhlis, A. Bakar, V. Terzija, and H. Illias, Application of firefly algorithm with online wavelet filter in automatic generation control of an interconnected reheat thermal power system, *International Journal of Electrical Power & Energy Systems*. **63**, 401–413 (2014).
16. B. K. Sahu, S. Pati, P. K. Mohanty, and S. Panda, Teaching–learning based optimization algorithm based fuzzy-pid controller for automatic generation control of multi-area power system, *Applied Soft Computing*. **27**, 240–249 (2015).
17. S. P. Singh, T. Prakash, V. Singh, and M. G. Babu, Analytic hierarchy process based automatic generation control of multi-area interconnected power system using jaya algorithm, *Engineering Applications of Artificial Intelligence*. **60**, 35–44 (2017).

18. R. Rao, Jaya: A simple and new optimization algorithm for solving constrained and unconstrained optimization problems, *International Journal of Industrial Engineering Computations.* **7**(1), 19–34 (2016).
19. R. Rao, K. More, J. Taler, and P. Ocłoń, Dimensional optimization of a micro-channel heat sink using jaya algorithm, *Applied Thermal Engineering.* **103**, 572–582 (2016).
20. S. Mishra and P. K. Ray, Power quality improvement using photovoltaic fed dstatcom based on jaya optimization, *IEEE Transactions on Sustainable Energy.* **7**(4), 1672–1680 (2016).
21. H. Peng, J. Wang, and M. J. Pérez-Jiménez, Optimal multi-level thresholding with membrane computing, *Digital Signal Processing.* **37**, 53–64 (2015).

Part II
Applications

Chapter 5

Edge Detection in Underwater Image Based on Human Psycho Visual Phenomenon and Mean Particle Swarm Optimization (MeanPSO)

Hiranmoy Roy and Soumyadip Dhar*,†

RCC Institute of Information Technology
† *rccsoumya@gmail.com*

Underwater image edge detection becomes a difficult and challenging task due to various perturbations present in the water. Edge detection is a primary and important task in image processing. Here, a novel edge detection method on underwater image is proposed. The method is based on human psycho visual (HVS) phenomenon. The HVS imitates the original visual technique of a human being and it is used to divide each sub band into the Weber, De-Vries Rose and Saturation regions. The proposed methodology automatically detects the De-Vries Rose, Weber and Saturation regions in an image as an HVS system, based on image statistics using Mean particle swarm optimization algorithm (MeanPSO). This is followed by adaptive thresholding in each region to detect the edge points. The experimental results of the proposed method is found to be superior than that of the conventional and state-of-the-art method for edge detection on standard data set.

Keywords: Underwater Image, Edge Detection, HVS, MeanPSO.

1. Introduction

Underwater images are the images of the objects captured in the deep water. Recent years have witnessed rapidly increasing interest in underwater object detection and segmentation. It is motivated by the importance of different underwater applications such as underwater maintenance, repair of undersea structures, marine sciences, and homeland security, etc.

The propagation property of light in the water medium is different than that of the air medium.[1] The properties of the water medium cause degradation of the underwater captured images which is different from normal

---

*Corresponding Author.

113

images taken in the air. Deep inside the water, the amount of light starts decreasing and the image gets darker. Water is approximately 800 times denser than air, and this density absorbs light quickly. With the increase of depth the amount of light is reduced and it causes the colors to decrease. The decrease in color depends on the wavelengths of the light. The blue color has the shortest wavelength and it travels the longest in the water. On the other hand other colors are suppressed due to their long wavelengths. Due to the presence of more blue color, the underwater images are mainly dominated by blue color. The image under the water are basically attributed by their poor visibility due to dense water. The scenes deep in the water is not clear rather hazy. The visibility is limited by light attenuation, which is caused due to the scattering and absorption. In clear water the attenuation is less and light can travel up to twenty meters, on the other hand, in turbid water, it can travel up to only five meters or less. The absorption causes the reduction of light energy and scattering results the change of paths of light. These two perturbations affect the image capturing process at underwater. The underwater image is blurred due to the forward scattering, which is generated by randomly deviated light from an object to the camera. Again, another backward scattering is caused due to the reflection of light inside the water before reaching camera. The backward scattering is one of the main reasons behind the poor contrast of the underwater images. Due to the presence of dissolved organic materials and small floating objects in the water, the same two perturbations, absorption and scattering also occurs. In the deep water, the problem of floating particles increases the rate of attenuation of light. The limitation can be overcome by increasing artificial lighting inside the deep water. But, the artificial lighting also suffers from the same scattering and absorption. In addition, the artificial light gives a non uniform illumination of the scene. Due to this varying illumination, a halo effect of the image is produced. All the reasons mentioned above make the underwater image edge detection a challenging task.

An edge in an image is a noteworthy change in the local gray level intensity of an image. Edge detection is the basic tool for feature detection and extraction from an image by identifying the change in the pixel values in an image. The detection of meaningful and perfect edges determines the success of many computer vision and image processing tasks. Not only in low level image processing field, but also in the case of color images where multi dimensional color information is present, detection of edge is a difficult problem. Color images provide more accurate and multi dimensional object information in the images. This information becomes highly useful for further operations than the grayscale images. The extraction of complete and perfect edge becomes very much difficult due to the following unavoidable reasons such as noise, distortion, segmentation errors, intensity variations, overlap (large number of clutter objects), and occlusion. The output image with inadequate edge information is not pleasing visually. In literature, quite a lot number of methods are available to detect edges from images. No doubt that the edge detection task is difficult one, but at the same time a very important one because, the edge information of an image can be used for higher-level image processing tasks and object recognition systems. Due to varying reasons such as distortion, intensity variation and overlapped boundaries, it becomes very much difficult to detect the proper edges of the image. So detecting the proper edges in an image is a challenging task.

In this book chapter, we proposed a new edge detection method using HVS. In the proposed method the three regions (De Vries-Rose, Weber, and Saturated) in an underwater image are estimated to adopt the efficiency of a human visual system and locate the edge points correctly. The threshold values for the edge detection are chosen adaptively in the three regions. But the exact estimation of the three regions demands the correct determination of the parameters involved with the regions. The parameters depend on the image statistics. The incorrect estimation of the parameters may lead to poor performance. Thus, an efficient evolutionary algorithm is required to find the parameters and the regions correctly and adaptively. Hence in the proposed method an evolutionary algorithm is required to choose the parameters correctly. Nowadays, apart from genetic algorithm,[2] several evolutionary algorithms have been used by researchers for optimization[3-6] as already discussed. In the proposed method we use the bio-inspired MeanPSO algorithm[7] to find the parameters optimally, regulated by the nature of a particular image. Thus, the novelty of the method is that it identifies the HVS regions adaptively depending on the image statistics and detects the edge points automatically. The performance of the proposed method is compared with some popular methods of edge detection and a state-of-the-art method and found to be superior to the other methods. The block diagram of the proposed method is shown in Figure 1.

The novelty of this chapter are as follows:

(1) In this chapter we propose a novel method for edge detection of an underwater image by HVS. The HVS imitates the human visual system and detect the edge points in the presence of different perturbations in an underwater image.

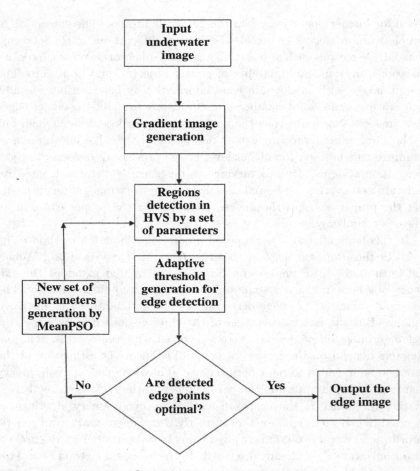

Fig. 1. Block diagram of the proposed method

(2) The De Vries-Rose, Weber, and Saturation regions in an underwater
    image are detected optimally by a bio-inspired MeanPSO. The proposed
    method is found to be efficient than that of the conventional methods.

2. Related Works

The methods for edge detection are quite rich in the literature. But it
is very difficult to propose a unified method which can detect edges in all
types of images. The popular conventional edge detection includes the edge
detection by Canny, Robert, Sobel and Prewitt.[8] Canny's method finds the

edges using the local maxima of the gradient. The gradient is calculated by the derivative of a Gaussian filter. Robert and Sobel's technique use 2D spatial gradient technique on an image and give more emphasis on the high frequency zones of the image, which represent the edges. The Prewitt Edge filter is used to detect edges based applying a vertical and horizontal filter in sequence. Those filters are convolved with the image to get the final result.

Apart from the conventional gradient based techniques described above, some researchers used different techniques for detecting the edges. Hu *et al.*[9] integrated multi-scale and orientation of structural elements and fuzzy properties of the image to detect the edges using mathematical morphology. Junna *et al.*[10] and Kaur *et al.*[11] proposed the edge detection technique based on mathematical morphology. A bilateral filtering technique for edge detection was proposed by Seelamantula *et al.*[12] and wavelet based approach for edge detection was adopted by An.[13] He *et al.*[14] used k-means algorithm for underwater edge detection. They used dark channel prior method as preprocessing steps before edge segmentation. The edge classification is done by Fatan *et al.*[15] for underwater cable detection by texture information . In the literature the recent papers are also found to be using the gradient based edge detection techniques.[16–18] Some of the proposed methods,[19–22] used neural network or membrane computing to detect the edges in an image. Uncertainty handing to detect the edges in an image also proposed by some researchers. They used powerful type-2 fuzzy systems to detect edges in an image,[16,23] by combing with the Sobel edge detector.

All the methods described above did not consider the property of the human visual system (HVS)[24] to detect the edges in an underwater image. As a result, the performances of the methods are still below the expectation. Kundu *et al.*[25] detected the edge points in an image by identifying the De Vries- Rose, Weber and saturated regions in HVS. Dhar *et al.*[26] used the HVS for detecting edges in non-destructive testing images.

In the literature, several methods were proposed to detect the edges in an image, though the methods for edge detection in an underwater image are limited. Since, an underwater image is subjected to different perturbations, it is logical and convenient to use the human visual model to detect the edges. The human visual system is one of most powerful edge detection system. But the proper identifications of the three regions in HVS are not fully adaptive and depends on human intervention. This is the major motivation for the current investigation for the best solution to detect the edges in an underwater image using HVS.

Though the human visual system (HVS) based method[25] improves the performance of edge detection, proper identifications of the regions automatically is very difficult. Moreover, the statistics of the underwater image changes due to different perturbations. Thus, to identify those regions properly as well as adaptively depending on the image in hand, we need some meta-heuristic techniques.

Glover[27] introduced the term meta-heuristic. The meaning of the Greek word meta is upper or beyond level and the meaning of the word heuristics is to find or to discover. For many complex problems, meta-heuristics play an important role as a technique of problem solving. It is a kind of algorithm, which does not consider all possible states of the problem. It only considers the feasible solutions and then select the global optimal one by overcoming the local optimal solutions. The nature-inspired algorithms are also called as meta-heuristics,[27–30] e.g., Genetic Algorithm (GA), Tabu Search (TS), Scatter Search (SS), Particle Swarm Optimization (PSO), Differential Evolution, Firefly algorithm (DEF), Ant Colony Optimization (ACO), Simulated Annealing (SA), and Bee Algorithm (BA).[27] All meta-heuristic algorithms consists of two important components, exploitation and exploration.[27,29] In exploitation, the algorithm aims to make different solutions to discover globally the search space, whereas in exploration the algorithm concentrates the search locally considering that the chance of getting a better solution is high in the region. The rate of convergence is guaranteed by selecting the best solutions through a good balance between exploitation and exploration. Meta-heuristic algorithms are mainly a kind of nature inspired algorithm and it can be easily applied either on a set of populations or a single solution to find the near optimal solution. Evolutionary computation is a biologically inspired evolution algorithm for global optimization, and it is considered as a subfield of artificial intelligence and soft computing for those interested in studying these algorithms. Technically, they belong to a family of problem solvers with a meta-heuristic characteristics. Evolutionary algorithms mainly involve biologically inspired techniques such as mutation, recombination, reproduction, natural selection and survival of the fittest.

In the 1970s, Holland[31] invented Genetic Algorithm. The progress of meta-heuristic algorithms attained its peak in between 1980 to 1990. In 1983, Kirkpatrick *et al.*[32] pioneered the first major step by developing Simulated Annealing, which was inspired by the metal annealing process.

Glover[30] introduced Tabu Search meta-heuristic algorithm by incorporating memory with search technique. In Tabu Search, the moves in the search are stored in a Tabu list. In future moves only new solutions are considered. A new field of machine learning has been opened from a book on Genetic Programming (GP), published by Koza.[33] In 1995, a new meta-heuristic method called PSO was introduced by Kennedy and Eberhart.[34] In 2004, an optimization technique for Internet hosting centers called Honey-Bee algorithm (BA) was introduced by Nakrani and Tovey.[35] In 2008, a Bio-Geography based optimization Algorithm (BGA) was proposed by Simon.[36] Again in 2008, a popular Firefly algorithm (FA) based on the flashing behaviour of fireflies was proposed by Yang.[37,38] In the next year 2009, an efficient Cuckoo Search algorithm (CS) was developed by Yang and Deb.[39,40] The output results of the FA and CS algorithms demonstrate that their searching process is efficient than all other meta-heuristic algorithms for various real time applications. Besides, in 2010, an interesting Bat algorithm (Bat), which is based on the echolocation behavior of bats, was proposed by Yang.[41]

Almost all the evolutionary algorithms are either similar to GA or PSO. From literature, it has been seen that PSO gives better results than GA in solving different optimization problems. In literature, there are many available modified varieties of PSO. The different categories of PSO algorithms are as follows:

- In this category, mainly the modifications based on new coefficients are considered. These modifications are done in terms of velocity and position of the search. The original PSO provides very poor local search capability.[42] An inertia weight based new concept was proposed for efficient control of the exploitation and exploration. In 1998, the first time the modification of the particle swarm optimization algorithm using an inertia weight called MeanPSO was reported in the literature.[43] Clerc and Kennedy[44] introduced a constriction factor, χ, to improve the ability of PSO algorithm through constrain and control velocities. Shi and Eberhart[43] showed that an improvement in global optimum selection is achieved by initializing the value of w to 0.9 and then linearly decreasing it to 0.4. Again, Eberhart and Shi[45] found that the performance of PSO can be improved significantly by combining the value of χ with constraints on Vmax. If we check the two versions, which are mentioned above, the speed of the constriction factor version of PSO is higher in convergence than that of the inertia weight version which decreases linearly. One problem with constriction factor version of PSO is that it probably get stuck locally in multi modal functions.

- This second category is mainly concentrated on the information regarding social sharing. Suganthan[46] proposed one variable neighborhood methodology. In this methodology, at first a neighborhood is considered for each particle, but in the next generations they included all the neighborhood particles. On the other hand, the Van Neumann neighborhood topology based PSO was introduced by Kennedy and Mendes.[47] They concluded that this method gives the better performance. A dynamically adjusted neighborhoods is proposed by Mohais et al.[48] In this method, the initial population was generated by the directed structures of the topology. Then, the edge structures were randomly moved from one source to another in the next generations. A novel utilization of the neighboring higher fitness particle was proposed by Peram et al.[49] Liang et al.[50] proposed a new method, where different particles have different learning strategies for each dimension. A frequent message passing between the modified PSO and FDR-PSO concurrently was simulated by Baskar and Suganthan.[51] The selection of fitness values was measured by fitness-distance ratio (FDR), which shows the improvement ratio of fitness over the respective distance. Van den Bergh and Engelbrecht[52] divided the decision vector into several sub vectors and then put them to the respective swarms. A simple modification of the velocity update equation using passive congregation was introduced by He et al.[53] To define the neighborhood structure, a dynamic hierarchy was proposed by Janson and Middendorf.[54]
- The third category is mainly a kind of hybridization with other EAs. At first, the selection operator of GA was combined with PSO.[55] PSO was extended by using genetic programming in.[56] Lovbjerg et al.[57] mixed the breeding concept and a subpopulation of GA with PSO. Differential evolution operator was merged into PSO in.[58] Inspired by the pheromone trails of ant colony optimization Hendtlass[59] extended the memory of the particles. A further step ahead, Krink and Lovbjerg[60] combined three different heuristic techniques such as PSO, GAs and hill climbing. In some papers,[61–63] the authors attempted a mutation based PSO.
- In the fourth category, the main concern was given to increase the diversity mechanism by preventing the convergence to local minima. Silva et al.[64] proposed a novel predator-pray model to maintain the diversity in the population. Lovbjerg and Krink[65] proposed a criticality based

self-organization. A predefined extension interval, for all the particles, is used to re-initialize the velocities by Zhang *et al.*[66] Krink *et al.*[60] suggested a set of collision strategies to avoid crowding of the swarm. To measure the diversity of the population, Riget and Vesterstrem[67] introduced two different phases: attractive phase and repulsive phase alternation. The modification of the velocity update equation is given in Refs. 47,51. In Refs. 68–70, a set of good review on PSO is available.

The organization of the paper is as follows: In Section 3, the edge detection using HVS, and the limitations of HVS in edge detection are explained in detail. Section 4 explains the PSO and mean-PSO algorithms. In Section 5, the proposed methodology is explained in detail. Experimental results of computational experiments, and performance measure are discussed in the Section 6. Finally, the conclusions on the chapter are derived in Section 7.

3. Edge Detection and Thresholding using HVS

For edge detection in an image different gradient operators are used.[71] These operators give detectable response at the edge points. Let X_{mn} be gray level value of $\{m, n\}$ th pixel of an image X of dimension $M \times N$. The edge intensity is represented by the gradient x'_{mn} and it is given by

$$x'_{mn} = (|G_1| + |G_2|)/2 \tag{1}$$

where G_1 and G_2 are the gradients along the row and column of the image respectively. The gradients can be ordinary gradient, Robert's gradient, Prewitt's gradient and Sobel's gradient. The ordinary gradients are given by

$$G_1 = x_{m,n} - x_{m,n+1}$$
$$G_2 = x_{m,n} - x_{m+1,n} \tag{2}$$

The Robert's gradient is given by

$$G_1 = x_{m,n} - x_{m+1,n+1}$$
$$G_2 = x_{m,n+1} - x_{m+1,n} \tag{3}$$

The Prewitt's gradient and Sobel's gradient are given by

$$G_1 = \frac{1}{2+W}[(x_{m+1,n+1} + Wx_{m+1,n} + x_{m+1,n-1})$$
$$- (x_{m-1,n+1} + Wx_{m-1,n} + x_{m-1,n-1})]$$
$$G_2 = \frac{1}{2+W}[(x_{m-1,n+1} + Wx_{m,n+1} + x_{m+1,n+1})$$
$$- (x_{m+1,n-1} + Wx_{m,n-1} + x_{m-1,n-1})] \tag{4}$$

For Prewitt's edge detection $W = 1$ and for Sobel's edge detection $W = 2$ are used. The second difference operator is Laplacian and it is given by

$$G_1 = \frac{1}{2}(x_{m-1,n} - x_{m+1,n} - 2x_{m,n})$$
$$G_2 = \frac{1}{2}(x_{m,n-1} - x_{m,n+1} - 2x_{m,n})$$

(5)

The limitation of simple and Robert's gradient is that they respond not only at the edges but also at isolated points. So, there is a chance of false detection of edges. On the other hand, Laplacian detects corners, line and line ends, prominently though it has a good edge detection capacity. Prewitt's and Sobel's gradient exhibit good response at noisy situation.

After the gradient detection by various operators, as described above the proper threshold value is chosen to find out the true edge pixel from the gradients. The threshold depends local and global statistical property of the image at hand. Thus, the finding out the accurate threshold value is a challenging task. The detection becomes difficult when an image is subject to various perturbations. As a result the edge detection in an underwater image is really a difficult process as the underwater image becomes corrupted by different perturbations which is already described.

To deal with the different perturbations it is natural and convenient that one should use some tool which imitate the human visual system. The human visual system can recognize the edges in an underwater image efficiently. In the next subsection we will discuss the HVS to find out the edges in the image.

3.1. *Human Psychovisual Phenomenon*

In HVS brightness is defined by a psychological effect. The sensation is related to light stimulus. As, the human eye has a powerful ability for adaption, the absolute brightness can not be quantified. It is a psychological sensation about the different gray value of pixels. To measure it quantitatively, contrast is used and it represents the difference between the illuminations of objects. The perception about the grayness of a pixel depends upon the local background. If the ratio between the local background and object remains unchanged, the perceived value remains also unchanged.[71]

The contrast C is the ratio of the difference between the object luminance B_0 and its local surroundings B_s. It is represented as

$$C = \frac{|B_0 - B_s|}{B_s}$$

(6)

The visual threshold $\triangle B_T$ is to be added in its immediate surroundings to make it recognizable by the human eye. That means if that amount of difference is added to local surrounding then the pixel can be deselected. This conception is used to recognize the edge points from the gradients.

The major problem in low intensity level image processing[72] like underwater image edge detection is that

(1) It is very difficult to detect the change between a pixel and its surrounding in a low steady but visible illumination.
(2) Detection of absolute visual threshold, which can distinguish an object and its background in the poor light condition.

In the underwater image edge detection, both the above mentioned problems are present prominently due to light scattering and poor contrast of the underwater image. The two problems also affect the features which are the scale space representation of the image. So it is better to use the adaptive threshold for edge detection by the human visual system.

On HVS the visual information is emphasized at large spatial points of light intensity.[24] The model to imitate the human visual system was proposed by Kundu *et al.*[25] as a human psycho visual phenomenon (HVS). The model was used successfully used for image edge thresholding by the authors.

In human visual system three regions can be found where the absolute visual threshold (the presence and absence of light intensity) varies differently with visual incremental threshold $\triangle B_T$. The three regions are called De Vries-Rose, Weber and Saturation regions. In visual system the visual increment $\triangle B_T$ is unchangeable. With the increase in B, $\triangle B_T$ converges non-linearly to B i.e $\triangle B_T \propto B$.

The characteristics response graph in the three regions is shown in $log\triangle B_T - logB$ plane at Figure 2. From the Figure it can be seen that the slope is $\frac{1}{2}$ in De Vries-Rose region. The Weber region exhibits the slope of 1. The actual case at the high visual intensity region the $\triangle B_T \propto B^2$. This region is called a saturation region.

From the Figure 2 it can be seen that the change in $\triangle B_T$ is slower in De Vries-Rose region than the Weber region. So, the discrimination ability of the De Vries-Rose region is more than that of the Weber region region. The $log\triangle B_T - logB$ curve can be treated as pairwise linear. The equations involving B and $\triangle B_T$ for Weber, De Vries-Rose and Saturation region can be written as

$$log\triangle B_T = logK_1 + logB \qquad (7)$$

$$log\triangle B_T = logK_2 + \frac{1}{2}logB \qquad (8)$$

$$log\triangle B_T = logK_3 + 2logB \qquad (9)$$

Here K_1, K_2 and K_3 are the constants of proportionality.

That means when the difference between the gray value of the pixel and its immediate surrounding B is greater than or equal to $\triangle B_T$, the point will appear above the curve and it is detectable from its surroundings. So, it will appear darker or brighter than its local surroundings. In the next section we will discuss how to find out the threshold value adaptively to find out the edge points using HVS.

3.2. Edge Detection using HVS

The main idea of edge detection is to find an accurate or near accurate threshold value, which may be local, global or dynamic. The value is considered in such a way that, if at a point the spatial difference exceeds the measured threshold, then it can be taken as a valid edge. Therefore, the threshold values for the edge detection should be chosen adaptively depending on the position of the gradient, i.e. whether the gradient is present in De Vries-Rose, Weber or Saturation regions.

Let us divide the background intensity B into the 4 regions after sorting them in ascending order. The $B_{x_1}, B_{x_2}, B_{x_3}$ represents the point of transition from low background intensity to De Vries-Rose, De Vries-Rose to Weber region and Weber region to Saturation region respectively. Kundu and Pal showed that the value of K_1, K_2 and K_3 can be calculated as

$$K_1 = \frac{1}{100}\beta\left(\frac{\triangle B}{B}\right)$$
$$K_2 = K_1\sqrt{B_{x_2}} \qquad (10)$$
$$K_3 = K_1/B_{x_3}$$

where the ratio $\frac{\triangle B}{B}$ remains constant at about $\beta\%$ of its maximum value over a wide range of B value. From the literature, we have found that the value of β is used to be .02. The minimum values of incremental threshold in the three regions can be given by

$$\triangle B_T = K_2\sqrt{B} = \frac{\sqrt{B}}{100}\beta\left(\frac{\triangle B}{B}\right)_{max}\sqrt{B_{x_2}} \qquad (11)$$

when $B_{x_2} \geq B \geq B_{x_1}$

$$\triangle B_T = K_1B = \frac{B}{100}\beta\left(\frac{\triangle B}{B}\right)_{max} \qquad (12)$$

when $B_{x_3} \geq B \geq B_{x_2}$ and

$$\triangle B_T = K_3 B^2 = \frac{B^2}{100} \beta \left(\frac{\triangle B}{B} \right)_{max} \frac{1}{B_{x_3}} \qquad (13)$$

when $B \geq B_{x_3}$.

Here the threshold values for detecting edges at three different regions are given in the Eq 11, Eq 12 and Eq 13. Kundu and Pal[25] showed that for a particular point in an image having intensity B_p if we have

$$\frac{\triangle B}{\sqrt{B}} \geq K_2 \quad \text{when} \quad \alpha'_2 B_1 \geq B \geq \alpha'_1 B_1 \qquad (14)$$

$$\frac{\triangle B}{B} \geq K_1 \quad \text{when} \quad \alpha'_3 B_1 \geq B \geq \alpha'_2 B_1 \qquad (15)$$

$$\frac{\triangle B}{B} \geq K_3 \quad \text{when} \quad B \geq \alpha'_3 B_1 \qquad (16)$$

with $\triangle B = |B_p - B|$ where B_p is the intensity at the point p, B is the background intensity of the point, then and only then it can be considered as a detectable edge point having edge intensity $\triangle B$. The B is calculated for each pixel by taking the weighted average of its 8 neighborhood pixels and B_1 represents the maximum value of B. In the above equations $\alpha'_2 B_1 \geq B \geq \alpha'_1 B_1$, $\alpha'_3 B_1 \geq B \geq \alpha'_2 B_1$ and $B \geq \alpha'_3 B_1$ represent the background intensity in the De-Vries rose, Weber and Saturation region respectively for $0 < \alpha'_1 < \alpha'_2 < \alpha'_3 < 1$.

The background intensity B of an $M \times N$ image at the coordinates m, n denoted by B_{mn} is calculated as

$$B_{mn} = \left\{ \frac{1}{2} \left(\frac{1}{4} \sum_Q x_{ij} + \frac{1}{4\sqrt{2}} \sum_{Q'} x_{kl} + x_{mn} \right) \right\} \bigg/ 2 \qquad (17)$$

where $(i, j) \in Q$ and $(k, l) \in Q'$. Q and Q' are the set of neighboring pixels x_{ij} and x_{jk} which are in the distance 1 and $\sqrt{2}$ distances respectively from x_{mn}.

3.3. *Limitation of HVS for Edge Detection*

Although the edges are detected using adaptive thresholding at the three different regions, accurate demarcations (shown in Figure 2) of the three regions are difficult. This is due to the difficulty in finding the proper combinations of α'_1, α'_2 and α'_3. In the underwater image the statistics of the image are changed due to different perturbations. Due to scattering

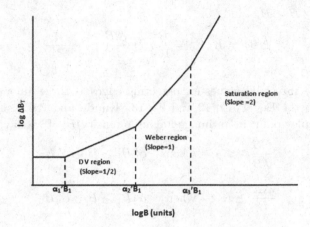

Fig. 2.   The incremental threshold $\triangle B$ vs background intensity B with the demarcation by α_1', α_2' and α_3'

of light and light attenuation the regions are difficult to detect accurately and the regions depend on the image in hand. So, it is obvious that finding the three regions properly is a challenging task. Moreover, it logical to determine the three regions adaptively with the image in hand. To find the parameters adaptively with the underwater image in hand, we use an evolutionary Mean particle swarm optimization(MeanPSO). The algorithm finds the optimal combinations of the parameters based on image statistics to identify the three regions and detects the edge points automatically in the underwater image. For solving the optimization problem Mean PSO is taken as it outperformed the other meta-heuristic methods[7] in terms of accuracy and robustness. In the next section we will discuss about the MeanPSO.

4. Particle Swarm Optimization

Particle swarm optimization (PSO) is an efficient optimization technique. The optimization technique is based on evolution of population. Nowadays, the PSO gained the popularity over other evolutionary techniques like genetic algorithm (GAs). The PSO was proposed by Kennedy and Eberhart[34] in the year 1995 as a stochastic search technique. The advantages of PSO is that it requires less memory. Also, it is very efficient and simple to implement than that of the other evolutionary techniques. The

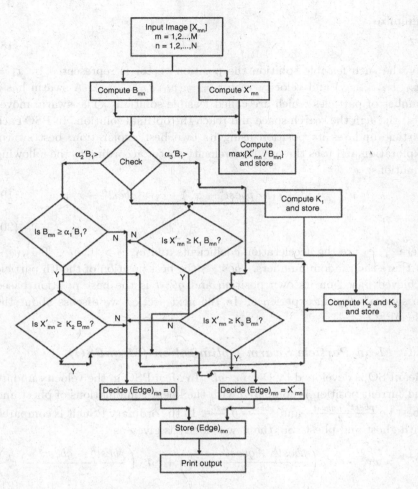

Fig. 3.   Schematic diagram of edge detection by HVS[25]

algorithm is follows the social behaviour of fish schools and bird. Though, PSO is mainly designed for optimization problems which are continuous, but in recent years it has been used to solve various types of problems in science and engineering applications.

The PSO is popular to the science community due its simple implementation. In PSO each particle in a PSO is a possible solution. The position vector and velocity vector represent the coordinates of each particle. In n dimensional optimization problem the objective is to optimize the function, minimize

$$f : R^n \to R \tag{18}$$

For the each feasible solution the position vector is represented by $x_i = (x_{i1}, x_{i2}, ..., x_{in})$ and velocity vector $v_i = (v_{i1}, v_{i2}, ..., v_{in})$. A swarm has a number of particles which are called feasible solutions. The swarm moves (fly) through the search space and reach the optimal solution. In PSO each particle updates its position using its own best exploration, best swarm exploration and uses the previous velocity vector according to the following equations:

$$v_i^{k+1} = v_i^k + c_1 r_1 (pbest_i^k - x_i^k) + c_2 r_2 (gbest^k - x_i^k) \tag{19}$$

$$x_i^{k+1} = x_i^k + v_i^{k+1} \tag{20}$$

Here c_1, c_2 are the acceleration coefficients and $c_1, c_2 > 0$. $r_1 \in [0\ 1], r_2 \in [0\ 1]$ are the random numbers. $pbest_i$ is the best position of the ith particle achieved based on its own position and $gbest$ is the best position based on swarm's overall experience. In the next section we discuss about the MeanPSO.

4.1. *Mean Particle Swarm Optimization (MeanPSO)*

MeanPSO is developed by Deep *et al.*[7] In MeanPSO in the velocity update the current position is compared with the linear combinations of pbest and gbest i.e $\frac{pbest_i^k + gbest^k}{2}$ and $\frac{pbest_i^k - gbest^k}{2}$. In the ordinary PSO it is compared with gbest and pbest. So, the new velocity is given as

$$v_i^{k+1} = wv_i^k + c_1 r_1 \left(\frac{pbest_i^k + gbest^k}{2} - x_i^k \right) + c_2 r_2 \left(\frac{pbest_i^k - gbest^k}{2} - x_i^k \right) \tag{21}$$

In the equation above, the current particles' velocity is the first term and the second term represents particles current position. Here the current position is the mean of the best position (pbest) and global best position (gbest). The third term is used for the attraction of particles current position. w represents an inertia factor. It is used to overcome the premature convergence of PSO.

The algorithm of MeanPSO is shown below:

Algorithm :: MeanPSO:

    for (t=1; t¡=Maximum Iterations; t++)

        for (i=1; i¡=Swarm size; i++)

for (j=1; j¡=Dimension numbers; j++)
    The updating of velocity is done using Eq 21;
    The updating of position is done using Eq 20;
End of j
The fitness of the new position is computed
The previous values of the pbest and the gbest are updated
  End of i
    Stop when termination criteria for gbest is reached;
  End of t
End of MeanPSO.

5. Proposed Methodology

In this section, we will discuss the proposed methodology where the edge detection is considered as constraint optimization problem and used of MeanPSO for edge detection (see Figure 3).

5.1. *Edge Detection as Constraint Optimization Problem*

In the previous section we have seen that it is logical to determine the three regions of HVS in an underwater image adaptively. So, edge detection in an underwater image becomes a constraint optimization problem. For constraint optimization using an evolutionary algorithm we have to find out the α'_1, α'_2 and α'_3. in such a way that the equations are satisfied with the constraint $0 < \alpha'_1 < \alpha'_2 < \alpha'_3 < 1$ and $\sum_{i=1}^{3} \alpha'_i = 1$. Now, we need an evaluation function to quantify the the the total variation V_T is given by

$$V_T = var(eg) + var(neg) \tag{22}$$

where $var(eg)$ and $var(neg)$ represent the variations of the edge pixels and non-edge pixels respectively. Where eg and neg represent the set of edge and non-edge pixels. Here we consider the edge detection in an underwater image as a two class problem. One class is the edge class and other class is the variance class. The correct classification of the classes will result minimum total variations among the member of the classes. So the objective of the MeanPSO is to construct the parameters for the three regions depending on image statistics with least variance. So, the reciprocal of evaluation function is used as the fitness function, where MeanPSO will try to find out the maximum value of it. In the next section we will discuss the PSO.

5.2. *Proposed Algorithm for Edge Detection using MeanPSO*

In the proposed method the underwater image is taken as input image. The parameters for the three regions are detected using the evolutionary MeanPSO. The threshold value for edge points are then detected based on the three regions. For this at first the background intensity B at each pixel position, maximum background intensity B_1 and $\triangle B$ is calculated. Now the following steps are executed. The initial swarm population P = 50 and total number of iterations = 40.

- **Step 1** Input image and, initialize the parameter vectors of $x_i = (\alpha'_1, \alpha'_2, \alpha'_3)$ and initialize c_1, c_2, r_1 and r_2.
- **Step 2** For each x_i divide the image into three different regions using the ranges in the Eq(11), Eq(12) and Eq(13).
- **Step 3** Threshold each pixel for edge point detection Eq(14), Eq(15) and Eq(16) by checking their background intensity for each region
- **Step 4** Merge the edge pixel for making *eg* and non-edge pixel for making *neg* and calculate E.
- **Step 5** Repeat step 6-step 9 until no change in evaluation function or the number of iterations completes.
- **Step 6** Generate new solutions by updating velocity and Position by the Eq 21, 20.
- **Step 7** Compute fitness by $\frac{1}{E}$ for the updated positions.
- **Step 8** Terminate if $|gbest_{k+1} - gbest_k| \leq \varepsilon$ where ε is a small positive quantity.
- **Step 9** Find the best solution v_i corresponding to *gbest*.
- **Step 10** Use the three parameters α'_1, α'_2 and α'_3 to find the De-Verse, Weber and Saturation regions and threshold the underwater image to generate the edge pixels.

6. Experimental Results and Discussion

In this section, we tested the proposed method on the underwater images from Sun dataset.[71] From the dataset we used 100 images for segmentation. The image size varies from 200×200 to 500×500. The uncertainties in underwater images are more due to inherent noise in the image during capturing of the image and during analog to digital conversion. The initial population was taken as 300 and the algorithm ran for 100 iterations. The inertia weight w was taken as 0.7 and the coefficient of accelerations for the

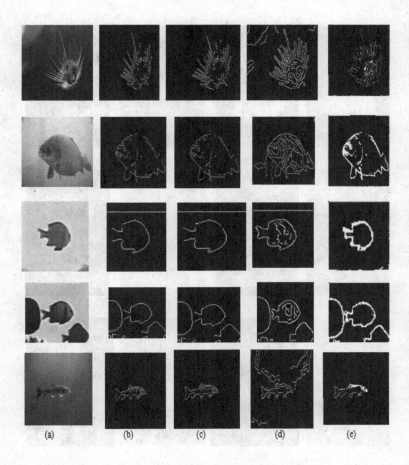

Fig. 4. Qualitative performances (a) Original test image (b) edge detection by He (c) edge detection by Ann (d) edge detection by Canny (e) edge detection by proposed method

MeanPSO were taken as $c1 = c2 = 2$. The proposed method was compared with four methods Canny, Soblel, He[14] and Ann.[13] The quantitative performance of the proposed segmentation method and all the methods compared here are measured using widely used for quantitative performance measure we used the figure of merit of Pratt (IMP) by Abdou and Pratt.[73] The IMP measures the contour similarity. It is defined as

$$IMP = \frac{1}{max(N_I, N_B)} \sum_{1}^{N_B} \frac{1}{1 + \nu \times d_i^2} \tag{23}$$

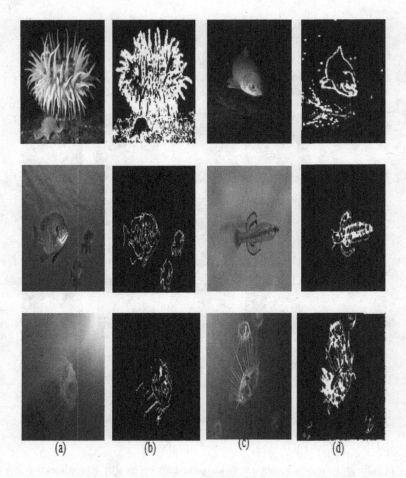

Fig. 5.   Additional results by the proposed method (a) Original underwater test images
(b) Edge detection by the proposed method (c) Another set of test images (d)Edge
detection by the proposed method

Table 1.   Quantitative performance of the results in Figure 4

Performance	Canny	He	Ann	Proposed
IMP	0.7123	0.7912	0.8013	0.8232

Where N_I and N_B and are the edge points in the test image and its corresponding ground truth. d_i represents the distance between corresponding edge pixel's of resultant and ground truth images. ν is an calibration

constant and here the applied value is $\nu = 1/9$. Abdou and Pratt[73] measured the optimal value. The value of IMP varies from [0 1] where 1 represents the optimal truth i.e. the result coincides with ground truth.

In the proposed method the edge points were detected based on the De Vries-Rose, Weber or Saturation regions of the HVS. In these three regions the threshold for the edge points were detected adaptively. The parameters α'_1, α'_2 and α'_3 were detected automatically depending on the image in hand. The underwater image suffers from different perturbations as described earlier. Due to the perturbation the statistics of an image changes and as a result the three region changes. So, the detection of the three regions should not be ad-hoc rather adaptive. Since, the three regions were detected adaptively, the proposed method performed better than the conventional edge detection methods. Table 2 shows the value of the parameters α'_1, α'_2 and α'_3 for the test images shown in Figure 4.

Table 2. Detection of the three regions of the test images row wise in Figure 4 by the proposed method

Image	α'_1	α'_2	α'_3
1(a)	0.21	0.30	0.49
1(b)	0.22	0.28	0.50
1(c)	0.14	0.24	0.62
1(d)	0.31	0.34	0.35
1(e)	0.21	0.32	0.47

The qualitative results of the proposed method and all the methods compared here are shown in Figure 4. The corresponding quantitative results are shown in Table 1. Additional qualitative results by the proposed method are shown in Figure 5. The quantitative results on Sun dataset[74] and Turbid dataset[75] are shown in Table 3. Since, MeanPSO is meta-heuristic search technique, it may give slightly different results at different iterations. So for measuring the quantitative performance we ran the algorithm for 50 times and took the average of it. taken the average of 300 iterations. Both from qualitative and quantitative results it is clear that the proposed method is quite efficient in determining the edge points from the underwater images. The reason can be explained in the following way. He used a dark channel method prior to the edge detection to remove the haze. But, the haze reduction may cost the positional accuracy of the edge points. So, the edge pixels which was found out finally by the k-means algorithm may not be accurate. Ann used wavelet transform for the edge detection. The wavelet transform is a scale space transformations of the underwater images. The transform captures the edges in an image in different scale and orientations. But, the transform is not robust to different perturbations of an underwater image. The threshold for the gradients in Canny's edge detection method did not take into account the local statistics of the image. The statistics of the underwater images changes due to different perturbations. So, detecting the edge points from the gradients it required that the thresholds are selected adaptively. The thresholds are values are dependent on the three region detected by HVS. The regions get distorted by the different perturbations. Hence, the MeanPSO helps to optimal detection of the three regions depending on the image in hand. So, the proposed method can efficiently detect the edges in the underwater image. No, other methods have the provision for detecting the the edge points adaptively and hence the performance are low for underwater images. We also compared the proposed method with the edge detection methods by Zhang et al.[17] and Xu et al.[18] The method by Zhang used a scale invariant detectors for edge detection. The Clifford gradient was used by Xu for detection of edges in an image. The quantitative results are shown in Table 3. From the results it can be said that that the proposed method is quite efficient than that of the methods mentioned above.

Table 3. Average performance of different methods on the underwater image from SUN dataset(100 images) and Turbid dataset(100 images)

Methods	Canny	He[14]	Ann[13]	Zhang[17]	Xu[18]	Proposed
Sun dataset	0.8039	0.8210	0.8121	0.8157	0.8201	0.8553
Turbid dataset	0.8144	0.8245	0.8221	0.8278	0.8301	0.8572

6.1. *Comparisons with Other Evolutionary Algorithms*

In this sub-section we compared the proposed constraint optimization problem for edge detection with other evolutionary algorithm. For, comparison we used the genetic algorithm with elitist model[76] and traditional particle swarm optimization.[34] For comparisons we applied the algorithms on the set of underwater images for SUN dataset. The quantitative results are shown in Table 4. For the genetic algorithm the crossover probability and mutation probability are taken as 0.2 and .03 respectively. All the algorithms were executed 30 times and average performances were used for comparisons. From the table it clear that the proposed underwater image edge detection is better that that of the other methods compared here.

Table 4. Average performance of different evolutionary methods for edge detection methods on the underwater image from Sun dataset and Turbid dataset

Methods	GA(Eletist model)	PSO	MeanPSO
Sun dataset	0.8311	0.8399	0.8553
Turbid dataset	0.8204	0.8311	0.8504

7. Conclusion

In this chapter, we have proposed a novel method for edge detection in underwater images. The method uses the human psycho visual phenomenon for edge points detection in an image. The De-Vries Rose, Weber and Saturation regions detected by the human visual system is determined here and the edge points are generated automatically from the regions based on the underwater image statistics. For automatic and optimal detection of the three regions MeanPSO algorithm is used judiciously. The proposed method performs better both qualitatively and quantitatively than the other conventional and state-of-the-art methods for edge detection. Current research is going on for the detection of the edge points from the color images.

References

1. R. Schettini and S. Corchs, Underwater image processing: state of the art of restoration and image enhancement methods, *EURASIP Journal on Advances in Signal Processing.* **2010**(1), 746052 (2010).
2. D. Bhandari, C. A. Murthy, and S. K. Pal, Genetic algorithm with elitist model and its convergence, *International Journal of Pattern Recognition and Artificial Intelligence.* **10**(06), 731–747 (1996).
3. T. Kurban, P. Civicioglu, R. Kurban, and E. Besdok, Comparison of evolutionary and swam based computational techniques for multilevel color image segmentation, *Applied soft Computing.* **23**, 128–143 (2014).
4. R. E. Precup, R. C. David, E. M. Petriu, S. Preitl, and M. B. Radac, Fuzzy logic-based adaptive gravitational search algorithm for optimal tuning of fuzzy controlled servo systems, *IET Control Theory and Applications.* **7**(1), 99–107 (2013).

5. D. Azar, K. Fayad, and C. Daoud, A combined ant colony optimization and simulated annealing algorithm to assess stability and fault-proneness of classes based on internal software quality attributes, *International Journal of Artificial Intelligence.* **14**(2), 137–156 (2016).

6. X. Yang., A new metaheuristic bat-inspired algorithm, *International journal of Bio-inspired Computation.* **3**(5), 267–274 (2011).

7. K. Deep and J. C. Bansal, Mean particle swarm optimisation for function optimisation, *International Journal of Computational Intelligence Studies.* **01**(01), 72–92 (2009).

8. N. Senthilkumaran and R. Rajesh, Edge detection techniques for image segmentation — a survey of soft computing approaches, *International Journal of Recent Trends in Engineering.* **1**(2), 250–254 (2009).

9. D. Hu and X. Tian. A multi-directions algorithm for edge detection based on fuzzy mathematical morphology. In *Artificial Reality and Telexistence–Workshops, 2006. ICAT'06. 16th International Conference on*, pp. 361–364 (2006).

10. J. Shang and F. Jiang. An algorithm of edge detection based on soft morphology. In *Signal Processing (ICSP), 2012 IEEE 11th International Conference on*, vol. 1, pp. 166–169 (2012).

11. B. Kaur and A. Garg. Mathematical morphological edge detection for remote sensing images. In *Electronics Computer Technology (ICECT), 2011 3rd International Conference on*, vol. 5, pp. 324–327 (2011).

12. A. Jose and C. S. Seelamantula. Bilateral edge detectors. In *Acoustics, Speech and Signal Processing (ICASSP), 2013 IEEE International Conference on*, pp. 1449–1453 (2013).

13. N. V. An, Edge detection using wavelets, *VNU Journal of Science: Natural Sciences and Technology.* **29**(2) (2016).

14. Y. He, B. Zheng, Y. Ding, and H. Yang. Underwater image edge detection based on k-means algorithm. In *Oceans-St. John's, 2014*, pp. 1–4 (2014).

15. M. Fatan, M. R. Daliri, and A. M. Shahri, Underwater cable detection in the images using edge classification based on texture information, *Measurement.* **91**, 309–317 (2016).

16. P. Melin, C. I. Gonzalez, J. R. Castro, O. Mendoza, and O. Castillo, Edge-detection method for image processing based on generalized type-2 fuzzy logic, *IEEE Transactions on Fuzzy Systems.* **22**(6), 1515–1525 (2014).

17. X. Zhang and C. Liu, An ideal image edge detection scheme, *Multidimensional Systems and Signal Processing.* **25**(4), 659–681 (2014).

18. C. Xu, H. Liu, W. Cao, and J. Feng, Multispectral image edge detection via clifford gradient, *Science China Information Sciences.* **55**(2), 260–269 (2012).

19. D. Naidu, C. S. Rao, and S. Satapathy. A hybrid approach for image edge detection using neural network and particle swarm optimization. In *Emerging ICT for Bridging the Future-Proceedings of the 49th Annual Convention of the Computer Society of India (CSI) Volume 1*, pp. 1–9 (2015).

20. D. Díaz-Pernil, A. Berciano, F. PeñA-Cantillana, and M. A. M. A. Gutiérrez-Naranjo, Segmenting images with gradient-based edge detection using

membrane computing, *Pattern Recognition Letters.* **34**(8), 846–855 (2013).

21. J. Gu, Y. Pan, and H. Wang, Research on the improvement of image edge detection algorithm based on artificial neural network, *Optik-International Journal for Light and Electron Optics.* **126**(21), 2974–2978 (2015).

22. Y. Guo and A. Şengür, A novel image edge detection algorithm based on neutrosophic set, *Computers & Electrical Engineering.* **40**(8), 3–25 (2014).

23. C. Gonzalez, P. Melin, J. R. Castro, O. O. Mendoza, and O. Castillo. Color image edge detection method based on interval type-2 fuzzy systems. In *Design of Intelligent Systems Based on Fuzzy Logic, Neural Networks and Nature-Inspired Optimization*, pp. 3–11. Springer (2015).

24. G. Buchsbaum, An analytical derivation of visual nonlinearity, *IEEE Transactions on biomedical engineering.* **27**(5), 237–242 (1980).

25. M. K. Kundu and S. K. Pal, Thresholding for edge detection using human psychovisual phenomena, *Pattern Recognition Letters.* **4**(6), 433–441 (1986).

26. S. Dhar, S. Alam, M. Santra, P. Saha, and S. Thakur. A novel method for edge detection in a gray image based on human psychovisual phenomenon and bat algorithm. In *Computer, Communication and Electrical Technology: Proceedings of the International Conference on Advancement of Computer Communication and Electrical Technology (ACCET 2016), West Bengal, India, 21-22 October 2016*, p. 3 (2017).

27. F. Glover, Future paths for integer programming and links to artificial intelligence, *Computer Operation Research.* **13**(5), 533–549 (1986).

28. K. Dejong, *Evolutionary computation a unified approach.* MIT press, Cambridge, USA (2006).

29. F. Glover, M. Laguna, and M. R. Marti, Fundamentals of scatter search and path relinking, *Control Cybernetics.* **39**(3), 653–684 (2000).

30. F. Glover and M. Laguna, *Tabu Search.* Kluwer Academic, Norwell (1997).

31. J. Holland, *Adaption in Natural and Artificial Systems.* The University of Michigan Press, Ann Harbor (1975).

32. S. Kirkpatrick, C. D. Gelatt, and M. P. Vecchi, Optimization by simulated annealing, *Science.* **220**(4598), 671–680 (1983).

33. J. R. Koza, *Genetic programming: On the programming of computers by means of natural selection.* MIT press, Cambridge, USA (1992).

34. J. Kennedy and R. Eberhart. Particle swarm optimization. In *Neural Networks, 1995. Proceedings., IEEE International Conference on*, vol. 4, pp. 1942–1948 (1995).

35. S. Nakrani and C. Tovey, On honey bees and dynamic server allocation in internet hosting centers, *Adaptive Behavior.* **12**(34), 223–240 (2004).

36. D. Simon, Biogeography-based optimization, *IEEE Transaction of Evolutionary Computation.* **12**(6), 702–713 (2008).

37. X. S. Yang, *Nature-Inspired Metaheuristic Algorithms.* Luniver Press, Frome (2008).

38. X. S. Yang. Firefly algorithms for multimodal optimization. In O. Watanabe, and T. Zeugmann (eds.) *Stochastic Algorithms: Foundations and Applications. Lecture Notes in Computer Science*, vol. 5792, pp. 169–178 (2009).

39. X. S. Yang and S. Deb. Cuckoo search via lvy flights. In *World Congress on Nature and Biologically Inspired Computing*, pp. 210–214 (2009).

40. X. S. Yang and S. Deb, Engineering optimization by cuckoo search, *International Journal of Mathematical Modeling and Numerical Optimization*. $1(4)$, 330–343 (2010).

41. X. S. Yang. A new metaheuristic bat-inspired algorithm. In *Nature Inspired Cooperative Strategies for Optimization: Studies in Computational Intelligence*, vol. 284, pp. 65–74 (2010).

42. P. J. Angeline. Evolutionary optimization versus particle swarm optimization philosophy and performance differences. In *Lecture Notes in Computer Science*, vol. 1447, pp. 601–610 (1998).

43. Y. Shi and R. C. Eberhart. A modified particle swarm optimizer. In *Proceedings of the IEEE International Conference on Evolutionary Computation*, pp. 69–73 (1998).

44. M. Clerc and J. Kennedy, The particle swarm explosion, stability and convergence in a multi dimensional complex space, *IEEE Transaction of Evolutionary Computation*. **6**, 58–73 (2002).

45. R. C. Eberhart and Y. Shi. Comparing inertia weights and constriction factors in particle swarm optimization. In *Proceedings of the Congress on Evolutionary Computation*, pp. 84–88 (2000).

46. P. N. Suganthan. Particle swarm optimizer with neighborhood operator. In *Proceedings of the Congress on Evolutionary Computation*, pp. 1958–1962 (1999).

47. J. Kennedy and R. Mendes. Population structure and particle swarm performance. In *Proceedings of the Congress on Evolutionary Computation*, pp. 1671–1676 (2002).

48. A. Mohais, C. Ward, and C. Posthoff. Randomized directed neighborhood with edge migration in particle swarm optimization. In *Proceedings of the IEEE International Conference on Evolutionary Computation*, pp. 548–555 (2004).

49. T. Peram, K. Veeramachaneni, and C. K. Mohan. Fitness-distance-ratio based particle swarm optimization. In *Proceedings of the IEEE Swarm Intelligence Symposium*, pp. 174–181 (2003).

50. J. J. Liang, A. K. Qin, P. N. Suganthan, and S. Baskar. Particle swarm optimization algorithms with novel learning strategies. In *Proceedings of the IEEE International Conference on Systems, Man and Cybernetics*, pp. 3659–3664 (2004).

51. S. Baskar and P. M. Suganthan. A novel concurrent particle swarm optimization. In *Proceedings of the Congress on Evolutionary Computation*, pp. 792–796 (2004).

52. F. V. den Bergh and A. P. Engelbrecht, A cooperative approach to particle swarm optimization, *IEEE Transaction of Evolutionary Computation*. $8(3)$, 225–239 (2004).

53. S. He, Q. H. Wu, J. Y. Wen, J. R. Saunders, and R. C. Paton, A particle swarm optimizer with passive congregation, *Biosystems*. **78**, 135–147 (2004).

54. S. Janson and M. Middendorf, A hierarchical particle swarm optimizer and its adaptive variant, *IEEE Transaction on System, Man and Cybernetics: Part B.* **38**, 1272–1282 (2005).

55. P. J. Angeline, Using selection to improve particle swarm optimization. In *Proceedings of the IEEE International Conference on Evolutionary Computation*, pp. 84–89 (1998).

56. R. Poli, W. B. Laugdon, and O. Holland. Extending particle swarm optimization via genetic programming. In *Proceedings of the Eighth European Conference on Genetic Programming*, pp. 291–300 (2005).

57. M. Lovbjerg, T. K. Rasmussen, and T. Krink. Hybrid particle swarm optimizer with breeding and subpopulation. In *Proceedings of the Third Genetic and Evolutionary Computation Conference*, pp. 469–476 (2001).

58. W. J. Zhang and X. F. Xie. Depso: hybrid particle swarm with differential evolution operator. In *Proceedings of the IEEE International Conference on Systems, Man and Cybernetics*, pp. 3816–3821 (2003).

59. T. Hendtlass. Preserving diversity in particle swarm optimization. In *Lecture Notes in Computer Science*, vol. 2718, pp. 31–40 (2003).

60. T. Krink and M. Lovbjerg. The lifecycle model: combining particle swarm optimization, genetic algorithms and hill climbing. In *Proceedings of Parallel Problem solving from Nature*, vol. 7, pp. 621–630 (2002).

61. A. Stacey, M. Jancic, and I. Grundy. Particle swarm optimization with mutation. In *Proceedings of the Congress on Evolutionary Computation*, pp. 1425–1430 (2003).

62. S. C. Esquivel and C. A. C. Coello. On the use of particle swarm optimization with multi modal functions. In *Proceedings of the Congress on Evolutionary Computation*, pp. 1130–1136 (2003).

63. N. Higasbi and H. Iba. Particle swarm optimization with Gaussian mutation. In *Proceedings of the IEEE Swarm Intelligence Symposium*, pp. 72–79 (2003).

64. A. Silva, A. Neves, and E. Costa. An empirical comparison of particle swarm and predator-pray optimization. In *Lecture Notes in Computer Science*, vol. 2464, pp. 103–110 (2002).

65. M. Lovbjerg and T. Krink. Extending particle swarm optimizers with self-organized criticality. In *Proceedings of the Congress on Evolutionary Computation*, p. 15881593 (2002).

66. W. J. Zhang, X. F. Xie, and Z. L. Yang. Hybrid particle swarm optimizer with mass extinction. In *International Conference on Communication, Circuits and Systems*, pp. 1170–1173 (2002).

67. J. Riget and J. S. Vesterstrem, *Technical Report: A diversity-guided particle swarm optimizer the ARPSO*. EVALife, Department of Computer Science, University of Aarbus (2002).

68. A. Banks, J. Vincent, and C. Anyakoha, A review of particle swarm optimization, part ii: hybridisation, combinatorial, multicriteria and constrained optimization and indicative applications, *IEEE Transaction on System, Man and Cybernetics: Part B.* **7**(1), 109–124 (2008).

69. A. Banks, J. Vincent, and C. Anyakoha, A review of particle swarm optimization, Part I: background and development, *Natural Computing: an International Journal.* **6**(4), 467–484 (2007).
70. X. Hu, Y. Shi, and R. C. Eberhart. Recent advances in particle swarm. In *Proceedings of the Congress on Evolutionary Computation*, pp. 90–97 (2004).
71. E. L. Hall, Computer image processing and recognition, *Academic Press, New York* (1979).
72. P. Zuidema, J. J. Koenderink, and M. A. Bouman, A mechanistic approach to threshold behavior of the visual system, *IEEE Trans. Systems, Man, and Cybernetics.* **13**, 923–934 (1983).
73. I. E. Abdou and W. K. Pratt, Quantitative design and evaluation of enhancement/thresholding edge detectors, *Proceedings of the IEEE.* **67**(5), 753–763 (1979).
74. SUN Dataset, `https://groups.csail.mit.edu/vision/SUN/`(2003).
75. TURBID Dataset, `http://amandaduarte.com.br/turbid/`(2016).
76. D. Bhandari, C. A. Murthy, and S. K. Pal, Genetic algorithm with elitist model and its convergence, *International Journal of Pattern Recognition and Artificial Intelligence.* **10**(06), 731–747 (1996).

Chapter 6

Quantum Inspired Non-dominated Sorting Based Multi-objective GA for Multi-level Image Thresholding

Sandip Dey

Department of Computer Science & Engineering,
OmDayal Group of Institutions, Birshibpur,
Howrah-711316, India
dr.ssandip.dey@gmail.com

Siddhartha Bhattacharyya

Department of Computer Application,
RCC Institute of Information Technology,
Canal South Road, Beliaghata, Kolkata-700015, India
dr.siddhartha.bhattacharyya@gmail.com

Ujjwal Maulik

Department of Computer Science & Engineering,
Jadavpur University, Kolkata-700032, India
ujjwal_maulik@yahoo.com

In this paper, a new quantum behaved multi-objective method for multi-level image thresholding has been introduced. This method exploits the fundamentals of quantum computing by using a popular multi-objective framework, called NSGA-II for better usability and efficiency. A number of conflicting objective functions are employed to determine the set of non-dominated solutions. Subsequently, these solutions are used by a popular thresholding method, called Kittler's method for different levels of image thresholding. The accuracy and stability (robustness) of the proposed approach are exhibited through the average fitness value and standard deviation of fitness. The usefulness of the proposed approach is also established visually and computationally on three real life images and three Berkeley images (Benchmark dataset). In multi-objective point of view, the performance of each method is evaluated with reference to two different measures viz., Inverted Generational Distance and Hypervolume. In addition, a statistical comparison methodology has also been introduced to find the number of participants which are significantly dominated by the selected method in the same perspective. The usefulness of the proposed method is finally exhibited by using a statistical superiority test, known as Friedman test. As a matter of comparative analysis, the proposed method has been compared with two popular evolutionary algorithms, called NSGA-II and SMS-EMOA. Results prove that the proposed approach is more efficient comparable to the others.

Keywords: multi-objective optimization, quantum computing, genetic algorithm, Friedman test, kittler's method.

1. Introduction

Optimization is a popular method used to attain for best combination of feasible solutions of a specific problem. The search space is first explored to determine the possible solutions any given problem and later optimized within a nominal time period. A single-objective optimization problem has only one objective, whereas multi-objective optimization (MOO) problem deals with a number of objectives concurrently. In principle, in case of former type of optimization, the attention is usually fixed towards discovering solution which attains global optima. Since a MOO generally optimizes multiple objectives simultaneously, it is not always possible to find a solution in search space, which produces best fitness values with regard to each objective. In the given search space, there may subsist a group of solutions which has better fitness with respect to a set of objectives and worse value for the rest as compared to other solutions. These non-dominated set of solutions are basically known as Pareto-optimal solutions. Since, there exists no solution in Pareto-optimal set, which holds superiority for all objectives, there must lie a few problem specific knowledge and decision making capability for selecting preferred solutions in MOO [1]. Over the last few decades, some methods have been introduced in the literature that have coped with multi-objective optimization problems in different facets [2].

An evolutionary algorithms (EA) emulates the mechanism of natural evolution towards the goal of global optimization. EA is population based stochastic type optimization procedure which can simultaneously handle multiple solutions at a single run. It is usually utilized as a powerful effectual tool to solve various optimization problems. It has been already proved to be highly effective specially for searching Pareto optimal set of solutions in MOO problem. At each generation, it tries to find the best possible solutions as far as possible and produces a new population for further improvement. As compared to other comparable methods, EA is the most easiest method to implement and entails no other derivative information for execution. The inherent flexibility of EA inspires the researchers to espouse it in a variety of domain of applications. The efficacy of solving any complex MOO problem is exceptionally higher for EAs compared to other equivalent methods. Thus far, a variety of evolutionary-based methods have been used to solve different MOO problems. Some of them are presented in [3, 4].

A basic part of image processing is image segmentation. Fundamentally, it bifurcates an image into number of homogenous, non-overlapping regions based on the basic features like color, texture and other image attributes. Every segmented region must contain one or more attributes in common. In the literature, image segmentation has been efficiently and successfully applied in multidimensional applications. A few examples in this direction include image retrieval [5], face detection [6] and object recognition [7] to name a few. In [7], a variety of segmentation methods has been reported. Among different segmentation methods available in these days, thresholding is used as one of the popular and most powerful tools in this regard. Basically, it helps to extract object (foreground image) from the corresponding background image. Thresholding is simple to implement, provides highest level of accuracy and is robust in nature. The computational complexity increases with the increase of level of thresholding. To date, thresholding has been widely used in various domains successfully. A few of them are available in [8, 9]. A brief review on different thresholding methods has been presented by Sezgin and Sankar in their survey paper [10].

Quantum mechanics is in essence known to be the basis of quantum computing (QC). The operations in QC are performed according to the rules of quantum mechanics. Feynman [11] has first presented an exhaustive investigation on QC. Later, a number of researchers from different branches has drawn their intensive attentions for conducting comprehensive investigations on QC. The thought of QC has been successfully applied in computer science, artificial intelligence and many other fields [12]. The capability of parallel computation in quantum computing helps to decrease computational complexity almost exponentially [13–16]. Till date, many researches have been proposed in this direction.

In this paper, a quantum inspired multi-objective genetic algorithm for multi-level image thresholding has been presented. The Kittler's method [17] has been employed as a fitness function to determine optimal thresholds values from test images. For this reason, this method uses non-dominated set of solutions at different levels of computation. Using the concept of quantum computing (QC), qubit encoded scheme (real coded) has been implemented to perform experiments. The performance of the proposed method has been compared with NSGA-II [18] based and SMS-EMOA [19] based multi-objective methods by utilizing different performance metrics of multi-objective optimization procedure. Several metrics of this category have been used for this purpose to establish the dominance of the proposed method.

The paper is organized as follows. The background on different multi-objective algorithms is illustrated in Section 2. The theory of multi-objective optimization is briefly discussed in Section 3. The concepts of genetic algorithm and also the basic quantum computing are elaborately presented in Section 4. A popular thresholding method has been used as the objective function for each of the participating methods. This method is briefly described in Section 5. Thereafter, the proposed methodology is described elaborately in Section 6. In Section 7, various experimental results are presented. Finally, the paper ends with some relevant conclusions in Section 8.

2. Background

To date, a large number of researchers have expressed their profound interest in a variety of MOO problems. A brief review of different evolutionary algorithms has been reported in [1]. A number of Pareto-based methods on genetic algorithm is available in the literature. Shaffer [20] has developed a multi-objective evolutionary algorithm (MOEA), called vector-evaluated genetic algorithm (VEGA). VEGA performs efficiently for number of generations but fails to provide unbiased solution for a few occasions. Fonseca and Fleming [21] have proposed a variant MOEA, entitled as Multi-Objective Genetic Algorithm (MOGA). The concept of MOGA is that all non-dominated chromosomes in the population are allotted the best possible objective value and the remaining chromosomes in the dominated group are reprimanded in accordance with the population density of the respective regions of these chromosomes. Horn et al. [22] have proposed another multi-objective optimization method, called Niched-Pareto Genetic Algorithm (NPGA). Srinivas and Deb [23] have developed a variant MOO algorithm, popularly known as Non-dominated Sorting Genetic Algorithm (NSGA). The NSGA was designed according to the classification theory as proposed by Goldberg [24]. The backbone of NSGA is said to be pareto ranking of population at different generations. This makes NSGA a less efficient algorithm compared to other contemporary algorithms. Tanaka and Tanino later integrated the user's association into an evolutionary multi-objective optimization to propose a new system [25]. Instead of searching the entire pareto front, user may be interested in only putting effort on a little segment of it. Deb *et al.* [18] have introduced a second edition of NSGA [23] called, Non-dominated Sorting Genetic Algorithm II (NSGA-II). A speedy nondominated sorting strategy was adopted in this algorithm. Unlike the normal selection procedure, a variant operator was used for the selection purpose. The population for next generation is produced by coalescing chromosomes (equal to the population size) from parent and offspring pool with respect to best fitness values. Zitzler and Thiele [26] have suggested another multi-objective optimization algorithm, called Strength Pareto Evolutionary Algorithm (SPEA). This algorithm can be visualized as an approach of amalgamating multiple evolutionary multi-objective optimization algorithms. Zitzler and Thiele [27] have introduced a second version of SPEA named as Strength Pareto Evolutionary Algorithm 2 (SPEA2). This algorithm is more efficient with regards to search capability compared to SPEA. Pareto Archived Evolution Strategy (PAES) Algorithm is a well-admired MOO algorithm presented by Knowles and Corne [28]. In PAES algorithm, one offspring agent is being created from one parent agent. This algorithm uses crowding method to segregate objective space recursively. Corne *et al.* [29] have introduced a popular MOO algorithm known as Pareto Envelope based Selection Algorithm (PESA). They have adopted the good features from both SPEA and PAES to construct PESA. In the literature, a few bio-inspired methods e.g. ant colony optimization [30] and artificial immune systems [31] have been successfully implemented to solve different MOO problems. Simulated annealing has also been used in different aspects for solving various MOO problems. Emmerich *et al.* [19] used a novel idea to introduce a popular evolutionary multi-objective optimization algorithm, where authors used Hypervolume measure as the selection criterion. Some distinctive examples may be presented in [32, 33] in this regard.

3. Multi-objective Optimization

Unlike a single-objective optimization problem, a group of objective functions are considered simultaneously for optimization in multi-objective optimization problem. Initially, the decision space is explored to find the vector of decision variables and henceforth the objective functions are simultaneously optimized. In addition, there may have few constraints, which must be satisfied by any solution in multi-objective optimization problem. The formal definition of a MOO problem can be presented as follows:

$$\mathcal{M} \; \mathbf{y} = f(\mathbf{x}) = [f_1(\mathbf{x}), f_2(\mathbf{x}), \dots, f_p(\mathbf{x})]^T$$
$$\text{subject to } \phi_i(\mathbf{x}) \geq 0, \qquad i = 1, 2 \dots, q \qquad (1)$$
$$\psi_j(\mathbf{x}) = 0, \qquad j = 1, 2 \dots, r$$

According to the nature of optimization, $\mathcal{M}$ is considered as either a minimization or a maximization problem. Here, $\mathbf{x} = (x_1, x_2, \dots, x_s) \in X$ denotes a vector or sometimes called a decision vector comprising s number of decision variables whereas, $\mathbf{y} = (y_1, y_2, \dots, y_t) \in Y$ is the called objective vector. X and Y denote the parameter space and the objective space, respectively. As mentioned in equation (1), the decision vector must satisfy q number of inequality constraints and r number of equality constraints for MOO.

The thought of dominance is exceedingly significant in the perspective of MOO. For the sake of clarity, in a minimization framework, let us assume that $\mathcal{Z} = \{z_1, z_2, \dots, z_u\}$ be the set of solution for a MOO problem comprising $\mathcal{H}$ number of objective functions.

The solution $z_i \in \mathcal{Z}$ dominate the solution $z_j \in \mathcal{Z}$ if both of the following criteria are satisfied.

(1) $f_l(z_i) \leq f_l(z_j), \forall \ell \in 1, 2, \dots, \mathcal{H}$.
(2) $f_l(z_i) < f_l(z_j)$, if $\exists$ at least one $\ell \in 1, 2, \dots, \mathcal{H}$.

As a general rule, a MOO algorithm acknowledges a set of non-dominated solutions.

4. Fundamental Concepts

4.1. *Genetic Algorithm*

John Holland [34] from University of Michigan, has first introduced a popular evolutionary algorithm called, Genetic algorithm (GA) in 1970. It is generally used for discrete optimization. GA is a population based adaptive heuristic optimization method. The primary spur of GA was from biological admiration. It is basically inspired from Darwin's principle, known as "survival of the fittest" and is used to generate offsprings of chromosomes in population [35]. GA may be very useful for solving different complex problems which need large search space to be walked through. As the population is formed with multiple chromosomes, it can explore large amount of search space at each single run, which increases the possibility of attaining global optima in a lesser span of time. At each generation, three genetic operators namely, selection, crossover and mutation are successively applied to have population assortment. Based on a given fitness function, solution space is being created using the participating chromosomes in population to find the best individual. To date, a number of researchers have effectively used GA in different applications. Some distinctive examples of such applications may include portfolio management [36], project management, data clustering [37] and image processing [5].

4.2. *Quantum Computing*

The facet of quantum computing is basically focused on developing computer technology on the basis of principles of quantum theory. The quantum theory describes the nature and behavior of energy and matter on the quantum (atomic/subatomic) level. The quantum computer follows the laws of quantum physics. It would gain massive processing power through the ability to be in multiple states, and to accomplish tasks using all possible permutations concurrently. A quantum computer (QC) is fundamentally a computer machine which exploits the features of quantum theory. Since QC performs at atomic and/or subatomic level, this ability helps QC to enhance its computational potential beyond the limit of traditional computer [38–46]. Since the last few years, its increasing popularity has drawn favorable attention for the new researchers in different fields. A few examples are given in [47, 48] in its favor. Theoretically, the fundamental constituent of QC is known as quantum bit or in short qubit, which is basically a unit vector represented in a 2D Hilbert space system [12, 49–51]. The superposition of states (considering one qubit having length 2) is generally represented by

$$|\psi\rangle = d_1|0\rangle + d_2|1\rangle \tag{2}$$

where, $|0\rangle$ and $|1\rangle$ represent the "ground state" and "excited state", respectively and $(d_1, d_2) \in \mathbb{C}$. More generally, a r-state system must satisfy the quantum orthogonality as given by

$$\sum_{i=1}^{r} d_i^2 = 1 \tag{3}$$

One fascinating feature of QC is quantum entanglement. Basically, if there exists an unique correlation between the participating quantum states in quantum system, the states may be named as quantum entangled states. Mathematically, these states are symbolically defined as a tensor product between the quantum states as $|v_1\rangle \otimes |v_2\rangle$.

In QC, p number of qubits can concurrently represent a sum of 2^p states in 2^p dimensional quantum space. The states in superposed form are collapsed into a single state for quantum measurement. With reference to equation (2), the required probability for transforming $|\psi\rangle$ into $|0\rangle$ is $|d_1|^2$ and that of $|1\rangle$ is $|d_2|^2$ [13, 52].

A quantum register $(\mathcal{Q}_r)$ is formed with a group of qubits. The size of $\mathcal{Q}_r = n$ signifies that there exists n number of qubits in $\mathcal{Q}_r$. The decimal value of qubits in $\mathcal{Q}_r$ can be derived as

$$\underbrace{|1\rangle \otimes |0\rangle \otimes \cdots \otimes |0\rangle \otimes |1\rangle}_{n\ qubits} \equiv |\underbrace{10\cdots 01}_{n\ bits}\rangle \equiv |\mathcal{D}\rangle$$

where, $\mathcal{D}$ is the equivalent decimal number of the qubits in $\mathcal{Q}_r$ and $\otimes$ denotes tensor product.

In a quantum system, quantum gates may be significantly useful for updating quantum bits where prompt convergence is the necessary condition. These are basically hardware devices, operated into coherent period of time. To get the n number of outputs, a quantum gate of n number of inputs must be incorporated. A quantum gate must satisfy the following equation

$$U^+ = U^{-1}, UU^+ = U^+U = I \text{ and } U = e^{iHt} \tag{4}$$

where, U is popularly known as unitary operator and H is the so called Hermitian operator in the basic mathematical notations. A typical example of quantum rotation gate is as follows:

$$\begin{bmatrix} \alpha'_k \\ \beta'_k \end{bmatrix} = \begin{bmatrix} cos(\theta_k) & -sin(\theta_k) \\ sin(\theta_k) & cos(\theta_k) \end{bmatrix} \begin{bmatrix} \alpha_k \\ \beta_k \end{bmatrix} \tag{5}$$

where, k^{th} qubit (α_k, β_k) is updated to (α'_k, β'_k) using the rotation angle, θ_k [12, 49]. Some popular and widely used quantum gates include NOT gate, Hadamard gate, C-NOT, Toffoli gate, Fredkin gate, controlled phase-shift gate etc.

5. Segmentation Criteria

In the proposed approach, Kittler's method [17] has been used as the objective function to find the optimal threshold values of gray scale images. A brief overview of Kittler's method [17] is presented in the following subsection.

5.1. *Kittler's Method*

Kittler's method is a popular thresholding method proposed by Kittler and Illingworth [17]. This method computes the histogram of the foreground and background image and then formulates the corresponding Gaussian models. It has been noticed that a threshold has an adequate influence on the overlapping area between the Gaussian models for the object and background parts. With the change of threshold values, the model of the probability distribution of the object and background image is changed accordingly. The vital challenge remains in finding the optimum threshold value which is best fitted in Gaussian models having smallest overlapping area as mentioned above and thereby minimizes the classification error. Kittler's method is very effective in bi-level image thresholding. It can be extended to multi-level domain if necessary. For the sake of clarity, let an image is segmented into $\mathcal{C}$ number of classes using $(\mathcal{C} - 1)$ number of threshold values, namely $\{\theta_1, \theta_2, \cdots, \theta_{\mathcal{C}-1}\}$. Formally, Kittler's method can be defined as follows [17]

$$\mathcal{F} = \gamma^2 \{\theta_1, \theta_2, \cdots, \theta_K\}$$
$$= 1 + 2 \times \sum_{i=1}^{\mathcal{C}} (v_i(\log \omega_i - \log v_i)) \tag{6}$$

where,

$$p_i = f_i/N, \ v_k = \sum_{i \in \mathcal{C}_k} p_i, \ \mu_k = \sum_{i \in \mathcal{C}_k} \frac{p_i \times i}{v_k}$$

$$\text{and } \omega_k^2 = \sum_{i \in \mathcal{C}_k} \frac{p_i \times (i - \mu_k)^2}{v_k} \tag{7}$$

Note that, k is a positive integer and $k \in [1, \mathcal{C}]$, f_i is the frequency of ith pixel whereas, p_i represents the probability of this pixel. N is the total number of pixels in the image. v_k, ω_k and μ_k represent the priori probability, standard deviation and mean in class $\mathcal{C}_k$, respectively.

6. Proposed Method

In this section, the fundamental principles of QC are explored to introduce a novel method known as, quantum inspired nondominated sorting genetic algorithm for multi-objective multi-level thresholding (QINSGA-II). The proposed method is developed to find the predefined number of optimum threshold values from gray scale image. The details of QINSGA-II is explained in Algorithm 1. At the beginning, the population of chromosome (POP) is filled with $\mathcal{A}$ number of chromosomes. The length of each chromosome in POP is taken as $\mathcal{L} = \sqrt{L}$, where, L represents the maximum intensity value of the image. A real encoding scheme using the basic features of QC is employed to encode real numbers between (0, 1) for each image pixel in POP. This results in an encoded population matrix, called POP'. At each generation, POP' passes through quantum rotation gate to ensure faster convergence. Successively, each element in POP' must ensure the fundamental property of QC, known as quantum orthogonality, which produces POP''. Three basic genetic operators (selection, crossover and mutation) are successively applied in POP', which results in a offspring population ($OPOP'$) of size $\mathcal{A}$. Thereafter, the parent population is combined with its offspring population to have a combined population matrix (FP) of size $2 \times \mathcal{A}$. This combined population is then sorted according to its non-domination. A fast non-dominated sorting strategy (as used in NSGA-II [18]) is applied for this purpose. This sorting approach finds the following measures:

- X_k: It represents a set all individuals which are dominated by k.
- c_k: It stands for the number of individuals which dominates k.
- F_j: It signifies the set individuals in jth front.

The motto of this sorting strategy is to assign a rank for each solution according to non-domination level. For an example, rank 1 is assigned to the solutions at the best level, likewise, rank 2 to the second-best level and so on. In the next phase, crowding distances for every fronts are computed. Since the individuals are selected based on rank and crowding distance, all the individuals in the population are assigned a crowding distance value.

Algorithm 1. Steps of QINSGA-II for multi-objective multi-level thresholding
 Input: Generation number: $\mathcal{G}$
Population size: $\mathcal{A}$

No. of thresholds: K
Output: Optimal threshold values: θ

1: Firstly, pixel intensity values from input image are randomly selected to generate $\mathcal{A}$ number of chromosomes (POP). Here, each chromosome in POP is of length $\mathcal{L} = \sqrt{L}$, where, L stands for maximum intensity value of the input image.

2: Using the fundamental concept of quantum computing, each pixel in POP is encoded with a positive real number less than unity. Let us assume that POP becomes POP' after this real encoding.

3: Set the number of generation, $g = 1$.

4: The quantum rotation gate is employed to update POP' as explained in equation (5).

5: Each chromosomal ingredient in POP' endures *quantum orthogonality* to form POP''.

6: Using a probability criteria, K number of thresholds as pixel intensity are found from population. Let it creates POP^*.

7: Evaluate fitness of each chromosome in POP^* using the equation (6).

8: Three basic operators namely, selection, crossover and mutation are successively applied in POP'' to generate its offspring population of size $\mathcal{A}$. Let it be called as $OPOP'$.

9: Repeat steps 4-5 to generate $OPOP''$.

10: $FP = POP''g \cup OPOP''g$.

11: **repeat**

12:     Use fast-non-dominated-sort mechanism to create F_j (say, j number of front).

13:     Set $POP_{g+1} = \emptyset$.

14:     Use crowding-distance-computation mechanism in F_d, $d \in [1, j]$ to populate POP_{g+1}.

15:     Use crowded-comparison operator ($\prec_n$) to sort F_d in descending order (assuming maximization problem).

16:     $POP_{g+1} = POP_{g+1} \cup F_d[1 : (\mathcal{A} - |POP_{g+1}|)]$.

17:     Use equation (6) to evaluate POP_{g+1}. The threshold value of the input image is recorded in T_C.

18:     The thresholds possessing best fitness value is recorded in T_B.

19:     Repeat step 6: to generate a new population $OPOP_{g+1}$.

20:     $FP = POP_{g+1} \cup OPOP_{g+1}$.

21:     Repeat steps 4-5 for the chromosomes in FP.

22:     $g = g + 1$.

23: **until** $g < \mathcal{G}$
24: The optimal threshold values for MOO algorithm is reported in $\theta = T_B$.

6.1. *Analysis of Time Complexity*

The time complexity (worst case) of QINSGA II is presented elaborately in this section. The stepwise complexity analysis is given below.

(1) Suppose, the population contains $\mathcal{V}$ number of chromosomes. The time complexity to generate initial population, becomes $O(\mathcal{V} \times \mathcal{L})$. Note that, $\mathcal{L}$ represents maximum pixel intensity value of the image.

(2) Using basic principle of qubit, each image pixel is encoded with a real number between $(0,1)$, which leads the time complexity as $O(\mathcal{V} \times \mathcal{L})$.

(3) For implementing quantum rotation gate and applying the property, called quantum orthogonality in each member in the population, the time complexity for each operation require $O(\mathcal{V} \times \mathcal{L})$.

(4) Since the method finds predefined number of threshold values from POP'' and produces POP^*. The time complexity for this process turns into $O(\mathcal{V} \times \mathcal{L})$.

(5) Again, to compute fitness values using POP^*, the time complexity becomes $O(\mathcal{V} \times \mathcal{C})$. Note that, $\mathcal{C}$ is the required number of classes.

(6) Three genetic operators viz., selection, crossover and mutation are applied in sequence in POP'' to generate $OPOP'$. The time complexity for performing each operation turns out to be $O(\mathcal{V} \times \mathcal{L})$.

(7) In the next step, steps 4-5 are repeated to generate $OPOP''$. The time complexity for each operation is $O(\mathcal{V} \times \mathcal{L})$.

(8) POP'' and $OPOP''$ are combined together to form FP. The time complexity to produce FP becomes $O(2 \times \mathcal{V})=O(\mathcal{V})$.

(9) For fast-non-dominated-sort, one individual can only be a member of a single front. Suppose, maximum $(\mathcal{Y})$ number of comparisons is required for each domination checking in the population. Hence, to perform the fast-non-dominated-sort, the time complexity becomes $O(\mathcal{V} \times \mathcal{Y}^2)$.

(10) The crowding-distance-computation in any single front may require at most $\mathcal{Y}$ number of sorting for $\frac{\mathcal{V}}{2}$ solutions. Therefore, the time complexity becomes $O(\mathcal{Y} \times \mathcal{V} \times \log(\mathcal{V}))$.

(11) The crowded-comparison operator $(\prec_n)$ is used for sorting, which requires $O(\mathcal{V} \times \log(\mathcal{V}))$ computational complexity.

(12) The algorithm runs for predefined number of generations $(\mathcal{G})$. Hence, the overall time complexity to run the proposed algorithm turns into $O(\mathcal{V} \times \mathcal{L} \times \mathcal{Y}^2 \times \mathcal{G})$.

Therefore, summarizing the over discussion stated above, the worst case time complexity of QINSGA-II happens to be $O(\mathcal{V} \times \mathcal{L} \times \mathcal{Y}^2 \times \mathcal{G})$.

7. Results of Simulation

In this section, the performance of QINSGA-II has been assessed with reference to optimal threshold values of three real life gray scale images and three Berkeley images [53]. The proposed method has been constructed using NSGA-II [18] as a reference method. The relevant discussion for this part is confined on basis of following facets.

7.1. *Experimental Settings*

For experimental purpose, the system with the configuration "Toshiba Intel(R) Core (TM) i3, 2.53GHz PC with 2GB RAM" has been used. The parameter specification (best combinations) for the all methods is listed in Table 1. The experiment has been conducted on six test images; (a) Lena, (b) Peppers, (c) Cameraman, and (d) ♯38092 [53], (e) ♯147091 [53] and (f) ♯220075 [53]. The dimension of real life images and Berkeley images are selected as 256×256 and 120×80, respectively. The original test images are depicted in Figures 1(a)-(f).

7.2. *Experimental Results*

In this paper, the experiments have been conducted for the proposed QINSGA-II, NSGA-II [18] proposed by Deb *et al.* and SMS-EMOA [19] proposed by Emmerich *et al.* Each method has been evaluated for 30 different runs. The optimum threshold values for different gray scale images have been documented at various levels using multi-objective flavour. At the outset, two different conflicting type objective functions have been evaluated for determining the non-dominates set of solutions. Thereafter, Kittler's method [17] has been used as a third objective function for final assessment. In this section, the experimental results would be reported on

Table 1.   Parameters specification for QINS-GA-II, NSGA-II and SMS-EMOA

QINSGA2/NSGA2/SMS-EMOA
Number of generations: $\mathcal{G} = 100/500/1000$
Population size: $\mathcal{S} = 20$
Crossover probability: $\varsigma = 0.95$
Mutation probability: $\varrho = 0.05$
No. of thresholds: $K = 3, 5, 7$

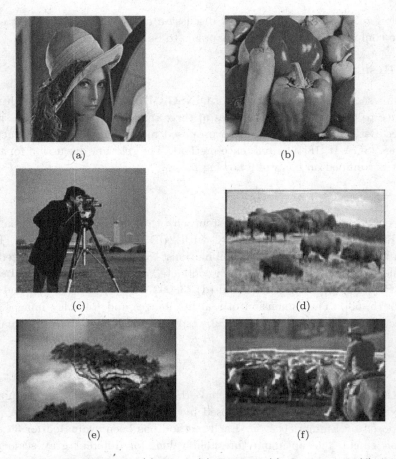

Fig. 1. Original test images (a) Lena, (b) Peppers, (c) Cameraman, (d) ♯38092, (e) ♯147091 and (f) ♯220075

the basis of following facets: (1) the results of multilevel thresholding for Kittler's method [17], (2) the stability of each of them; and finally, (3) their performance evaluation.

7.2.1. *The results of multi-level thresholding for QINSGA-II, NSGA-II and SMS-EMOA*

The best results for different images have been reported in reference to optimum thresholds (θ) and objective (fitness) value ($\mathcal{F}_{best}$) in Table 2. The time for computations (t) (in seconds) for each of them in presented

Table 2. Best Experimental Results for QINSGA-II, NSGA-II and SMS-EMOA of Lena, Peppers, Cameraman, ♯38092, ♯147091 and ♯220075

K	QINSGA-II θ	QINSGA-II $\mathcal{F}_{best}$	NSGA-II θ	NSGA-II $\mathcal{F}_{best}$	SMS-EMOA θ	SMS-EMOA $\mathcal{F}_{best}$
Lena						
4	68,94,114	9.560	64,93,115	9.645	66,87,109	9.614
6	71,93,111,127,144	10.566	58,79,111,130,161	11.069	84,118,139,151,161	10.956
8	67,89,108,127,139,156,170	11.747	75,100,104,137,145,158,183	12.549	46,77,97,111,126,150,165	12.307
Peppers						
4	64,97,116	9.770	56,95,122	9.859	64,98,117	9.775
6	62,93,110,131,152	10.806	27,63,93,119,151	11.204	49,77,102,127,148	11.042
8	62,84,104,115,142,160,178	12.038	56,92,116,145,167,173,189	12.466	56,86,102,128,150,165,186	12.271
Cameraman						
4	22,93,126	9.331	26,91,126	9.349	30,95,127	9.388
6	25,81,115,135,152	10.385	28,77,115,130,152	10.491	27,87,128,152,169	10.604
8	19,71,117,127,144,157,169	11.681	11,22,69,106,121,139,149	12.063	24,44,61,115,129,148,155	12.228
♯38092						
4	84,134,177	4.757	104,145,188	4.769	79,133,167	4.765
6	67,113,150,194,229	6.587	70,115,144,173,208	6.600	27,64,102,147,184	6.587
8	53,88,121,145,171,210,241	8.501	49,100,133,158,182,207,234	8.524	60,87,103,139,166,196,228	8.520
♯147091						
4	50,112,154	4.734	43,93,143	4.748	51,114,160	4.739
6	34,70,120,151,193	6.554	27,71,102,138,170	6.602	38,61,112,147,183	6.572
8	32,54,96,127,153,180,220	8.494	39,63,106,133,162,211,232	8.524	33,73,104,129,159,201,252	8.510
♯220075						
4	49,86,124	4.706	50,94,139	4.714	50,90,129	4.707
6	41,67,97,126,165	6.553	40,67,103,145,209	6.566	38,70,101,119,147	6.573
8	27,48,74,94,122,153,212	8.490	25,55,75,94,112,144,207	8.501	30,44,58,88,115,159,224	8.505

in Table 3. The experimental results have been reported for four-level, six-level and eight-level of computation (K). The thresholded images for QINSGA-II have been presented in Figure 2.

Table 3. Execution time (t) of QINSGA-II, NSGA-II and SMS-EMOA for multi-level thresholding of Lena, Peppers, Cameraman, ♯38092, ♯147091 and ♯220075

K	Lena			Peppers		
	(a)	(b)	(c)	(a)	(b)	(c)
4	04.59	06.36	06.17	04.09	06.14	05.20
6	07.39	09.10	08.09	06.24	08.12	09.01
8	08.46	12.27	11.03	08.12	11.01	10.30
K	Cameraman			♯38092		
	(a)	(b)	(c)	(a)	(b)	(c)
4	04.27	05.56	05.02	02.49	03.10	03.13
6	06.19	08.16	07.25	05.50	06.35	06.24
8	08.26	10.24	10.49	06.25	10.03	09.11
K	♯147091			♯220075		
	(a)	(b)	(c)	(a)	(b)	(c)
4	02.11	04.04	03.23	02.22	03.16	03.27
6	04.56	05.38	05.55	05.14	06.12	06.01
8	06.03	09.25	08.04	06.23	09.21	08.12
(a):→ **QINSGA-II**		(b):→ **NSGA-II**				
(c):→ **SMS-EMOA**						

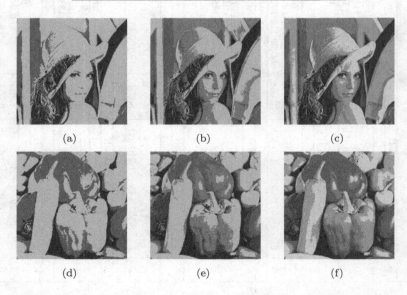

(a)   (b)   (c)

(d)   (e)   (f)

Fig. 2. For $K = 4, 6$ and 8, images (a)-(c), for Lena, (d)-(f), for Peppers, (g)-(i), for Cameraman, (j)-(l), for ♯38092, (m)-(o), for ♯147091 and (p)-(r), for ♯220075, after using QINSGA-II, for multi-level thresholding

Fig. 2.   (Continued)

7.2.2. *The stability of the comparable methods*

The stability and accuracy of each method is examined in terms of mean fitness ($\mathcal{F}_{avg}$) value and standard deviation (σ) over different runs. These results are reported in Table 4. As the level increases, the values of ($\mathcal{F}_{avg}$) and (σ) varies significantly. The proposed method possesses lowest (σ) value for all level of thresholding, which proves that QINSGA-II is the most stable method among others. Moreover, from Tables 2 and 4, it can be found that QINSGA-II has a very little deviation in $\mathcal{F}_{avg}$ values for each case. Hence, the proposed method possesses highest level of accuracy compared to others.

Table 4. Average fitness ($\mathcal{U}_{avg}$) and standard deviation (σ) of QINSGA-II, NSGA-II and SMS-EMOA for multi-level thresholding of Lena, Peppers, Cameraman, ♮38092, ♮147091 and ♮220075

Lena					
K	QINSGA-II		NSGA-II		SMS-EMOA	
	$\mathcal{F}_{avg}$	σ	$\mathcal{F}_{avg}$	σ	$\mathcal{F}_{avg}$	σ
4	9.579	0.013	10.389	0.734	10.209	0.474
6	10.635	0.089	12.147	0.770	11.751	0.559
8	11.937	0.094	13.483	0.650	13.291	0.501

Peppers					
K	QINSGA-II		NSGA-II		SMS-EMOA	
	$\mathcal{F}_{avg}$	σ	$\mathcal{F}_{avg}$	σ	$\mathcal{F}_{avg}$	σ
4	9.782	0.010	10.521	0.366	10.348	0.454
6	10.876	0.035	12.055	0.698	11.732	0.389
8	12.187	0.082	13.332	0.614	13.049	0.335

Cameraman					
K	QINSGA-II		NSGA-II		SMS-EMOA	
	$\mathcal{F}_{avg}$	σ	$\mathcal{F}_{avg}$	σ	$\mathcal{F}_{avg}$	σ
4	9.337	0.003	9.744	0.311	9.671	0.227
6	10.444	0.035	11.205	0.617	11.225	0.485
8	11.816	0.082	12.812	0.453	12.868	0.463

♮38092					
K	QINSGA-II		NSGA-II		SMS-EMOA	
	$\mathcal{F}_{avg}$	σ	$\mathcal{F}_{avg}$	σ	$\mathcal{F}_{avg}$	σ
4	4.757	0.001	4.796	0.033	4.791	0.023
6	6.592	0.002	6.662	0.038	6.651	0.034
8	8.512	0.003	8.572	0.028	8.569	0.023

♮147091					
K	QINSGA-II		NSGA-II		SMS-EMOA	
	$\mathcal{F}_{avg}$	σ	$\mathcal{F}_{avg}$	σ	$\mathcal{F}_{avg}$	σ
4	4.735	0.001	4.766	0.021	4.766	0.020
6	6.561	0.004	6.627	0.026	6.619	0.041
8	8.503	0.004	8.541	0.020	8.550	0.025

♮220075					
K	QINSGA-II		NSGA-II		SMS-EMOA	
	$\mathcal{F}_{avg}$	σ	$\mathcal{F}_{avg}$	σ	$\mathcal{F}_{avg}$	σ
4	4.706	0.001	4.758	0.042	4.734	0.019
6	6.555	0.004	6.610	0.030	6.597	0.022
8	8.494	0.003	8.527	0.019	8.540	0.028

7.2.3. *Performance evaluation*

In this subsection, the performance of the proposed approach has been evaluated into two directions. Firstly, two convergence-diversity based metrics, known as Inverted Generational Distance (IGD) and Hypervolume (HV) are introduced to establish the superiority of the proposed method on

Table 5.   IGD and HV values of QINSGA-II, NSGA-II and SMS-E-MOA for multi-level thresholding of Lena, Peppers, Cameraman, ♯38092, ♯147091 and ♯220075

K	QINSGA-II		NSGA-II		SMS-EMOA	
	IGD	HV	IGD	HV	IGD	HV
4	0.06200	21.476	0.00480	12.089	0.00210	2.568
6	0.00004	21.045	0.00032	17.088	0.00015	3.208
8	0.00009	39.838	0.00024	2.944	0.00013	2.236

Lena (above)

K	QINSGA-II		NSGA-II		SMS-EMOA	
	IGD	HV	IGD	HV	IGD	HV
4	0.00598	4.578	0.00747	1.170	0.00133	1.538
6	0.00010	26.029	0.00019	1.116	0.00031	1.428
8	0.00015	3.500	0.00018	1.634	1.358	0.00045

Peppers (above)

K	QINSGA-II		NSGA-II		SMS-EMOA	
	IGD	HV	IGD	HV	IGD	HV
4	0.00273	5.579	0.00562	3.031	0.00284	1.894
6	0.00054	1.849	0.00092	1.071	0.00093	1.653
8	0.00025	2.588	0.00028	1.924	0.00034	2.465

Cameraman (above)

K	QINSGA-II		NSGA-II		SMS-EMOA	
	IGD	HV	IGD	HV	IGD	HV
4	0.00067	7.626	0.00086	3.285	0.00014	4.974
6	0.00009	6.691	0.00028	4.784	0.00031	3.984
8	0.00240	5.222	0.00017	1.925	0.00039	3.129

♯38092 (above)

K	QINSGA-II		NSGA-II		SMS-EMOA	
	IGD	HV	IGD	HV	IGD	HV
4	0.00129	5.293	0.00057	1.628	0.00055	5.014
6	0.01073	6.254	0.00280	1.377	0.00168	4.437
8	0.00331	8.066	0.00025	1.675	0.00023	3.376

♯147091 (above)

K	QINSGA-II		NSGA-II		SMS-EMOA	
	IGD	HV	IGD	HV	IGD	HV
4	0.01530	20.872	0.02441	1.939	0.08618	13.531
6	0.00482	20.370	0.00927	4.114	0.00070	15.013
8	0.00008	24.722	0.00005	1.719	0.00001	12.965

♯220075 (above)

multi-objective viewpoint. In addition, in connection with multi-objective optimization, a statistical comparison methodology has also been used for that perspective. IGD and HV are basically used to judge the quality of the optimal set of solutions with regard to convergence and diversity. This statistical comparison test finds the number of participating methods significantly dominating the selected method. Later, the effectiveness of the

Table 6.   Statistical comparison of QINS-GA-II to NSGA-II and SMS-EMOA with reference to the hypervolume indicator of Lena, Peppers, Cameraman, ♯38092, ♯147091 and ♯220075. The number reveals the performance score $\mathcal{P}$

	Lena			Peppers		
K	(a)	(b)	(c)	(a)	(b)	(c)
4	0	2	1	0	2	1
6	0	2	1	0	2	1
8	0	2	1	0	2	1
	Cameraman			♯38092		
K	(a)	(b)	(c)	(a)	(b)	(c)
4	0	1	2	0	2	1
6	0	1	2	0	1	0
8	0	1	2	0	2	1
	♯147091			♯220075		
K	(a)	(b)	(c)	(a)	(b)	(c)
4	0	2	1	0	2	1
6	0	2	1	0	1	2
8	0	2	1	0	1	2
(a):→ QINSGA-II, (b):→ NSGA-II						
(c):→ SMS-EMOA						

proposed method has also been statistically proved by using a statistical superiority test, called Friedman test [54, 55]. Generally, this test is conducted for comparing the performance of several methods using a group of data set. This test determines the average rank of the comparing methods. The results of this test is presented in Table 7. This test finds the lowest average rank value for the proposed method in each case as compared to NSGA-II [18] and SMS-EMOA [19]. A brief overview of IGD, HV and statistical comparison test in connection with multi-objective optimization is discussed below.

(1) Inverted Generational Distance: IGD [56, 57] is a superior version of Generational Distance [18, 56, 58], which considers solutions with reference to the diversity and convergence. IGD considers the obtained solution set and sample points from Pareto front, and thereafter computes the average nearest distance between them. Formally, IGD can be defined by

$$IGD(P, S) = \frac{\left[\sum_{j=1}^{|P|} d_j^q \right]^{\frac{1}{q}}}{|P|} \tag{8}$$

Table 7. Data sets used in QINSGA-II, NSGA-II and SMS-E-MOA for Friedman test for K=4, 6 and 8, respectively. The value in parentheses signifies the rank of the respective method

SN	Image	QINSGA-II	NSGA-II	SMS-EMOA
For K=4				
1	Lena	9.560 (1)	9.645 (3)	9.614 (2)
2	Peppers	9.770 (1)	11.204 (3)	11.042 (2)
3	Cameraman	9.331 (1)	9.349 (2)	9.388 (3)
4	♯38092	4.757 (1)	4.769 (3)	4.765 (2)
5	♯147091	4.734 (1)	4.748 (3)	4.739 (2)
6	♯220075	4.706 (1)	4.714 (3)	4.707 (2)
Average rank		1.00	2.83	2.16
For K=6				
1	Lena	10.566 (1)	11.069 (3)	10.956 (2)
2	Peppers	10.806 (1)	11.204 (3)	11.042 (2)
3	Cameraman	10.385 (1)	10.491 (2)	10.604 (3)
4	♯38092	6.587 (1.5)	6.600 (3)	6.587 (1.5)
5	♯147091	6.554 (1)	6.602 (3)	6.572 (2)
6	♯220075	6.553 (1)	6.566 (2)	6.573 (3)
Average rank		1.08	2.66	2.25
For K=8				
1	Lena	11.747 (1)	12.549 (3)	12.307 (2)
2	Peppers	12.038 (1)	12.466 (3)	12.271 (2)
3	Cameraman	11.681 (1)	12.063 (2)	12.228 (3)
4	♯38092	8.501 (1)	8.524 (3)	8.520 (2)
5	♯147091	8.494 (1)	8.524 (3)	8.510 (2)
6	♯220075	8.490 (1)	8.501 (2)	8.505 (3)
Average rank		1.00	2.66	2.33

where, S represents the optimal set of solution and P is the finite number of pareto-optimal set of solutions that approximates the true Pareto front. d_j is the smallest Euclidean distance of a point in P to the nearest solutions in S.

(2) Hypervolume: Zitzler *et al.* [26, 59] introduced the most popular performance metric, called Hypervolume (HV). In this metric, firstly, a set of hypercubes (HC_j) is formed by using a nadir point and a solution j from its non-dominated solution set. To determine HV value, volume of each member of HC_j is accounted separately and added together. Formally, HV can be defined as follows:

$$HV = volume \left[\bigcup_{j=1}^{|Q|} HC_j \right]$$

(9)

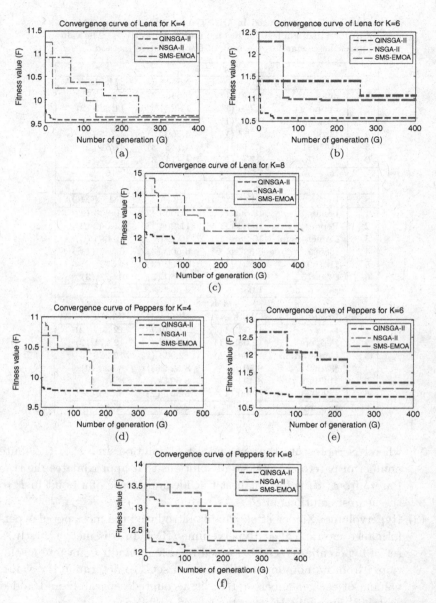

Fig. 3. For $K = 4, 6$ and 8, convergence curves (a)-(c), for Lena, (d)-(f), for Peppers, (g)-(i), for Cameraman, for QINSGA-II, NSGA-II and SMS-EMOA

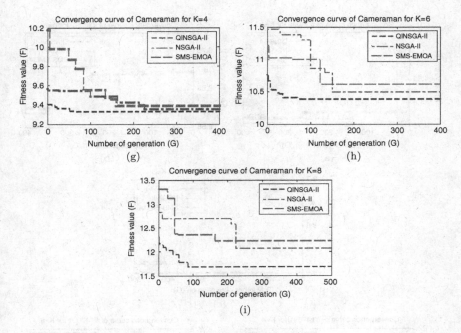

Fig. 3.   (Continued)

where, Q denotes the solution set. Higher HV value designates a better solution as regards convergence and diversity. Note that, a nadir
point is created by considering the worst objective values from the non-
dominated solution set.

(3) Statistical Comparison Methodology: The hypervolume indicator can
be used to judged the quality of the Pareto-set of solutions. In case of
multi-objective problems dealing with less than 6 objectives, the values
of this hypervolume indicator are computed exactly according to the
HV values. Otherwise, the concept of Monte Carlo sampling [60] is used
for this approximation. Let $\mathcal{B}_k$ denotes the set of participating methods
to be compared, where $1 \leq k \leq m$ and m is the number of methods.
Each method $\mathcal{B}_k$ has been executed for 30 number of independent runs
for 500 generations. Investigation is carried out about the statistical superiority among the participating methods. The null hypothesis
(H_0) for this statistical test establishes the equality in approximation of
Pareto-opimal set of solutions. To reject this hypothesis, an alternative
hypothesis (H_1) is introduced, which establishes the unequal behaviour
in approximation of Pareto-opimal solution set.

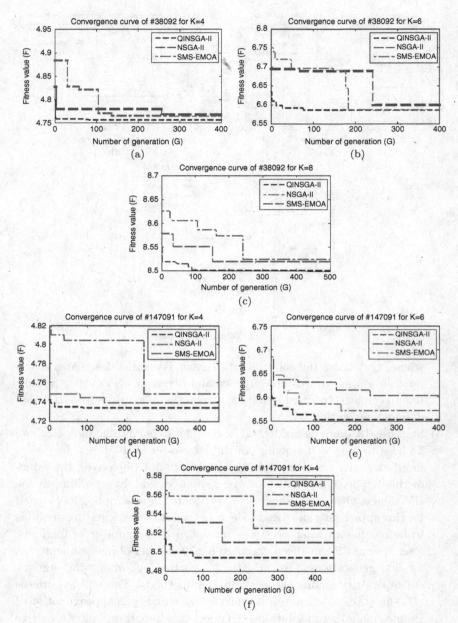

Fig. 4.   For $K = 4, 6$ and 8, convergence curves (a)-(c), for ♯38092, (d)-(f), for ♯147091, (g)-(i), for ♯220075, for QINSGA-II, NSGA-II and SMS-EMOA

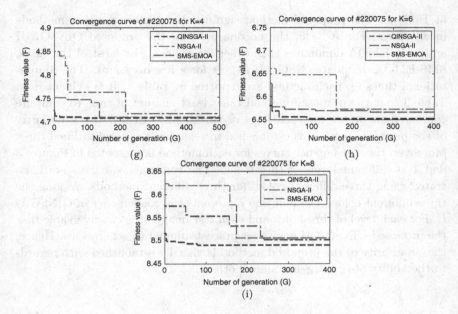

Fig. 4.   (Continued)

Thereafter, the median of the HV values for each pair of methods is compared. The significance of this difference is tested by using Conover-Inman method [61]. To judge this significance, a performance index $P(\mathcal{B}_k)$ is introduced. This index is formally defined by

$$P(\mathcal{B}_k) = \sum_{k=1, q \notin p}^{m} \delta_{p,q} \tag{10}$$

Let $B_i, B_j \in \mathcal{B}_k$. If B_i is significantly better than B_i, $\delta_{p,q}$ is 1, otherwise, $\delta_{p,q}$ is 0. This value finds the number of better performing methods than the corresponding method for a particular test case. Note that, the smaller is the performance index value, the better is the method. A zero index indicates a significantly best approximation for Pareto-set with reference to hypervolume indicator.

The values for IGD and HV for different methods have been reported in Table 5. Compared to other methods, the proposed method possesses better performance metric values in all respects except for a very few occasions. For statistical comparison among the participants, a performance index is introduced indicating the number of other participating methods significantly dominating the selected method. These index values are reported in Table 6. The proposed method significantly dominates other methods in all cases. For $K = 6$, the no one between the proposed QINSGA-II and SMS-EMOA dominates each other for ♯38092. For most of the cases, SMS-EMOA dominates NSGA-II expect for a few occasions. The computational times for each method are reported in Table 3. It is evident from Table 3 that the proposed method takes least amount of time to compute compared to others for each level of thresholds. Hence, the superiority of the proposed method is established in reference to computational time. Moreover, the convergence curves for each method is presented in Figures 3 and 4 at different levels of thresholds. The convergence curves are illustrated using three different colors for three different methods. Among the three different colors, the blue one represents the convergence of QINSGA-II. For each level of thresholds and each test image, it is clearly visible that the proposed QINSGA-II converges in least number of generations. Hence, the superiority of the proposed method is visually established with regards to the ability of convergence among others.

8. Conclusion

In this paper, a computationally fast quantum inspired multi-objective approach has been developed. This proposed method uses basic principles of quantum computing on the backbone of a well-known multi-objective method (NSGA-II) [18] and is applied for multi-level image thresholding. The parameters have been tuned for several times to get the best set of results. The results of QNSGA-II have been compared with the existing multi-objective optimization methods, referred to as NSGA-II [18] and SMS-EMOA [19] for performance evaluation. The superiority of the proposed method is established in terms of fitness measure, standard deviation of fitness measures, average fitness value and computational time. Finally, the performance of different methods is also evaluated using two different performance metrics and using an statistical comparison methodology on multi-objective point of view. The results of Friedman test also finds the proposed method as the best performing method. Hence, the effectiveness of the proposed method is established in all facets for each level of thresholds.

The authors are presently working on developing an automatic quantum inspired multi-objective optimization method for multi-level image thresholding.

References

[1] K. Deb, *Multi-objective optimization using evolutionary algorithms.* John Wiley & Sons Ltd., Chichester, UK (2001).

[2] K. M. Miettinen, *Nonlinear Multiobjective Optimization.* Kluwer Academic Publishers, Boston, MA (1998).

[3] C. M. Fonseca and P. J. Fleming, An overview of evolutionary algorithms in multiobjective optimization, *Evolutionary Computation.* **3**(1), 1–16 (1995).

[4] D. A. V. Veldhuizen and G. B. Lamont, Multiobjective evolutionary algorithms: Analyzing the state-of-the-art, *Journal of Evolutionary Computation, The MIT Press.* **8**(2), 125–147 (2000).

[5] A. A. Younes, I. Truck, and H. Akdaj, Color image profiling using fuzzy sets, *Turk J Elec Engin.* **13**(3), 343–359 (2005).

[6] L. Lanzarini, J. L. Battaglia, J. Maulini, and W. Hasperue, Face recognition using sift and binary pso descriptors, *32nd International Conference on Information Technology Interfaces (ITI).* pp. 557–562 (2010).

[7] N. R. Pal and S. K. Pal, A review on image segmentation techniques, *Pattern Recognition.* **9**(26), 1277–1294 (1993).

[8] P. S. Liao, T. S. Chen, and P. C. Chung, A fast algorithm for multilevel thresholding, *Journal of Information Science and Engineering.* **17**, 713–727 (2001).

[9] A. Nakiba, H. Oulhadja, and P. Siarry, Image thresholding based on pareto multiobjective optimization, *Engineering Applications of Artificial Intelligence.* **23**(3), 313–320 (2010).

[10] M. Sezgin and B. Sankur, Survey over image thresholding techniques and quantitative performance evaluation, *Journal of Electronic Imaging.* **13**(1), 146–165 (2004).

[11] R. Feynman, Simulating physics with computers, *International Journal of Theoretical Physics.* **21**, 467–488 (1982).

[12] D. Mcmohan, *Quantum computing explained.* John Wiley & Sons, Inc., Hoboken, New Jersey (2008).

[13] S. Bhattacharyya and S. Dey, An efficient quantum inspired genetic algorithm with chaotic map model based interference and fuzzy objective function for gray level image thresholding, *Proc. 2011 International Conference on Computational Intelligence and Communication Systems (CICN 2011), Gwalior, India.* pp. 121–125 (2011).

[14] S. Dey, S. Bhattacharyya, and U. Maullik, *Chaotic Map Model based Interference Employed in Quantum Inspired Genetic Algorithm to Determine the Optimum Gray Level Image Thresholding.* Global Trends in Intelligent Computing Research and Development (2013).

[15] S. Dey, S. Bhattacharyya, and U. Maulik, Quantum inspired meta-heuristic algorithms for multi-level thresholding for true colour images, *Proceedings of the IEEE Indicon 2013, Mumbai, India.* pp. 1–6 (2013).

[16] P. W. Shorr, Polynomial-time algorithms for prime factorization and discrete logarithms on a quantum computer, *Quantum computing.* p. 467486 (1978).

[17] J. Kittler and J. Illingworth, Minimum error thresholding, *Pattern Recognition.* **19**(1), 41–47 (1986).

[18] K. Deb, A. Pratap, S. Agarwal, and T. Meyarivan, A fast and elitist multiobjective genetic algorithm: Nsga-II, *IEEE Transactions on Evolutionary Computation.* **6**(2), 182–197 (2002).

[19] M. Emmerich, N. Beume, and B. Naujoks, *An EMO Algorithm Using the Hypervolume Measure as Selection Criterion.* Springer-Verlag, Berlin, Heidelberg (2005).

[20] J. D. Shaffer, *Some Experiments in Machine Learning Using Vector Evaluated Genetic Algorithms.* Ph. D. Thesis, Vanderbilt University, Nashville, TN (1984).

[21] C. M. Fonseca and P. J. Fleming, Genetic algorithms for multiobjective optimization: Formulation, discussion and generalization, *in Proceedings of the Fifth International Conference on Genetic Algorithms, S. Forrest, Ed. San Mateo, CA: Morgan Kauffman.* pp. 416–423 (1993).

[22] J. Horn, N. Nafpliotis, and D. E. Nafpliotis, A niched pareto genetic algorithm for multiobjective optimization, *In proc. of the First IEEE Conference on Evolutionary Computation, IEEE World Congress on Computational Intelligence, Piscataway, New Jersey, IEEE Service Center.* **1**, 82–87 (1994).

[23] N. Srinivas and K. Deb, Multiobjective optimization using nondominated sorting in genetic algorithms, *Evolutionary Computation Journal.* **2**(3), 221–248 (1994).

[24] D. E. Goldberg, *Genetic Algorithms in Search.* Optimization and Machine Learning, Reading, Mass, Addison Wesley (1989).

[25] M. Tanaka and T. Tanino, Global optimization by the genetic algorithm in a multi-objective decision support system, *In Proc. of the 10th International Conference on Multiple Criteria Decision Making.* **2**, 261–270 (1992).

[26] R. Zitzler and L. Thiele, Multiobjective evolutionary algorithms: A comparative case study and the strength pareto approach, *IEEE Transactions on Evolutionary Computation.* **3**(4), 257–271 (1999).

[27] E. Zitzler, M. Laumanns, and L. Thiele, Spea2: Improving the strength pareto evolutionary algorithm, *In: EUROGEN 2001. Evolutionary Methods for Design, Optimization and Control with Applications to Industrial Problems, Athens, Greece.* pp. 95–100 (2002).

[28] J. D. Knowles and D. W. Corne, Approximating the nondominated front using the pareto archived evolution strategy, *Evolutionary Computation.* **8**(2), 149–172 (2000).

[29] D. W. Corne, J. D. Knowles, and M. J. Oates, The pareto envelope-based selection algorithm for multi-objective optimization, *In: PPSN, LNCS, Springer, Heidelberg.* **1917**, 839–848 (2000).

[30] M. Gravel, W. L. Price, and C. Gagné, Scheduling continuous casting of aluminium using a multiple objective ant colony optimization metaheuristic, *European Journal of Operational Research.* **143**(1), 218–229 (2002).

[31] C. A. Coello and N. CruzCortes, Solving multiobjective optimization problems using an artificial immune system, *Genetic Programming and Evolvable Machines.* **2**, 163–190 (2005).

[32] B. Suman, Study of self-stopping pdmosa and performance measure in multiobjective optimization, *Comput. Chem. Eng.* **29**(5), 1131–1147 (2005).

[33] B. Suman and P. Kumar, A survey of simulated annealing as a tool for single and multiobjective optimization, *J. Oper. Res. Soc.* **57**(10), 1143–1160 (2006).

[34] J. Holland, *Adaptation in Natural and Artificial Systems.* Ann Arbor: University of Michigan Press (1975).

[35] C. Reeves, Using genetic algorithms with small populations, *Proceedings of the Fifth International Conference on Genetic Algorithms, Morgan Kaufman, San Mateo, CA.* pp. 92–99 (1993).

[36] C. Aranha, Portfolio management by genetic algorithms with error modeling, *Inform. Sci.* pp. 459–465 (2007).

[37] M. Paulinas and A. Uinskas, A survey of genetic algorithms applications for image enhancement and segmentation, *Inform. Technol. Control.* **36**(3), 278–284 (2007).

[38] S. Dey, S. Bhattacharyya, and U. Maulik, Quantum inspired genetic algorithm and particle swarm optimization using chaotic map model based interference for gray level image thresholding, *Swarm and Evolutionary Computation.* **15**, 38–57 (2014).

[39] S. Dey, I. Saha, S. Bhattacharyya, and U. Maulik, Multi-level thresholding using quantum inspired meta-heuristics, *Knowledge-Based Systems.* **67**, 373–400 (2014).

[40] S. Dey, S. Bhattacharyya, and U. Maulik, New quantum inspired tabu search for multi-level colour image thresholding, *Proceedings of 8th International Conference On Computing for Sustainable Global Development (INDIACom-2014), BVICAM, New Delhi.* pp. 311–316 (2014).

[41] S. Dey, S. Bhattacharyya, and U. Maulik, Quantum inspired automatic clustering for multi-level image thresholding, *Proceedings of the International Conference On Computational Intelligence and Communication Networks (ICCICN 2014), RCCIIT, Kolkata, India.* pp. 247–251 (2014).

[42] S. Dey, S. Bhattacharyya, and U. Maulik, Quantum behaved multi-objective pso and aco optimization for multi-level thresholding, *Proceedings of the International Conference On Computational Intelligence and Communication Networks (ICCICN 2014), RCCIIT, Kolkata, India.* pp. 242–246 (2014).

[43] S. Dey, S. Bhattacharyya, and U. Maulik, New quantum inspired meta-heuristic techniques for multi-level colour image thresholding, *Applied Soft Computing.* **46**, 677–702 (2016).

[44] S. Dey, S. Bhattacharyya, and U. Maulik, efficient quantum inspired meta-heuristics for multi-level true colour image thresholding, *Applied Soft Computing.* **56**, 472–513 (2017).

[45] S. Dey, I. Saha, S. Bhattacharyya, and U. Maulik, New quantum inspired meta-heuristic methods for multi-level thresholding, *Proceedings of the 2013 International Conference on Advances in Computing, Communications and Informatics (ICACCI), Mysore.* pp. 1236–1240 (2013).

[46] S. Bhattacharyya, P. Dutta, S. Chakraborty, R. Chakraborty, and S. Dey, Determination of optimal threshold of a gray-level image using a quantum

inspired genetic algorithm with interference based on a random map model, *Proceedings of the IEEE International Conference on Computational Intelligence and Computing Research (ICCIC 2010), Coimbatore, India.* pp. 422–425 (2010).

[47] D. Deutsch and R. Jozsa, Rapid solution of problems by quantum computation, *Proc. of the Royal Society of London. Series A, Mathematical and Physical Sciences.* **439**(1907), 553–558 (1992).

[48] P. Shor, Polynomial-time algorithms for prime factorization and discrete algorithms on a quantum computer, *Proc. of the 35th Annual Symposium on Foundations of Computer Science, IEEE Computer Society Press.* pp. 124–134 (1994).

[49] V. Vendral, M. B. Plenio, and M. A. Rippin, Quantum entanglement, *Physical Review Letters.* **78**(12), 2275–2279 (1997).

[50] C. Williams and S. Clearwater, *Ultimate Zero & One: Computing at the Quantum Frontier.* Copernicus Books, New York (1999).

[51] C. Williams and S. Clearwater, *Explorations in Quantum Computing.* Springer-Verlag, New York (1998).

[52] K. H. Han and J. H. Kim, Quantum-inspired evolutionary algorithm for a class combinational optimization, *IEEE Transaction on Evolutionary Computation.* **6**(6), 580–593 (2002).

[53] Benchmark dataset. URL `https://www.eecs.berkeley.edu/Research/Projects/CS/vision/bsds/` (Date last accessed 15-March-2016).

[54] M. Friedman, The use of ranks to avoid the assumption of normality implicit in the analysis of variance, *Journal of the American Statistical Association.* **31**(200), 675–701 (1937).

[55] M. Friedman, A comparison of alternative tests of significance for the problem of m rankings, *Annals of Mathematical Statistics.* **11**(1), 86–92 (1940).

[56] D. V. Veldhuizen and G. Lamont, Multiobjective evolutionary algorithm test suites, *Proceedings of ACM Symposium on Applied Computing.* pp. 351–357 (1999).

[57] E. Zitzler and L. Thiele, Performance assessment of multiobjective optimizers: An analysis and review, *IEEE Transactions on Evolutionary Computation.* **7**(2), 117–132 (2003).

[58] H. Li and Q. Zhang, Multiobjective optimization problems with complicated pareto sets, moea/d and nsga-ii, *IEEE Transactions on Evolutionary Computation.* **13**(2), 284–302 (2009).

[59] E. Zitzler and L. Thiele, *Multiobjective optimization using evolutionary algorithms: A comparative case study.* Springer-Verlag, London, UK (1999).

[60] J. Bader and E. Zitzler, *HypE: An Algorithm for Fast Hypervolume-Based Many-Objective Optimization.* TIK Report 286, Institut fr Technische Informatik und Kommunikationsnetze, ETH Zürich (2008).

[61] W. J. Conover, *Practical Nonparametric Statistics.* John Wiley, 3rd edition (1999).

Chapter 7

An Optimized Support Vector Regression Using Whale Optimization for Long Term Wind Speed Forecasting

Sarah Osama[*] and Essam H. Houssein[†]

*Scientific Research Group in Egypt (SRGE),
Faculty of Computers and Information, Minia University, Egypt
* sarahosama792@gmail.com; † essam.halim@mu.edu.eg*

Ashraf Darwish[‡]

*Scientific Research Group in Egypt (SRGE),
Faculty of Science, Helwan University, Egypt
‡ ashraf.darwish.eg@ieee.org*

Aboul Ella Hassanien[§] and Aly A. Fahmy[¶]

*FCI-Cairo University, Scientific Research Group in Egypt (SRGE),
Faculty of Computers and Information, Cairo University, Egypt
§ aboitcairo@gmail.com; ¶ a.fahmy@fci-cu.edu.eg*

In this chapter, support vector regression and whale optimization algorithm (WOA) are presented for long-term prediction of wind speed. The WOA is adapted for optimizing the support vector regression (SVR) parameters so that the prediction error can be reduced. The rendering of the proposed algorithm is evaluated using three different measurements including forecasting based-measurements, statistical analyses, and stability. The daily average wind speed data from Space Weather Monitoring Center (SWMC) in Egypt was selected in the experiments. The experimental results showed that the suggested WOA algorithm is eligible for finding the best values of SVR parameters, avoiding local optima issue and it is competitive for wind speed forecasting. The result also demonstrates lower classification error rates compared with traditional SVR algorithm. The experimental result also proved that the WOA-SVR algorithm utilizing Linear kernel accomplished lesser classification fault rates than RBF kernel.

Keywords: Whale optimization algorithm (WOA); Support vector regression (SVR); Wind speed; Forecasting.

1. Introduction

There are different forms of sources such as wind, solar, hydropower, biomass, fuel cells, and tides. However, renewable sources such as wind are everywhere and environmentally friendly. On the arrival of the 21st century, Egypt has increased financial investments in the use and development of wind energy due to the lack of electricity resources. Egypt has one of the world's best and most predictable wind resources in the Gulf of Suez with average wind speed and average energy density of $7e^{10.5}$ m/s and $350e^{900}$ W/m^2 respectively.[1,2] So the wind industry is expanding quite rapidly. However, expansion of the wind energy industry has faced some challenges and troubles in the development of large current wind power in Egypt. Meanwhile, in the process of planning and design of , the assessment of wind resources potential is strictly necessary, which represents the key to earning future investment income, especially in renewable energy.[3]

The wind energy is a new option to fulfill the energy demand and is one of the most outstanding energy sources. Using wind power as a renewable source of energy has become increasingly popular because of its environment friendly nature. Modeling the wind speed is the first step to design a system according to the different parameters to predict the wind speed. We always view as a variable random, to determine the potential of wind energy resources in the region, the statistical analysis of wind speed is necessary. In recent years, assessing wind power sources has become a heated topic of research.[4] Normally, forecasting wind speed is split into three classes; their names are, short, medium, and long term predication. The short term predication could show us forecasting data for a few hours in advance no more. Theme demurrage forecasts are for a duration that varies from about a few hours to three days ahead. Longterm forecasts point to a duration more than three days to come; yet, there is no end of the duration.[5]

The is a very important scope of study in the energy sector. There are various studies in literature that suggest some methods that are suggested to predict wind speed as in Refs. 6–10. It is worth mentioning that wind speed varies from time to time, seasons, and even by the year. Also, the wind is never steady all the time. Moreover, the wind pattern usually, repeats over a year.

In the past years, revolutionary computations, which are a subfield of the computational intelligence that involves combinatorial optimization problems, have received much attention. These algorithms have been inspired by creating a relation between the power of natural evolutionary mechanisms and the nature of the solving problem.

The ant colony algorithm is to simulate the of the ant's colony in nature, and the improved particle swarm optimization (PSO) is based on predatory position studies of fish and birds, and acquisition of the cuckoo search (CS) acquisition acquired from the spawning behavior to detect the nest. Because of the simplicity and efficiency of solving optimization problems, these clustering optimization algorithms such as PSO, CS, simulated annealing (SA), genetic algorithm (GA), ant colony algorithm (ACA) and bat algorithm (BA) are increasingly becoming tools for effective optimization. Meta-Heuristic algorithms deliver competitive results when optimized solution problems including parameter setting problem.[6,9] Now, researchers and applications of meta-optimization algorithms are exceptionally inadequate in estimating parameters of wind speed distribution models. Once you get the unknown parameters of the density function, we can determine the specific shape of the wind speed distribution model. Therefore, the estimation and improvement of unknown parameters are of great importance in determining the wind speed distribution model.

In the past years, has been applied to forecast the speed of the wind. SVR is equipped with the 'Kernel Substitution' and other optimization features and is based on the principle of the structure error minimization.[11] SVR can perform a noise robust, non-linear regression. The accuracy and stability of SVR depend on various factors including feature selection, and parameter tuning is the most important factor.

The kernel is defined as an inner product in a feature space using the kernel trick, which we define as the kernel substitution.[12] The main idea is that, if an algorithm is formulated in a way that the input vector x enters only in the way of scalar products, then scalar product could be substituted with some other option of the kernel. Thus, the kernel trick is the technique of utilizing the kernel function as a substitute for the internal product of two vectors in the mapping of higher dimensional space. The main advantage of the kernel trick is that we can improve the higher dimensional space without a clear mapping function to draw arbitrary vector map of the space-dimensional feature to the higher dimensional space.[13,14] Some well-known utilized kernel functions are polynomial kernels, Gaussian RBF kernels, and Mercer kernels.[15]

The major objective of this chapter is to utilize whale optimization algorithm (WOA) to present a new WOA-SVR model for parameters optimization of SVR that include kernel function parameter, penalty factor C and best feature subset which both fulfill data description with least redundancy and improves the classification performance by reduced classification error.

This chapter is arranged as follows: Section 2 in brief, the definition of wind speed prediction problem. In Section 3 in brief, introduces the related work. In Section 4 the wind speed and fifteen meteorological factors from wind dataset are approached. In Section 5, offers a general description of Support Vector Regression and Whale Optimization Algorithm. The proposed forecasting algorithm is demonstrated in Section 6. Section 7 presents the experimental results and discussion. The conclusions had been shown in Section 8. Lastly, the acknowledgment in Section 8.

2. Problem Statement

In this chapter, we are paying a special attention to the case of relatively data because it is applicable to the planning and operation of wind energy generation in Egypt. SVR parameters has a great influence on the complexity and precision of model predication. The used wind speed data in this chapter is measured on an average daily basis at the height of 30 m from a meteorological station at Helwan University, Cairo, Egypt and were collected for 1 year (2016).

3. Literature Review

Several models have been applied in the state-of-art to improve the performance of wind speed forecasting approaches. Literature reviews explained to us that although a large number of forecasting methods have been studied, no one is found certain to be appropriate for all sets of data. As a point of explanation, in Ref. 16, the active learning approach for forecasting speed of the wind have been introduced. To be particular, three various active learning strategies had been proposed, developed for kernel ridge regression (KRR). Also, in Ref. 10, authors have proposed a time series model predication is based on structural break modeling and Bayesian theory to forecast the speed of the wind. Also, in Ref. 17, authors test a recent way for short term speed of the wind forecasting furthermore stated on gray model to minimize the error of short term wind speed predication, one of the most successful approaches is particle swarm optimization algorithm, which chooses the parameters of gray model to avoid the man-made blindness and strengthens the efficiency and capability of forecasting. In Ref. 18, Ahmed et al. had suggested a hybrid predication model based on

Krill-ANFIS for forecasting speed of the wind. There are different neural network algorithms that we applied to predication the speed of the wind, in Ref. 8, where researchers had presented an artificial neural network method for short-term power of the wind predication. The reliability of forecasting power of the wind gained with the proposed approach is rated against persistence, and ARIMA approaches. Also, in Ref. 19, Liu *et al.* have presented a forecasting model by using neural networks, then the model tested using wind power for the plant. Moreover, in Ref. 20, authors have developed a prediction model depend on artificial neural networks and fuzzy logic. Furthermore, in Ref. 21, authors had presented a Back Propagation neural network based on PSO (PSO-BP), the paper proposed a model named ISPSO-BP that join PSO-BP with comprehensive parameter selection. Which is a short for Input Parameter Selection. In Ref. 6, Wang *et al.* have proposed a hybrid prediction technique based on optimized support vector regression (SVR) and recurrence plot (RP). After that, the SVR model is utilized to forecast the speed of the wind, in which the input variables are chosen by RP, and two parameters, involving the penalties agent and gamma of the, are optimized by, and cuckoo optimization algorithm (COA). In Ref. 9, Chen *et al.* had proposed an ensemble approach by 5-3 Hanning filter and wavelet denoising techniques, conjunction with artificial intelligence optimization based SVR and NN model. These models optimized by GA, PSO, and COA and then applied the optimized models to speed of the wind predication series. According to Ref. 11, a hybrid methodology for wind speed predication based on SVR had been proposed. The autoregressive model called Time Delay Coordinates is utilized, feature selection is provided by the Phase Space Re-construction procedure. Then, SVR model is trained using wind speed time series and parameters of SVR which are tuned by a GA. Finally, Ref. 22, has used Evolutionary Programming algorithm (EP) and PSO to optimize the hyperparameters in SVR. Then, SVR model is utilized for speed of the wind predication.

From the literature review, the SVR forecasting results are better than other techniques. When utilizing SVR, we face two issues: how to select the optimal input feature subset of SVR and how to set the best parameters of SVR kernel function. The values of the two parameters interact and vice versa. These problems rise the complexity of the proposed model and lead to reduce the ability of the SVR predication that will influence on testing results and classifier accuracy. In this chapter, the WOA meta-heuristic algorithm is introduced to overcome these problems, by getting as much information as possible from a data set while utilizing the least number of features and carefully determining kernel function, penalty factor C and kernel parameter.This way you can save time calculation and build models that better circulate invisible data points.

4. Description of the Data Set

The data of the wind can be described with different agents, like the wind direction,humidity and air temperature, i.e., the variation of speed of the wind is affected by meteorological agents. In that chapter, sixteen meteorological factors (including: Outside Temperature (OutTemp),Hi Temperature (HiTemp), Low Temperature (LTemp), Outside Humidity (OutHum), Dew Point(DewP), Wind Run, Hi Speed, Wind Chell, Heat Index(HInd), THW Index(THWInd), Barometric Pressure(BarPress), Rain, Rin Rate, Hi Direction (HiDir), Wind Direction (WindDir) and Wind Speed (WindS)), the first fifteen factors have been utilized as the inputs to forecast the speed of the wind parameter and to prepare experimental data for the modeling and testing of the developed models. This data is completed with daily average weather data that is collected and employed from the Space Weather Monitoring Center (SWMC).The time of the study ranges from January 1, 2016, to December 22, 2016, except some missing days. The data set includes 197 wind samples.

Table 1 summarizes the sixteen meteorological factors, including the mathematical view for each variable.

A collected sample from data set with 15 wind data is shown in Table 2.

5. Preliminaries

5.1. *Wind Speed and Wind Direction*

Speed of the wind is the major parameter necessary for the evaluation of the wind as a source of . The overall annual mean wind speed is extremely important as well as the different period; daily, monthly, seasonal. It is crucial to estimate the overall of energy over a certain period. It is clear that the windiest month is August with the mean speed of the wind is 8.65 m/s at 25 m (a.g.l.). On the other hand, the least windy month is November with a mean wind speed of 5.24 m/s at the same height. To generate more electricity, the turbines should be perpendicularly adjusted to the wind direction to optimally extract maximum wind energy. In this

Table 1.   The input/output variables of wind dataset to facilitate the presentation of the subsequent analysis and results

Meteorological Factors (Input or Output Variables)	Mathematical Representation
Outside Temperature	X_1
Hi Temperature	X_2
Low Temperature	X_3
Outside Humidity	X_4
Dew Point	X_5
Wind Run	X_6
Hi Speed	X_7
Wind Chell	X_8
Heat Index	X_9
THW Index	X_{10}
Barometric Pressure	X_{11}
Rain	X_{12}
Rain Rate	X_{13}
Hi Direction	X_{14}
Wind Direction	X_{15}
Wind Speed	Y

chapter, we focus on the main parameters; namely wind speed and wind direction to build the new approach that is presented in this chapter.

5.2. *Support Vector Regression (SVR)*

The SVM proposed by Vapnik,[23] had been used successfully for pattern recognition, regression, and classification. SVM is based on the theory of statistical learning, the Vapnik-Chervonenkis dimension theory, and the principle of the structural risk minimization (SRM). Support vector regression (SVR), also founded by Vapnik and mates,[24] is an extension of SVM. In comparison with SVM, the generalized error bound instead of minimizing the observed training error had been reduced by SVR. To have the optimum generalization ability, the basic principle of SVR is to map the main data into a high dimensional feature space by nonlinear mapping.[10] Assume that the training data are $(x_1, y_1), \ldots, (x_n, y_n)$, the regression formula can be defined as:

$$f(x) = \sum_{i=1}^{D} \omega_i \Phi_i(x) + b, \Phi_i : R^n \to F, \omega_i \in F, b \in R \tag{1}$$

where $\{\omega_i\}_{i=1}^n$ weights evaluated from the training data, b is the threshold value and $\{\Phi_i\}_{i=1}^n$ nonlinear mapping functions which map the data to a

Table 2. A sample from wind dataset

X_1	X_2	X_3	X_4	X_5	X_6	X_7	X_8	X_9	X_{10}	X_{11}	X_{12}	X_{13}	X_{14}	X_{15}	Y
16.39	16.47	16.32	65.59	9.60	0.62	2.95	16.39	15.92	15.92	1018.52	0.00	0.00	45.94	33.75	1.02
17.21	17.28	17.13	63.69	9.99	0.72	3.13	17.21	16.72	16.71	1017.87	0.00	0.00	79.53	67.81	1.18
16.61	16.70	16.53	60.96	8.73	0.30	1.46	16.61	15.99	15.99	1016.47	0.00	0.00	149.53	156.72	0.49
16.51	16.59	16.43	64.97	9.74	0.45	2.27	16.51	16.08	16.08	1016.95	0.00	0.00	132.19	147.97	0.74
15.84	15.92	15.76	59.81	7.77	0.59	2.79	15.84	15.14	15.14	1017.88	0.00	0.00	127.81	122.97	0.96
16.07	16.14	15.99	61.48	8.44	0.73	3.02	16.06	15.47	15.46	1013.86	0.00	0.00	89.22	106.25	1.19
16.31	16.40	16.23	46.99	4.51	1.51	6.32	16.04	15.21	14.94	1008.94	0.00	0.00	205.47	208.59	2.50
12.41	12.46	12.35	46.98	1.12	1.86	6.88	11.27	11.37	10.23	1013.35	0.00	0.00	230.00	218.91	3.10
12.48	12.55	12.40	56.35	3.80	0.66	2.72	12.34	11.70	11.56	1018.96	0.00	0.00	185.16	188.28	1.10
12.57	12.74	12.45	64.19	5.58	0.21	1.05	12.57	12.07	12.07	1020.68	0.00	0.00	164.03	163.31	0.34
16.55	16.67	16.43	49.56	5.63	0.50	2.11	16.54	15.50	15.49	1013.99	0.00	0.00	184.14	191.16	0.81
16.19	16.27	16.12	56.30	7.14	1.69	5.46	15.36	15.35	14.52	1016.11	0.00	0.00	269.06	273.75	2.80
12.31	12.39	12.24	65.69	5.83	1.47	5.42	11.59	11.80	11.08	1018.27	0.00	0.00	282.19	292.19	2.45
13.24	13.30	13.20	54.69	4.20	0.77	3.38	13.10	12.36	12.22	1021.06	0.00	0.00	248.28	276.09	1.27
13.29	13.37	13.22	54.02	3.85	0.46	2.11	13.29	12.39	12.39	1021.34	0.00	0.00	61.41	61.09	0.75

high-dimensional feature space F. Based on the SRM principle, the weights $\{\omega_i\}_{i=1}^n$ can be gained from the given data by minimizing the following problem of the quadratic programming:

$$min\frac{1}{2} = \|\omega\|^2 + C\sum_{i=1}^n (\xi_i - \xi_i^*) \tag{2}$$

Subject to:

$$|y_i - \omega \cdot \Phi(x_i) - b| \le \varepsilon + \xi_i, \xi_i, \xi_i^* \ge 0, i = 1, 2, 3, \ldots, n \tag{3}$$

where constant C, also named the penalties factor, is greater than zero and determines the trade off by decreasing the training error and minimizing the complexity of the model. ξ_i and ξ_i^n are the slack variables. $\varepsilon(\cdot)$ is the ε-intensive loss function and is consider as follows:

$$\varepsilon(y_i) = \begin{cases} 0, |f(x_i - y_i)| < \varepsilon \\ |f(x_i) - y_i| - \varepsilon, otherwise \end{cases} \tag{4}$$

Through fixing the optimization problem, the estimation function could be gained as:

$$f(x, \alpha, \alpha^*) = \sum_{i=1}^n (\alpha_i - \alpha_i^*)K(x_i, x_j) + b \tag{5}$$

Subject to:

$$\sum_{i=1}^n (\alpha_i - \alpha_i^*) = 0, 0 \le \alpha_i, \alpha_i^* \le C \tag{6}$$

where $K(x_i, x_j)$ is a kernel function which represents the inner product in the D-dimensional feature space. SVR is described by the usage of kernel substitution to apply linear rating techniques to nonlinear rating issues.

$$K(x_i, x_j) = \sum_{i=1}^D \Phi(x_i) \cdot \Phi(x_j) \tag{7}$$

In machine learning theories, the famous kernel functions are three which are:

(1) Linear kernel:

$$K(x_i, x_j) = x_i^T x_j \tag{8}$$

(2) Polynomial kernel:

$$K(x_i, x_j) = (1 + x_i \cdot x_j)^d \tag{9}$$

(3) Radial Basis Function (RBF);

$$K(x_i, x_j) = e^{-\gamma\|x_i \cdot x_j\|^2} \tag{10}$$

where d indicates the degree of polynomial kernel function, γ indicates the gamma of RBF kernel function.

5.3. Feature Selection

Features selection (FS) is an important task before the classification phase. More features extracted often result in irrelevant and redundant features. This large features number, known as *the curse of dimensionality*, can have a grater part in the performance and strength of the system. Also it's considered a serious challenge to the learning methods that exists now.[25] Feature selection algorithms could solve that issue by choosing only relevant features (see Fig. 1).

Also, it could lessen the training computational time and simplify the learned classifier.[26] Four main steps are necessary for a typical features selection process 1. These basic steps are features subset generation, features subset evaluation, stopping/convergence criteria and finally feature subset 'result' validation. First, many features subsets are generated according to some criteria, then each feature subset is evaluated and compared to the previous one based on certain evaluation.[27] If the novel features subset is better than the previous one, it will replace as the first one. This procedure including features subsets generating and evaluation are repeated until convergence is reached. Finally the best features subset is evaluated

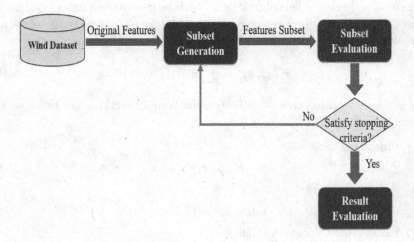

Fig. 1.   The main steps of features selection algorithm

using different measurements. For the feature selection issue, the aim is to find out the most important subset of features that represent the original features in wind datasets. The selected features are used in optimization of a certain fitness function, so the feature selection issue could be seen as an optimization problem.

5.4. *Whale Optimization Algorithm*

5.4.1. *Inspiration analysis*

Whales are superb mammals that are believed to be the biggest creatures in the earth. The adult whale could grow to 180 t in weight and 30 m in length. The WOA had been considered as a new nature-inspired meta-heuristic optimization algorithm that simulates the manner of humpback whales. Authors in Ref. 28 have proposed an optimization algorithm which simulates the hunting manner of humpback whales. The presented optimization algorithm in this chapter; named as the Whale Optimization Algorithm (WOA) considered one of three operators to mimic looking for the victim, surrounding the victim, and bubble-net for aging manner of humpback whales.

5.4.2. *Mathematical model and optimization algorithm*

This section highlights the mathematical model in three stages; surrounding victim, spiral bubble-net feeding maneuver, and looking for the victim.

Encircling prey The whale optimization algorithm assumes that the best solutions chosen are objective victims or close to optimal ones. In this case, humpback whales have identified the best seeking agent. The other search agents then seek to change their attitudes toward the best search agent. This position can be explained by the following equations:

$$\vec{D} = \left| \vec{C}.\vec{X^*}(t) - \vec{X}(t) \right| \tag{11}$$

$$\vec{X}(t+1) = \vec{X}(t) - \vec{A}.\vec{D} \tag{12}$$

In which t refer to the iteration of the current position, $\vec{A}$ and $\vec{C}$ are coefficient vectors, X^* is the position vector of the optimal solution which can gained so far, $\vec{X}$ is the position vector, $||$ can be defined as the absolute value. It is important to notice that, X^* should be updated for every iteration if there exists better solution. The vectors $\vec{A}$ and $\vec{C}$ could be estimated according to the following equations:

$$\vec{A} = 2\vec{a}.\vec{r} - \vec{a} \tag{13}$$

$$C = 2.\vec{r} \tag{14}$$

where $\vec{a}$ could be reduced from 2 to 0 over the iterations course, and $\vec{r}$ is a random vector in $[0,1]$. The humpback whales could raid the victim with the bubble-net method.

Bubble-net argument attacking method (exploitation stage): Their are two approaches are designed here to model mathematically the bubble-net attitude of humpback whales as follows:

Shrinking encircling mechanism:
This attitude is accomplished by reducing the value of $\vec{a}$ in the Equation (13). $\vec{A}$ is a random value in the interval $[-a, a]$ where a is reduced from 2 to 0 over the iterations course. By setting random values for $\vec{A}$ in [-1, 1], the new situation of a search agent could be known anywhere in between the original site of the agent and the site of the current best agent.

Spiral updating position:
A spiral equation is then evaluated between the position of whale and victim to mimic the helix-shaped movement of humpback whales as next:

$$\vec{X}(t+1) = \vec{D}'.e^{bl}.\cos(2\Pi l) + \overrightarrow{X^*}(t) \tag{15}$$

where $\vec{D} = \left| \overrightarrow{X^*}(t) - \vec{X}(t) \right|$ marks the distance between the i whale and the victim (best solution gained so far), b is a constant for defining the shape of the logarithmic spiral, l is a random number in [-1, 1], and is an element-by-element multiplication. During optimization phase; the mathematical model is as next:

$$\vec{X}(t+1) = \begin{cases} \overrightarrow{X^*}(t) - \vec{X}.\vec{D} & \text{if } p < 0.5 \\ \overrightarrow{D^*}.e^{bl}.\cos(2\Pi l) + \overrightarrow{X^*}(t) & \text{if } p \geq 0.5 \end{cases} \tag{16}$$

where p is a random number in $[0,1]$. In addition to the bubble-net method, the humpback whales looking for victim randomly. Finally, the mathematical model of the looking is as next.

Search for victim (exploration phase) The same approach depend on the variation of the $\overrightarrow{A}$ vector could be applied to search for victim. Humpback whales search randomly according to the sight of each other. We utilize $\overrightarrow{A}$ with the random values greater than 1 or less than 1 to impose search agent to shift further away from a reference whale. In contrast to the exploitation phase, the site of search agent had been updated in the exploration phase, according to a randomly selected search agent instead of the best search agent established till now. This mechanism and $\left|\overrightarrow{A}\right| > 1$ emphasize exploration and can permit the WOA algorithm to make a global search. The mathematical model can be described as follows:

$$\overrightarrow{D} = \left|\overrightarrow{C}.\overrightarrow{X_{rand}} - \overrightarrow{X}\right| \tag{17}$$

$$\overrightarrow{X}(t+1) = \overrightarrow{X_{rand}} - \overrightarrow{A}.\overrightarrow{D} \tag{18}$$

where $\overrightarrow{X_{rand}}$ is a random position vector which has been selected from the current population. The WOA algorithm begins with a set of random solutions. At every iteration, search agents upgrade their sites with respect to either a randomly selected search agent or the best solution obtained till now. The a parameter is reduced from 2 to 0 to allow exploration and exploitation, respectively. A random search agent is selected when $\left|\overrightarrow{A}\right| > 1$ while the best solution is chosen when $\left|\overrightarrow{A}\right| < 1$ for updating the site by the search agents. Depending on the value of p, WOA is capable to switch between either a spiral or circular movement. Finally, the WOA algorithm was ended by the satisfaction of a termination criterion.

6. The Proposed Forecasting Algorithm

Algorithms start from taking the wind dataset as input, then for missing values, we use linear interpolation to fill these gaps, then various meta-heuristic optimization algorithm are adopted to choose the best parameters of SVR. Finally, these selected parameters are evaluated using five measurements; forecasting based on measurements (including root mean square error (RMSE), mean square error (MSE), mean absolute percentage error (MAPE), and mean absolute error (MAE), convergence, computational time, statistical measurements (including the worst, best, mean fitness function and average of selected features) and stability. Figure 2 shows the proposed model architecture.

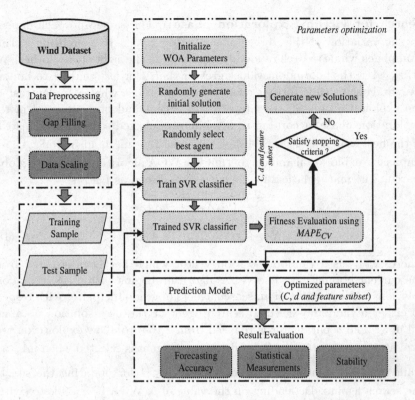

Fig. 2. · Block diagram of the proposed prediction architecture

6.1. *Data Preprocessing*

Preprocessing the input data set is considered a crucial task for a knowledge discovery goal.

(1) It was reported that the used dataset contains missing values (information) in some records. In this chapter, all missing values for a given features are replaced by the linear interpolation. between these points. If the two known values are X_1, X_3, the missing value X_2 is calculated as average of previous(X_1) and next(X_3) non-missing value.

(2) takes care of Data scaling (data normalization) for several reason: (a) to bypass numerical hardness through calculation,(B) to bypass features in greater numeric ranges masterful those in smaller numeric ranges,

(C) to help getting a higher classification accuracy. Generally, every feature could be scaled to the range linearly [-1, 1] or [0, 1].[29] Choosing the target range depends on the nature of the data. Consider

$$x_i^{scale} = \frac{x_i - x^{min}}{x^{max} - x^{min}} \tag{19}$$

where x_i^{scale} is a scaled value, x_i is an original value, x^{min} is the lower bounds of feature x and x^{max} is the upper bounds of the feature x.

6.2. *Parameters Initialization*

Each whale position represents a solution (penalty factor, kernel parameter and feature subset) in the search space. The parameters of proposed algorithm (dimension, maximum number of iterations, number of search agents size, lower and upper bounds were initialized. In the suggested algorithm, the WOA provides the SVR classifier with the values of C, kernel parameter (i.e. γ in RBF kernel) and features subset to train SVR utilizing the training set. So, there were only three parameters, i.e. $mathitC$, kernel parameter and features subset. Set the algorithm parameters involving a maximum number of iterations, locations, population size and dimension. Randomly generate initial agent population, positions, leader position and leader score.

6.3. *Fitness Function*

The fitness function is a standard that is used to determine the quality of each search agent or solution. Each frequency is evaluated by each search agent. The quality of search agents is evaluated by its ability to obtain the minimum error. In the suggested algorithm, the fitness had been defined by the k-fold cross validation method. In k-fold cross validation, the training data set randomly is divided into K mutually exclusive subsets of approximately similar size. The training data set is randomly subdivided into roughly equal K subgroups. With a given set of parameters, the regression function had been constructed, utilizing (K-1) subsets as the training set. By the mean abstract percent error (MAPE) on the last subset (testing set). The efficacy of the parameter set is evaluated. It was repeated K times the above-mentioned procedure, so each subset is utilized once for testing. Taking the MAE over the K trials. ($MPAE_{CV}$) gives an estimation of the predicated generalization error for testing on sets of size (K-1/K)l in which l is the number of testing data sets. Lastly, the optimal performing parameter set had been specified. Traditionally, the testing error of k-fold CV is applied to appreciate the generalization error where k = 3. So, that, the fitness function is known as follow:

$$minf = MAPE_{CV} = \frac{1}{m} \sum_{j=1}^{m} \left| \frac{A_j - F_j}{A_j} \right| \times 100 \tag{20}$$

In which the number of testing data samples is m, the actual value is A_j, and the forecasted value is F_j. The solution with a lesser ($MAPE_{CV}$) of the testing data set has a lesser fitness value, and so has a better chance of surviving in the successive generations.

6.4. *Termination Criteria*

When the termination criteria are satisfied, the process ends; otherwise, we continue with the next generating process. In the suggested model, the algorithm is ended when a maximum number of iterations which are reached

7. Experimental Results and Discussion

This chapter proposed model to predict wind speed. The SVR was repeatedly trained by WOA with different kernel functions in order to produce model that is more precise wind speed forecasting.

For all experiments, the parameters of the WOA algorithm are listed in Table 3.

Table 3.   Parameters setting for experiments

Parameter	Value	
	Linear	RBF
Maximum number of iteration(Generation)	20	20
Number of search agents size(Population)	200	200
Dimension	16	17
b	3	3
Lower bound of C	1	1
Upper bound of C	1000	1000
Lower bound of γ	—	1
Upper bound of γ	—	100
Lower bound of Feature	1	1
Upper bound of Feature	15	15

7.1. *Evaluation Metrics*

7.1.1. *Forecasting accuracy evaluation*

If forecast accuracy needs to be estimated, many performance measure ways had been used, but no one could be recognized as a global criterion method. Thus, some performance metrics should have been explained comprehensively to understand the algorithm characteristics. In this chapter four metrics are used: mean absolute percentage error (MAPE), root mean square error (RMSE), mean square error (MSE) and mean absolute error (MAE) to validate the difference between actual and predicted wind speed values:[6,10]

$$MAE = \frac{1}{m} \sum_{j=1}^{J} |A_j - F_j| \tag{21}$$

$$MSE = \frac{1}{m} \sum_{j=1}^{J} (A_j - F_j)^2 \tag{22}$$

$$RMSE = \left[\frac{1}{m} \sum_{j=1}^{J} (A_j - F_j)^2 \right]^{1/2} \tag{23}$$

$$MAPE = \frac{1}{m} \sum_{j=1}^{J} \left| \frac{A_j - F_j}{A_j} \right| \times 100 \tag{24}$$

where A_j and F_j represent observed value and predictive value of mth data and J is the total number of whole forecasting data utilized for performance evaluation.

7.1.2. *Stability measurements*

In this subsection, mean and standard deviation are utilized to determine the stability of the proposed algorithms. They are defined as following:

$$\mu = \frac{\sum_{i=1}^{MaxIter} B_i}{MaxIter} \tag{25}$$

$$Std = \sqrt{\frac{\sum_{i=1}^{MaxIter} (B_i - \mu)^2}{MaxIter}} \tag{26}$$

where *MaxIter* is the number of iterations and B_i is the best score obtained each time.

7.2. Statistical Measurements

In this subsection, four measurements are used such as the best, worst and mean fitness value. They are defined as following:

$$BestFitness = MIN_{i=1}^{MaxIter} B_i \tag{27}$$

$$WorstFitness = MAX_{i=1}^{MaxIter} B_i \tag{28}$$

$$MeanFitness = \frac{1}{MaxIter} \sum_{i=1}^{MaxIter} B_i \tag{29}$$

where *MaxIter* is the number of iterations and B_i is the best score obtained each time.

7.3. Results and Discussion

The platform has adopted to develop the WOA-SVR is a PC with the following features: Intel core 2.60 GHz CPU, 16.0 GB RAM, a Windows 10 operating system and the LIBSVM toolbox[30] and MATLAB R2016b development environment. The performance of proposed algorithm with many kernel function are compared to traditional SVR in three different aspects; forecasting based measurements (including mean absolute percentage error (MAPE), root mean square error (RMSE), mean square error (MSE) and mean absolute error (MAE), statistical measurements (including the worst, best and mean fitness function) and stability. The experiment was preformed to compare between the proposed algorithm with the traditional SVR algorithm when RBF and Linear kernels were used. In all experiments, 3-fold cross-validation with 10 repetitions had been utilized.

7.4. Statistical Analysis

Figures 3, 4 and 5 represent the scatter plots for each of the normalized meteorological factors with wind speed. These scatter plots show that any functional relationship between meteorological and wind speed factors is not trivial. This suggests that we can expect that classical learners such as linear classifier may not succeed in finding a precise graph of input variables for output variables. So, these plots intuitively justify the need to experiment with the linear classifier after applying the kernel trick.

The first step in most data analysis applications is to explore the statistical properties of the variables. This is usually done by plotting probability densities, which briefly summarize each variable for visualization.

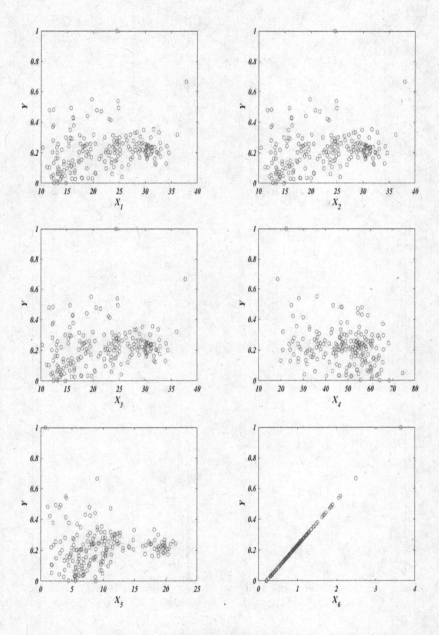

Fig. 3.   Scatter plot demonstrating input meteorological factors(X_1-X_{15}) and visually the normalized wind speed outputs

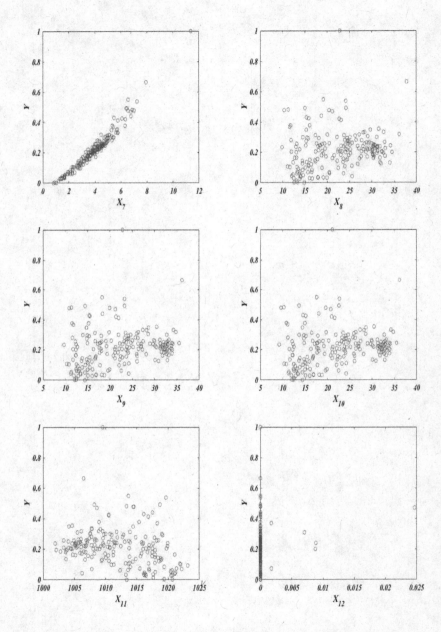

Fig. 4. Scatter plot demonstrating input meteorological factors(X_1-X_{15}) and visually the normalized wind speed outputs

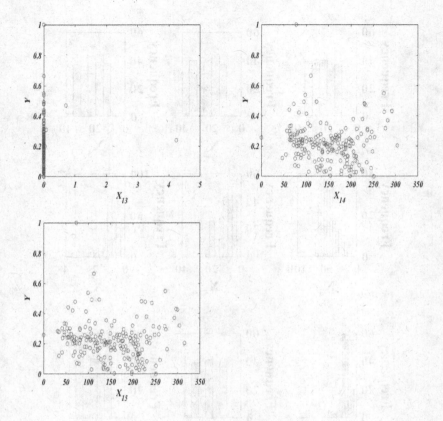

Fig. 5.   Scatter plot demonstrating input meteorological factors (X_1-X_{15}) and visually the normalized wind speed outputs

A method to obtain an experimental estimate of non-integer density is by using graphs. While raw graphs are believed to be the most advanced statistical applications, they had a great advantage of not having previous assumptions regarding the distribution of the examined variable which is very simple to calculate. Typically, this initial step can reveal whether the variable follows Gaussian distribution (normal), which features an unequal peak in the middle of a range of potential variable values, is quite symmetric, and particularly useful because a large number of mathematical functions are applicable.[31] The empirical probability distributions of all input meteorological factor presents in Fig. 6. These distributions shows that none of the variables follows the normal distribution.

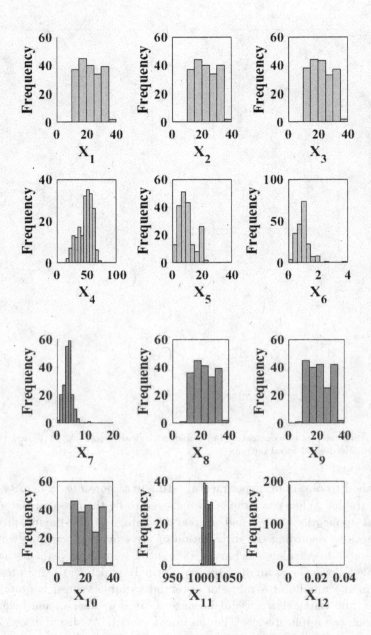

Fig. 6.   Probability density estimates utilizing histograms of the fifteen input variables

Table 4. Forecasting accuracy experimental

Kernel Function	Classifier	Measure			
		MAPE	MAE	MSE	RMSE
RBF	**SVR**	0.7010	0.5229	0.5380	0.7290
	WOA-SVR	0.1986	0.1766	0.1651	0.3732
Linear	**SVR**	0.3440	0.2628	0.2397	0.4687
	WOA-SVR	0.0217	0.0182	5.8826e-04	0.0238

Table 5. Performance evaluation of proposed approach using statistical measurements

Measure	Kernel Function	
	RBF	Linear
Best Fitness	0.1986	0.0217
Worst Fitness	0.7223	0.0255
Mean Fitness	0.2087	0.0220

7.4.1. *Comparison of forecasting accuracy measurements*

The prediction accuracy of suggested model is calculated with $MAPE_{CV}$. Table 4 compares the highest obtained tested results of WOA-SVR and traditional SVR with many kernels. What can be noticed is that WOA-SVR using linear kernel ranked first by achieved lower classification error rates, followed by WOA-SVR using RBF kernel.

7.4.2. *Comparison of statistical measurements*

In this section, three measurements are utilized to evaluate the performance of proposed WOA-SVR algorithm. Table 5 outline the best, worst and mean obtained fitness function ratio over all the iterations. As can be seen for wind dataset, in most cases the performance of WOA-SVR is superior in selecting the best SVR parameters with minimum $MAPE_{CV}$ with high classification performance in case of using linear kernel followed by WOA-SVR using RBF kernel.

7.4.3. *Comparison of stability*

To test robustness and stability of convergence of the suggested algorithm, mean and standard deviation of the obtained fitness values are calculated

Table 6. Stability of WOA-SVR Algorithm using various kernel functions

Measure	Kernel Function	
	RBF	Linear
Mean	0.2087	0.0220
Std.	0.0540	7.8659e-04

for 10 runs and outlined in Table 6. As can be observed WO-SVR using linear kernel has the best stability quality as it has minimum standard deviation. WOASVR using RBF is in second place.

8. Conclusion

In this chapter, whale optimization algorithm is suggested as parameters optimization and feature selection algorithm. The performance of this algorithm is evaluated using wind dataset. Also, SVR classifier is adopted using different kernel functions. The performance of each is compared and the best parameters of SVR using each kernel function are determined. The performance is compared with traditional SVR. From the experimental results, it can be concluded that the developed WOA-SVR algorithm giving lower classification error rate, yielded more appropriate parameters compared with traditional SVR. And also, WOA-SVR using Linear kernel is better than WOA-SVR using RBF kernel.

Acknowledgment

The authors of this chapter would like to thank Professor Ayman Mahrous, director of the Space Weather Monitoring Center at Helwan University for his support and recommendations.

References

1. H. S. Ramadan, Wind energy farm sizing and resource assessment for optimal energy yield in sinai peninsula, Egypt, *Journal of Cleaner Production*. **161**, 1283–1293 (2017).
2. E. H. Houssein, Particle swarm optimization-enhanced twin support vector regression for wind speed forecasting, *Journal of Intelligent Systems*. (2017).

3. S. Osama, A. Darwish, E. H. Houssein, A. E. Hassanien, A. A. Fahmy, and A. Mahrous. Long-term wind speed prediction based on optimized support vector regression. In *Intelligent Computing and Information Systems (ICI-CIS), 2017 Eighth International Conference on*, pp. 191–196 (2017).

4. H. Jiang, J. Wang, J. Wu, and W. Geng, Comparison of numerical methods and metaheuristic optimization algorithms for estimating parameters for wind energy potential assessment in low wind regions, *Renewable and Sustainable Energy Reviews.* **69**, 1199–1217 (2017).

5. H. B. Azad, S. Mekhilef, and V. G. Ganapathy, Long-term wind speed forecasting and general pattern recognition using neural networks, *IEEE Transactions on Sustainable Energy.* **5**(2), 546–553 (2014).

6. J. Wang, Q. Zhou, H. Jiang, and R. Hou, Short-term wind speed forecasting using support vector regression optimized by cuckoo optimization algorithm, *Mathematical Problems in Engineering.* **2015** (2015).

7. J. P. d. S. Catalão, H. M. I. Pousinho, and V. M. F. Mendes. An artificial neural network approach for short-term wind power forecasting in portugal. In *Intelligent System Applications to Power Systems, 2009. ISAP'09. 15th International Conference on*, pp. 1–5 (2009).

8. J. P. d. S. Catalão, H. M. I. Pousinho, and V. M. F. Mendes. An artificial neural network approach for short-term wind power forecasting in portugal. In *Intelligent System Applications to Power Systems, 2009. ISAP'09. 15th International Conference on*, pp. 1–5 (2009).

9. X. Chen, S. Jin, S. Qin, and L. Li, Short-term wind speed forecasting study and its application using a hybrid model optimized by cuckoo search, *Mathematical Problems in Engineering.* **2015** (2015).

10. Y. Jiang, Z. Song, and A. Kusiak, Very short-term wind speed forecasting with bayesian structural break model, *Renewable energy.* **50**, 637–647 (2013).

11. G. Santamaría-Bonfil, A. Reyes-Ballesteros, and C. Gershenson, Wind speed forecasting for wind farms: A method based on support vector regression, *Renewable Energy.* **85**, 790–809 (2016).

12. C. M. Bishop, Pattern recognition, *Machine Learning.* **128**, 1–58 (2006).

13. E. Gopi and P. Palanisamy, Neural network based class-conditional probability density function using kernel trick for supervised classifier, *Neurocomputing.* **154**, 225–229 (2015).

14. K. S. Parikh and T. P. Shah, Support vector machine — a large margin classifier to diagnose skin illnesses, *Procedia Technology.* **23**, 369–375 (2016).

15. Z. Zhang, D. Zhang, and Y. Tian, Kernel-based multiple criteria linear programming classifier, *Procedia Computer Science.* **1**(1), 2407–2415 (2010).

16. F. Douak, F. Melgani, and N. Benoudjit, Kernel ridge regression with active learning for wind speed prediction, *Applied energy.* **103**, 328–340 (2013).

17. M. Guo, Z. Wei, H. Zang, G. Sun, H. Li, and K. W. Cheung. Short term wind speed forecasting using wavelet transform and grey model improved by particle swarm optimization. In *Electric Utility Deregulation and Restructuring and Power Technologies (DRPT), 2015 5th International Conference on*, pp. 1879–1884 (2015).

18. K. Ahmed, A. A. Ewees, M. A. El Aziz, A. E. Hassanien, T. Gaber, P.-W. Tsai, and J.-S. Pan. A hybrid krill-anfis model for wind speed forecasting. In *International Conference on Advanced Intelligent Systems and Informatics*, pp. 365–372 (2016).

19. Z. Liu, W. Gao, Y.-H. Wan, and E. Muljadi. Wind power plant prediction by using neural networks. In *Energy Conversion Congress and Exposition (ECCE), 2012 IEEE*, pp. 3154–3160 (2012).

20. M. Monfared, H. Rastegar, and H. M. Kojabadi, A new strategy for wind speed forecasting using artificial intelligent methods, *Renewable energy*. **34**(3), 845–848 (2009).

21. C. Ren, N. An, J. Wang, L. Li, B. Hu, and D. Shang, Optimal parameters selection for bp neural network based on particle swarm optimization: A case study of wind speed forecasting, *Knowledge-Based Systems*. **56**, 226–239 (2014).

22. S. Salcedo-Sanz, E. G. Ortiz-Garcı, Á. M. Pérez-Bellido, A. Portilla-Figueras, L. Prieto, *et al.*, Short term wind speed prediction based on evolutionary support vector regression algorithms, *Expert Systems with Applications*. **38**(4), 4052–4057 (2011).

23. C. Cortes and V. Vapnik, Support-vector networks, *Machine learning*. **20**(3), 273–297 (1995).

24. V. Vapnik, S. E. Golowich, A. Smola, *et al.*, Support vector method for function approximation, regression estimation, and signal processing, *Advances in neural information processing systems*. pp. 281–287 (1997).

25. H. Liu and L. Yu, Toward integrating feature selection algorithms for classification and clustering, *IEEE Transactions on knowledge and data engineering*. **17**(4), 491–502 (2005).

26. I. A. Gheyas and L. S. Smith, Feature subset selection in large dimensionality domains, *Pattern recognition*. **43**(1), 5–13 (2010).

27. M. Dash and H. Liu, Feature selection for classification, *Intelligent data analysis*. **1**(1-4), 131–156 (1997).

28. S. Mirjalili and A. Lewis, The whale optimization algorithm, *Advances in Engineering Software*. **95**, 51–67 (2016).

29. A. Tharwat, E. H. Houssein, M. M. Ahmed, A. E. Hassanien, and T. Gabel, MOGOA algorithm for constrained and unconstrained multi-objective optimization problems, *Applied Intelligence*. 1–16 (2017).

30. C.-C. Chang and C.-J. Lin, Libsvm: a library for support vector machines, *ACM Transactions on Intelligent Systems and Technology (TIST)*. **2**(3), 27 (2011).

31. C. M. Bishop, *Pattern recognition and machine learning*. Springer (2006).

Chapter 8

A Hybrid Gray Wolf Optimization and Support Vector Machines for Detection of Epileptic Seizure

Asmaa Hamad* and Essam H. Houssein[†]

Scientific Research Group in Egypt (SRGE)
Faculty of Computers and Information, Minia University, Egypt
* asmaa_hamad222@yahoo.com; [†] *essam.halim@mu.edu.eg*

Aboul Ella Hassanien[‡] and Aly A. Fahmy[§]

Scientific Research Group in Egypt (SRGE)
Faculty of Computers and Information, Cairo University, Egypt
[‡] *aboitcairo@gmail.com;* [§] *a.fahmy@fci-cu.edu.eg*

Siddhartha Bhattacharyya[¶]

Scientific Research Group in Egypt (SRGE)
RCC Institute of Information Technology, India
[¶] *dr.siddhartha.bhattacharyya@gmail.com*

In this chapter, a hybrid classification approach is proposed using the gray wolf optimizer (GWO) integrated with support vector machines (SVMs) to automatically detect the seizure in EEG. The discrete wavelet transform (DWT) was utilized to decompose EEG into five sub-band components. The SVM classifier was trained using various parameters that were extracted and used as feature. GWO was used to select a sub-feature. As the EEG signal rating depends on the optimal parameters that have been selected, it is also integrated with SVM to obtain better resolution of the classification by selecting the best tuning parameters SVM. The experimental results showed that the proposed GWO-SVM approach, capable of detecting epilepsy, could therefore further enhance the diagnosis of epilepsy.

Keywords: EEG; Epilepsy; DWT; GWO; SVMS.

1. Introduction

One of the most common neurological diseases is epilepsy, which is characterized by frequent abnormal reactions of the brain such as epileptic seizures.[1] Nearly fifty million people around the world have epilepsy according to Wordpress Web and WebSite.[1] Therefore, the ability to seek prevention and treatment is more effective for patients is precisely through the diagnosis and prediction of epileptic seizures. To diagnose and predict epileptic seizures clinically, brain activity should be monitored through EEG signals that contain epileptic signs. Epilepsy can be detected by traditional methods by experienced neurologists by visual examination of long periods of EEG signals, that is dull and slow. Therefore, we need to develop a computer-assisted detection model of epileptic signals to overcome these limitations.

Perform electrical activity from the brain regularly through different electrodes in the scalp called brain electrophoresis (EEG). EEG is a very useful tool for understanding brain diseases, such as epilepsy, as it contains a lot of worthwhile information relating to many physiological conditions of the brain.[2] EEG signals from epileptic patients include two abnormal conditions of activity, interictal (free seizure) and ictal.[3] Interictal signals are sharp or spiky waves, transition waveforms and show screws. The ictal EEG signals are continuous waves with spikes and sharp wave sets.[4]

Each EEG is usually analyzed in five sub-bands: delta (0.5-4 Hz), theta (4-8 Hz), alpha (8-15 Hz), beta (15-30 Hz) and gamma (30-60 Hz). Alpha is rhythmic waves and its amplitude is low. Each region of the brain has the distinguishing marks of alpha rhythm but mostly it is recorded from parietal zone and the occipital. It oscillates from relaxed situation with eyes closed and an adult in the awake. Beta waves are irregular and its amplitude is very low. It is mainly recorded by the frontal and temporal lobes. It vibrates during deep sleep, mental activity and is connected with remembering. Theta waves are rhythmic waves and its amplitude is low-medium. It oscillates from drowsy adult, the children in a sleep state, and sentimental distress occipital lobe. Delta waves are slow and its amplitude is high. It differs from adult and normal sleep rhythm. Gamma waves are the rapid brainwave frequency with the smallest amplitude.[5] Table 1 shows the frequency range and amplitude for each type of waves.

In the analysis and processing the epileptic EEG signals; feature extraction, selection and function classification represent a significant challenge. For the classification problems there are many machine learning techniques

Table 1. Wave's frequency and amplitude.

Wave	Frequency range	Amplitude
Delta band	0.1-4 Hz	High
Theta band	4-8 Hz	Low-medium
Alpha band	8-15 Hz	Low
Beta band	15-30 Hz	Very low
Gamma band	30-100 Hz	Smallest

that are used. The success of any classification system depends on the selection of features and its parameters carefully. To solve the problem of epileptic classification of EEG signals, this research focuses on the use of support vector machines (SVM). SVM has showed its effectiveness as a classification method. However, SVMs face some challenges when they are applied in real practical applications. Tuning the best SVM parameters is one of these challenges.

This chapter proposes a method for selecting features that used as input data for classifiers and the optimal SVMS parameters via utilizing gray wolf optimizer. Choosing these parameters correctly ensures to get the best accuracy of classification.[6] SVMs have two types of parameters (kernel functions parameters and penalty constant C parameter), and these parameters values influence the SVMs performance.[7]

In this chapter, To analyze each EEG signal in five constitutive EEG subbands, DWT is utilized. The DWT is utilized for time-frequency analysis which provides a quantitative assessment of several frequency bands of the clinical brain wave. Using the wavelet function of Daubechies of the fourth order (db4) up to the fourth level of decomposition, the EEG signals were decomposed in different frequency bands. The parameter such maximum, minimum, Skewness, median, mean, variance, standard deviation, entropy, energy and Relative Wave Energy (RWE) were calculated for the extraction of feature. The SVM with RBF kernel function is utilized as the classifier. In this step, a gray wolf optimizer (GWO) is used to select the best feature subset and also to optimize the SVM parameter for maximizing the performance of the classifiers.

Consequently, this chapter adopts GWO to present a new optimized GWO-SVM hybrid classification model for classifying epileptic EEG signals. The proposed model implemented GWO in combination with SVM to get better EEG classification accuracy by choosing relevant features and optimal tuning of SVM parameters. The Gray Wolf optimizer (GWO) is a new metaheuristic method, inspired by gray wolves, which mimics the hierarchy of leadership and the hunting technique of gray wolves in nature. The suggested approach has four phases; That is, EEG pre-processing, feature extraction, feature selection by GWO, and GWO-SVM classification phases. The results clearly show significant improvements in the accuracy of classification achieved by the GWO-SVM classification model with respect to the accuracy of classification obtained from the SVM typical classification algorithm, SVM with practical swarm optimization algorithms (PSO-SVM) and SVM with genetic algorithms (GA-SVM).

The rest of the chapter is drawn as follows: the literature review is proposed in Section 2. The materials and methods is presented in Section 3. The proposed classification approach is provided in Section 4. the experimental results and discussion are presented in Section 5. The conclusion of this chapter is reported in Section 6.

2. Literature Review

Numerous algorithms have been developed in literature to improve the detection andíndexclassification of EEG signals. Authors in Ref. 8, proposed an epileptic seizure detection technique from brain EEG signals. The EEG time series are transformed into a weighted visibility graph (WVG). The modularity and average weighted degree are extracted based on WVG. Moreover, SVM and KNN are utilized for the classification process. Also in Ref. 9, authors proposed a multilateral EEG signal analysis framework. In this framework, DWT is utilized to analysis the signals into the frequency sub-bands and a set of features was extracted from the sub-bands to represent the distribution of wavelet coefficients. Linear discriminant analysis (LDA), linear discriminant analysis (LDA) and principal components analysis (PCA) are utilized for data reduction. Then SVM was used to classify EEG data to epileptic seizure or not. Also in Ref. 10, authors have proposed an automated approach for epileptic seizure prediction using Hilbert-Huang transform (HHT) and Bayesian classifiers from intracranial EEG signals. Then, the analysis of the signals into intrinsic mode functions is performed for getting features and the Bayesian networks (BN) are combined with correlation based feature selection for binary classification of preictal and interictal. Also in Ref. 11, authors presented statistical parameters from the decomposed wavelet coefficients that are obtained using wavelet transform for feature extraction. A feed-forward backpropagation artificial neural network (ANN) is used for the classification. In addition, authors in Ref. 12 proposed a hierarchical epileptic seizure detection approach. In this approach, the raw EEG signals are performed by wavelet packet coefficients using entropy as an advantageous feature. In the training phase, the k-nearest neighbor is used with cross-validation methods (CV), on the other hand, higher ranking discriminatory rules are used in the testing phase to calculate the rating accuracy and the rejection rate. Also, authors in Ref. 13 have proposed automated detection of epilepsy which uses reciprocal entropy (PE) as an advantageous feature. SVM is used to classify EEG into normal and epilepsy based on PE values. In the same way, in Ref. 14, the authors introduced the method of detection of epileptic seizure, which uses the almost entropy features extracted from multiwavelet transform. The artificial neural network (ANN) is combined with the entropy to classify EEG signaling to normal and epileptic signals.

Authors in Ref. 15 have presented a classification approach to detect epileptic seizures. Moreover, ANN is used for classification. Also in Ref. 16, authors proposed an automatic seizure detection method using sub-band nonlinear parameters and genetic algorithm (GA). In the experiment results, DWT was utilized to analysis EEG into five sub-band components and GA was used to select the effective feature subset. Non-linear parameters were extracted and employed as the features to train the SVM with linear kernel function and RBF kernel function classifiers. Moreover, in Ref. 17, authors presented a clustering-based least square support vector machine approach for the classification of EEG signals. The proposed approach comprises the following two stages. In the first stage, representative features of EEG data are extracted using clustering technique (CT). In the second stage, the extracted features of EEG signals are classified using least square support vector machine (LS-SVM). Finally, in Ref. 18, authors developed a scheme for exposing epileptic seizures from EEG signals taken from epileptic patients and normal persons. This scheme is based on DWT analysis and approximate entropy (ApEn) of EEG signals. SVM and (feedforward backpropagation neural network) FBNN are used for classification purpose.

3. Materials and Methods

This section produces the material and methods used in this chapter.

3.1. *Description of EEG Dataset*

The dataset used in this research was taken from publicly available data in University of Bonn.[19] This data set comprises five groups (designated

A, B, C, D and E), each of which includes 100 individual EEG segments of 23.6 seconds in length, with a sampling frequency of 173.6 Hz. Each segment of data contains N = 4097 data points accumulated at intervals of 1/173.61th of 1s.

The signals and parts of the continuous EEG multichannel records have been selected after visual artifacts, for example, due to eye movements and muscular activity. Datasets *A* and *B* to consist of slices extracted from surface EGG recordings performed in five healthy volunteers using a uniform locator positioning scheme. Volunteers were raised in case of the awakening of eyes (A) and closed eyes (B), respectively. Datasets *C*, *D*, and *E* are detected by epileptic subjects by intracranial electrodes for the epithelial and interictal activity. A summary of the data sets shown in Table 2.

Table 2. A summary of the clinical data.

Settings	Set A	Set B	Set C	Set D	Set E
Subjects	5 healthy	5 healthy	5 epileptic patients	5 epileptic patients	5 epileptic patients
Electrode placement	surface	surface	Hippocampal formation	Epileptogenic zone	Epileptogenic zone
Patient's state	Awake, eyes open	Awake, eyes closed	Seizure-free (Interictal)	Seizure-free (Interictal)	Seizure activity (Ictal)
Number of epochs	100	100	100	100	100
duration (s)	23.6	23.6	23.6	23.6	23.6

All EEG signals were taken with the same 128 channel system amplifier, using a common reference medium. After converting 12-bit analogy-to-digital data, it is continuously recorded on the disk of a computer system with 173.61 Hz sampling frequency data acquisition. The spectral frequency band of the acquisition system ranges from 0.5 to 85 Hz. Figure 1 shows examples of EEG signals for each set.

3.2. *Discrete Wavelet Transforms (DWT)*

For solving many real-life problems, Wavelet transforms are utilized. A wavelet is a short wave, which has its energy concentrated in time to give a tool for the analysis of non-linear and non-stationary signals. If a signal does not change much over time, its called a stationary signal. Fourier transform (FT) could be used to analysis the stationary signals easily and a good result can be taken. However, numerous signals such as EEG are

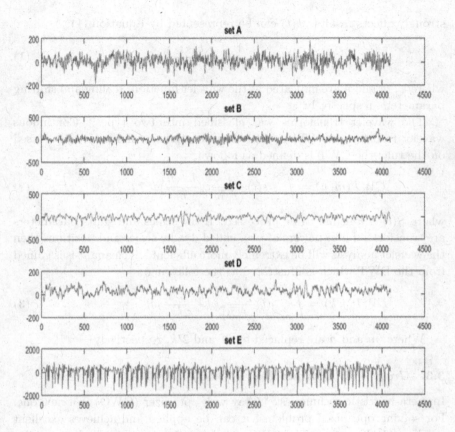

Fig. 1.   EEG signals from the five available sets.

non stationary signals; in such case FT cannot be used directly. But time-frequency methods can be utilized.[20] In this work, we used the DWT as a time-frequency method.

DWT can accurately show more details in both of the time and frequency domain from the signal. This makes it become a powerful tool in biomedical engineering, especially in detecting epileptic seizure. In this research, DWT is used to decompose EEG signals in different frequency bands. The DWT analyses a specific signal in detail and approximate coefficients at the first level. Then the coefficients of approximate are further subdivided into the next level of approximation and detail coefficients.[21]

In DWT, a wavelet called the mother wavelet $\psi(t)$ is the main controller of signal transformation, and a proper selection of such wavelet $\psi(t)$

strongly affects results. $\psi(t)$ can be represented by Equation (1):

$$\psi(t) = \frac{1}{\sqrt{m}} \psi\left(\frac{t-n}{m}\right) \tag{1}$$

where ψ, m and n are indicated as the wavelet function, scaling and shifting parameters, respectively.

The wavelet transforms was classified into two types: Continuous wavelet transform (CWT) and Discrete wavelet transform (DWT). Based on the rule, the CWT is defined as follows.[22]

$$CWT(m,n) = \int_{-\infty}^{\infty} s(t) \frac{1}{\sqrt{|m|}} \psi(\frac{t-n}{m}) dt \tag{2}$$

where $S(t)$ is a signal to be processed. If the scales and shifts parameters are transformed into powers of two, called dyadic scales and positions then the wavelet analysis will be extremely more efficient. Such analysis is gained from the DWT which is illustrated as the following:

$$DWT(j,k) = \int_{-\infty}^{\infty} s(t) \frac{1}{\sqrt{|2^j|}} \psi(\frac{t-2^jk}{2^j}) dt \tag{3}$$

Where, m and n are replaced by 2^j and 2^jk, respectively.

3.3. Gray Wolf Optimization (GWO)

In meta-heuristic techniques,[23] Gray wolf optimizer (GWO) is a new one. For solving optimized problems, it can be applied and achieves excellent results.[24-27] In nature, The GWO algorithm simulates the leadership hierarchy and hunting technique of gray wolves. Alpha (α), beta (β), delta (δ) and omega (ω) are four types of gray wolves which are used for mimicking the leadership hierarchy. In this algorithm, the optimization is guided by three wolves (alpha, beta and delta). The omega wolves follow these three wolves.[24]

3.3.1. Encircling prey

To hunt a prey, gray wolves encircle it. Mathematically, this encircling behavior is modeled by the following equations:[24,25]

$$\vec{D} = |\vec{C} \cdot \vec{X_p}(t) - \vec{X}(t)| \tag{4}$$

$$\vec{X}(t+1) = \vec{X_p}(t) - \vec{A} \cdot \vec{D} \tag{5}$$

where t is the current iteration, $\vec{C}$ and $\vec{A}$ are coefficient vectors, $\vec{X_p}$ is the prey position vector, and $\vec{X}$ indicates the gray wolf position vector. $\vec{A}$ and $\vec{C}$ vectors can be calculated as follows:

$$\vec{A} = 2\vec{a} \cdot \vec{r_1} - \vec{a} \tag{6}$$

$$\vec{C} = 2 \cdot \vec{r_2} \tag{7}$$

where components of $\vec{a}$ are linearly decreased from 2 to 0, over the course of iterations and $\vec{r_1}$, $\vec{r_2}$ are random vectors in [0, 1].

3.3.2. *Hunting*

To simulate the hunting procedure of gray wolves, assume that the alpha (the best candidate solution), beta and delta have better knowledge about the potential location of prey. Therefore, the optimal obtained three solutions are saved until now and force other search agents (inclusive omega) to update their locations according to the location of the optimal search agents. This updating for the gray wolves locations is as the following:[24]

$$\vec{D_\alpha} = |\vec{C_1} \cdot \vec{X_\alpha} - \vec{X}|, \vec{D_\beta} = |\vec{C_2} \cdot \vec{X_\beta} - \vec{X}|, \vec{D_\delta} = |\vec{C_3} \cdot \vec{X_\delta} - \vec{X}| \tag{8}$$

$$\vec{X_1} = \vec{X_\alpha} - \vec{A_1} \cdot (\vec{D_\alpha}), \vec{X_2} = \vec{X_\beta} - \vec{A_2} \cdot (\vec{D_\beta}), \vec{X_3} = \vec{X_\delta} - \vec{A_3} \cdot (\vec{D_\delta}) \tag{9}$$

$$\vec{X}(t+1) = \frac{\vec{X_1} + \vec{X_2} + \vec{X_3}}{3} \tag{10}$$

3.4. *Support Vector Machine (SVM)*

To distinguish the unknown verification set from the notes in their correct categories, the classification technique helps with that based on the set of training from known observations. The classifier is a mathematical function used by a classification technique to forecast the true class of unknown observation of validation data set. SVM proposed by Cortes and Vapnik.[28] To detect abnormal biomedical signal abnormalities, SVM is a powerful compendium in biomedical sciences. SVM is used to classify two different sets of observations in the appropriate category efficiently. It is capable of handling nonlinear and high dimensional data excellently.

In this chapter, to estimate the performance of the proposed model, we have four test cases with two sets of different categories, so we prefer this workbook to obtain better accuracy results. SVMs mechanism is based on the search for the best hyperplane that separates data from two different categories. The best hyperplane is that maximizes the margin, i.e., the distance from the nearest training points. The structural design of the SVM depends on the following: (1) The regulation parameter, c, is used to control the trade-off between margin optimization and some poor classification, (2) kernel functions of the non-linear SVM that are used to map the training data from the input space to the high-dimensional feature space. All kernel functions such as linear, polynomial, radial and radial basis function have some free parameters called hyperparameters. So far, the kernel used in the search between the brain and the computer has been the feature of the basic feature or Gaussian (RBF) with $t\sigma$[29]

$$K(a, yb) = \exp(-||a - b||^2/2\sigma^2) \tag{11}$$

where, K(a, b) is termed as the kernel function, which is built based the dot product of a and b. Suitable trade-off parameter C and the kernel parameter σ are required to train SVM classifier and usually obtained by the K-fold cross-validation technique.

3.4.1. K-fold cross-validation

Cross-validation is the statistical technique of dividing the data into subsets so that the training was initially executed in a single subset, while the other subsets are maintained for later use in validating or testing the initial subset. In K-fold cross validation, the original data is subdivided into sub-samples K. The K-1 sub-samples are used as training data, and a single sub-sample is maintained as validation data to test the model. The cross validation procedure is repeated K rounds, with each of the sub-samples K used exactly once validation data. K results, then, can be mediated to obtain a single assessment. The 10-fold cross validation technique is proper to estimate the accuracy of classification of a classifier in biomedical signals.[30]

3.5. Performance Evaluation Measurements

In this chapter, data set E is treated as the negative class and data sets A, B, C and D are treated positive class. To estimate the performance of classification for various test cases in this chapter, we used five measures, which are: 1) Accuracy (Acc), 2) Sensitivity (Sens), 3) Specificity (Spec),

4) Precision (Prec), and 5) F-Measure (F). In general, all mentioned performance measures depend on four main metrics of a binary classification result (positive / Negative); False Positive (FP), False Negative (FN), True Positive (TP) and True Negative (TN). Where the false identification of non-seizure activity is False Positive, the falsely recognized seizure activity is False Negative, correctly identified non-seizure activity is True Positive and the correctly identified seizure activity stands for True Negative. These Performance measures are defined in the following equations.

$$Acc = \frac{TP + TN}{TP + FN + TN + FP} * 100 \tag{12}$$

$$Sens = \frac{TP}{TP + FN} * 100 \tag{13}$$

$$Spec = \frac{TN}{TN + FP} * 100 \tag{14}$$

$$Prec = \frac{TP}{TP + FP} * 100 \tag{15}$$

$$F = 2 * \frac{Prec * Sens}{Prec + Sens} \tag{16}$$

4. The Proposed Classification Model: GWO-SVM

In this chapter, we proposed GWO-SVM model for the EEG signal classification. The goal of this model is to optimize the accuracy of the SVM classifier by automatically estimating the optimal feature subset and the best SVM parameters values for the SVM model. The proposed classification model consists of four main steps; namely, 1) EEG Pre-processing, 2) Feature extraction used to extract the EEG signal features from decomposed signal, 3) Feature selection and Parameters Optimization and 4) classification step that is mainly used to analyze and classify the EEG signal into normal or abnormal.

In the first stage, EEG datasets (A, B, C, D, and E) are pre-processed by DWT to decompose into five sub-band signals using four levels of degradation. In the second stage, useful features such as entropy, deviation, minimum, maximum, average, mean, standard deviation, energy, contrast and Relative Wave Energy are derived from each subset of wavelet coefficients. In the third stage, the relevant features of the extracted features and parameter values (C, σ) are selected from the SVM is dynamically optimized by the GWO to classify EEG signals. Next, selected features are applied as an input to the SVM-RBF for the epilepsy classification task with the optimal parameter values obtained. Finally, the results obtained are assessed using five different measures such as classification accuracy, sensitivity, specificity, precession, and F-Measure. The overall process of the proposed method is illustrated in Figure 2. Also algorithm 1 explains GWO-SVM classifier pseudo code.

Algorithm 1 GWO-SVM Algorithm.

1: **Input:** n Number of Wolves in the population(Search Agents), MaxIter (Maximum Number of iterations for optimization).
2: **Output:** Alpha_pos (Optimal wolf position):(SVM parameters / Selected Features), X_α Best fitness value: Classification Accuracy;
3: **Initialization:** $iter \leftarrow 1$, a population of n wolves positions: (SVM parameters / Selected Features), X_α, X_β, X_γ.
4: Compute the fitness of each wolf(Search Agent) by Eq. (17)
5: X_α = the best Search agent, X_β = the second best search agent, X_γ = the third best search agent.
6: **while** (iter < maximum number of iteration) **do**
7:     **for** each wolf i **do**
8:         update wolf position by Eq. 10.
9:     **end for**
10:    Compute the fitness of each wolf (Search Agent) by Eq. 17
11:    Evaluate the positions of individual wolves: Update X_α,X_β and X_γ.
12:    $iter \leftarrow iter + 1$
13: **end while**

4.1. *EEG Pre-processing*

For EEG pre-processing phase, DWT has been used as a pre-processing level for EEG epochs to derive five EEG sub-bands, gamma (30-60 Hz), beta (13-30 Hz), alpha (8-13 Hz), theta (4-8 Hz) and delta (0-4 Hz). In the first phase of DWT, The HP and LP filters are applied to pass the signal simultaneously. At the first level, the outputs of LP and HP filters are indicated as approximation (A1) and detailed coefficients (D1). Output signals that retain half the original frequency bandwidth of the original signal can be down-sampled by two due to Nyquist rules. The same process can be repeated for the approach of the first level approximation and detail coefficients had brought the second level coefficients. Through each step of this decomposition process, the frequency resolution is performed through multiple filtering and the time resolution is subdivided by sub-sampling. For this goal, we used four levels of DWT and Wavelet function with fourth order Daubechies (db4). Since our set of data is in the range 0-60 Hz, the

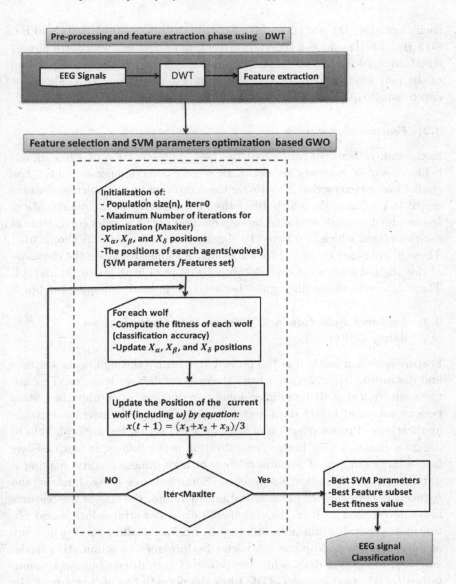

Fig. 2. Classification approach for SVM based on GWO.

coefficients D1, D2, D3, D4 and A4 corresponding to 30-60 Hz, 15-30 Hz, 8-15 Hz, 4-8 Hz and 0-4 Hz, respectively, were derived, which are almost standard physiological subbands. Figure 3 shows the wavelet decomposition of the four level of EEG signal. The complete analysis of EEG signals is coded using MATLAB (R2015a).

4.2. Feature Extraction

Extraction of features considered the best representation of EEG signals behavior and is necessary for automatic seizure detection performance. The goal of feature extraction is to obtain the significant and distinctive features exited in EEG signals, which affect the final accuracy of the classification. In our previous work, we extracted ten features of the wavelet coefficients of each sub-band which is selected to classify the EEG signals as shown in.[31] These features are extracted for all groups of signals to create the database of the original features of each decomposition level from D1 to D4 and A4. These are extracted to distinguish between the normal and epileptic signal.

4.3. Features Selection and Parameters Optimization using GWO

Feature selection method is the process to identify the significant features and discarding irrelevant ones from the original dataset features. The features selection aims to data dimensionality reduction, ameliorate the system performance and better data understanding for various machine learning applications. Proper selection of relevant EEG signal features can help to design a classifier with better generalization performance. In this case, we face a large number of features vectors of high dimensionality, making it difficult for the classification process. Some features are redundant and reduce the performance of classification; therefore, the size of the features must be reduced to help the classifier learn a powerful solution and obtain best generalization performance. In EEG, not all of the features are equally significant. You can get better performance by eliminating irrelevant and redundant data, while the power of data discrimination is maintained by selecting features. GWO has the potential to generate both the optimal subset of features and SVM parameters simultaneously. SVM tuning parameters have an important impact on their classification accuracy. Improper parameter settings lead to poor classification results. The parameters that need to be optimized include parameter C and parameters σ of the radial basis kernel function.

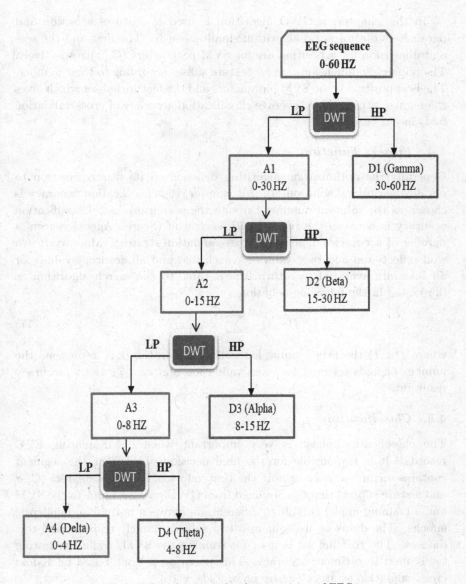

Fig. 3.   Four level wavelet decomposition of EEG.

In this chapter, a GWO algorithm is used as features selection and parameters optimization algorithm simultaneously. The first and the second dimension for a position are for SVM parameters (C, σ) respectively. The remaining dimensions are for feature subset according to their number. The best position is the SVM parameters and the feature subset which gives the highest fitness value (average classification accuracy of cross-validation folds in our case).

4.4. *Fitness Function*

Generally the optimization algorithm depends on its fitness function to obtain the optimal solution. In this chapter, the classification accuracy is chosen as the solution qualifier through the search process. Classification accuracy is between the range [0; 1], each wolf (Search Agent) reflects a number of accuracies depend on cross-validation strategy. Moreover, each wolf reflects ten accuracy values for each fold and all accuracy values for all folds are averaged to return fitness value to the search algorithm as illustrated in the following equation:

$$f(w,t) = \sum_{k=1}^{N} acc_{w,t,k}/N \qquad (17)$$

where $f(w,t)$ the fitness value for wolf w in iteration t, N represents the number of folds selected for cross validation and $acc_{w,t,k}$ is the accuracy resultant.

4.5. *Classification*

The classification phase is very important when discriminating EEG records. It is responsible for the final decision of whether the segment contains seizure activity or not. the best values of SVM parameters (C, σ and feature subset) that are obtained from GWO serve as input to the SVM and a training model is built to differentiate between normal and epileptic epochs. The datasets are split into two subsets namely training and test dataset. The training set is used for training the SVM, while the testing set is used to estimate accuracy. This partition is done based on K-fold cross validation strategy (where no of folds = 10).

5. Experimental Results and Discussion

5.1. *Original Feature Database*

To extract the main features of the Epileptic EEG, there are two stages.

In the first stage, a DWT is used to analyze the EEG signal in different sub-signals within various frequency bands. Selecting the number of decomposition levels and the wavelet function are significant for proper analysis of EEG signal with DWT. In this research, the number of decomposition levels is 4, which is recommended by other studies.[2] And the function selected is Daubechies wavelet of order 4, that demonstrated the best wavelet function for epileptic EEG signal analysis.[2] Frequency bands with four level DWT decomposition described in Table 3. The five different sub-signals (one approximation A4 and four details D1–D4 that correspond to delta (0-4 Hz), gamma (30-60 Hz), beta (13-30 Hz), alpha (8-13 Hz), and theta (4-8 Hz) respectively, of the sample EEG epoch derived from sets A, B, C, D and E are shown in Figures 4 to 8 respectively. The second stage, after the EEG signal, is broken down into five sub-signals, which correspond individually to various frequency bands, as described in Table 3. Ten classical features that shown in Ref. 31 are calculated from approximating coefficients and detail of all sub-bands of the entire 500 EEG epochs of five sets of A–E data sets to form the main features of the database using MATLAB (R2015a).

Table 3. Frequency bands of EEG signal with 4-Level DWT decomposition.

Decomposition level	Sub-band signal	Frequency band (Hz)
1	D1(gamma)	30–60
2	D2 (beta)	15–30
3	D3 (alpha)	8–15
4	D4 (theta)	4–8
4	A4 (delta)	0–4

5.2. *Experimental Results*

The proposed approach model is tested on the four different test cases as showed in Table 4. The input feature vector is randomly divided into training data set and testing data set based 10-fold cross-validation. The training data set is used to train the classifier, whereas the testing data set is used to satisfy the accuracy and performance of the trained classifier for the given EEG classification problem. Each row of the input data matrix is one observation and its column is one feature. In this work, the feature vector of data set A has 100 rows and 50 columns. Similarly, the feature vector of sets B, C, D and E individually have 100 observations and 50 features. The data set for the present binary classifier task consists of 200 observations of 50 features for case 1 to case 4. We implement the GWO-SVM algorithm

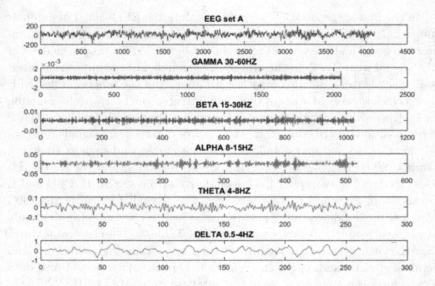

Fig. 4.   Approximate and detail coefficients are taken from a healthy subject (set A).

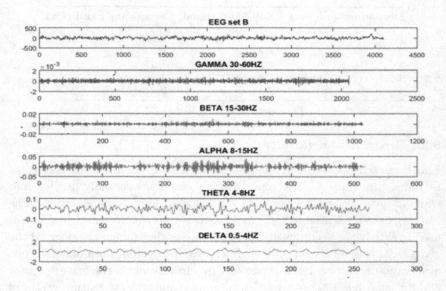

Fig. 5.   Approximate and detail coefficients for healthy subject (set B).

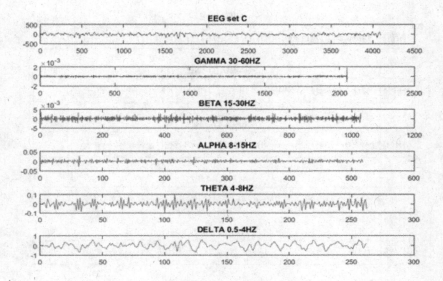

Fig. 6.   Approximate and detail coefficients for epileptic subject (set C).

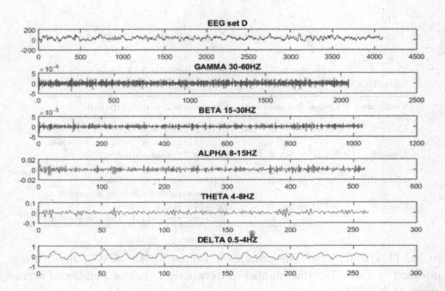

Fig. 7.   Approximate and detail coefficients for epileptic subject (set D).

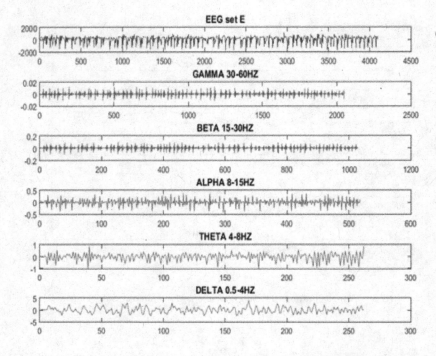

Fig. 8. Approximate and detail coefficients for epileptic subject (set E).

Table 4. The classification description of different test cases with their EEG data sets.

Test case	Cases for seizure	Classification description
Case 1	Set A vs Set E	Normal Persons with eye open vs Epileptic patients during seizure state
Case 2	Set B vs Set E	Normal Persons with eye close vs Epileptic patients during seizure state
Case 3	Set C vs Set E	Hippocampal seizure free vs Epileptic patients during seizure state
Case 4	Set D vs Set E	Epileptic seizure free vs Epileptic patients during seizure state

in MATLAB (R2015a).The parameter tuning for the GWO algorithm is outlined in Table 5. Same number of iterations and same number of agents are used for PSO and GA.

The experiments were performed to estimate the performance of the proposed GWO-SVM algorithm for SVM feature selection and SVM parame-

Table 5.   Parameter setting for GWO.

Parameter	Value
No of wolves	30
No of iterations	10
Penalty C range	[1,1000]
Kernel function parameters σ range	[1,100]
Feature subset range	[0, 1]

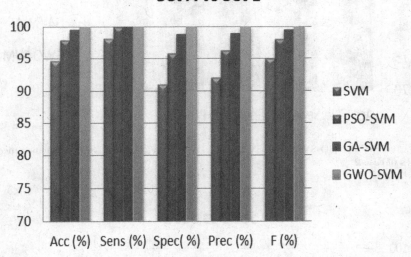

Fig. 9.   SVM, PSO-SVM, GA-SVM and GWO-SVM Comparative performance measures of case 1.

ters Optimization. Classification accuracy rate of the experiment was computed by averaging resultant accuracies from all 10-folds. Figures 9–12 show classification results obtained via applying the proposed GWO-SVM against traditional SVM classification approach, PSO-SVM and GA-SVM for RBF kernel function for case 1 to case 4 respectively. It is noticed from Figure 9 in case 1 that accuracy achieved by SVM without GWO is 94.643%, 97.979% using PSO-SVM, 99.422% using GA-SVM while 100% using GWO-SVM proposed approach, which means that the accuracy increased by 5.357% compared with SVM, 2.021% compared with PSO-SVM and 0.578% compared with GA-SVM. For case 2 in Figure 10, accuracy achieved with the

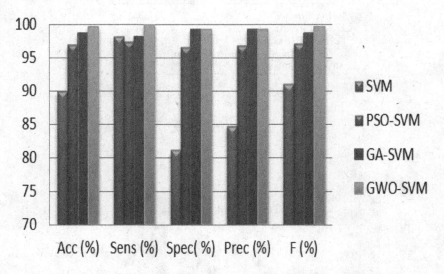

Fig. 10. SVM, PSO-SVM, GA-SVM and GWO-SVM comparative performance measures of case 2.

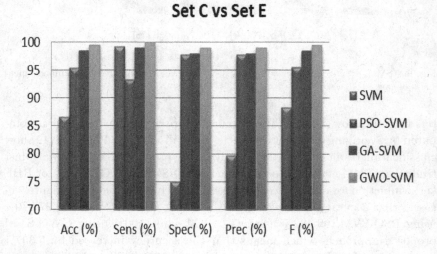

Fig. 11. SVM, PSO-SVM, GA-SVM and GWO-SVM comparative performance measures of case 3.

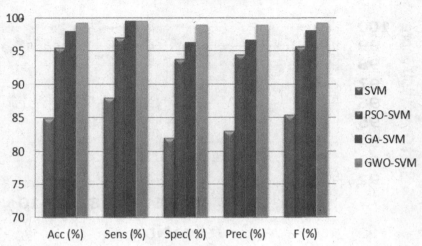

Fig. 12. SVM, PSO-SVM, GA-SVM and GWO-SVM comparative performance measures of case 4.

traditional SVM equals to 89.896%, 96.93% using PSO-SVM, 98.613% using GA-SVM, while it has increased to 99.577% using GWO-SVM proposed approach, which means that the accuracy increased by 10.104% compared with SVM, 2.647% compared with PSO-SVM and 0.964% compared with GA-SVM. Also, for case 3 in Figure 11, accuracy achieved with the traditional SVM equals to 86.594%, 95.468% using PSO-SVM, 98.362% using GA-SVM, while it has increased to 99.472% using GWO-SVM proposed approach, which means that the accuracy increased by 13.3% compared with SVM, 4.004% compared with PSO-SVM and 1.11% compared with GA-SVM. Finally, for case 4 in Figure 12, accuracy achieved with the traditional SVM equals to 85%, 95.541% using PSO-SVM, 97.945% using GA-SVM, while it has increased to 99.232% using GWO-SVM, which means that the accuracy increased by 14.232% compared with SVM, 3.691% compared PSO-SVM and 1.287% compared with GA-SVM.

Figures 13–16 show the convergence of optimization-based classifier GWO-SVM for case 1 to case 4 respectively over all iterations. It depicts the relation between the number of optimization iterations and the fitness value (classification accuracy). We note that when the number of iterations increases, the value of the fitness increases.

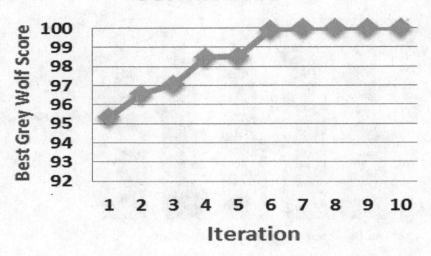

Fig. 13.   GWO convergence curve of case 1.

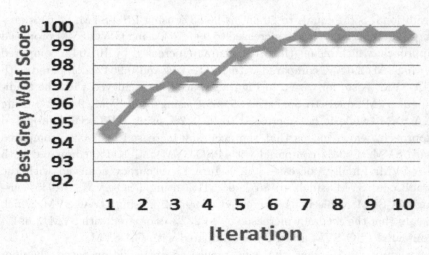

Fig. 14.   GWO convergence curve of case 2.

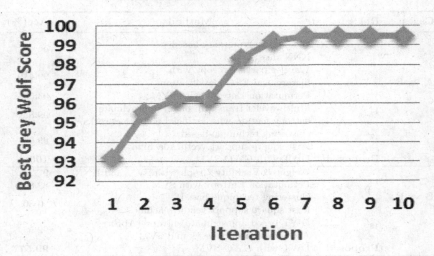

Fig. 15.   GWO convergence curve of case 3.

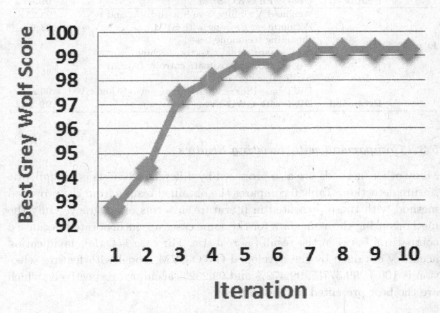

Fig. 16.   GWO convergence curve of case 4.

Table 6. A comparison of classification accuracy obtained by our proposed method and others method that used the same dataset for their experimentation.

Cases	Ref	Methods	Acc(%)
A vs E	2	Genetic programming-based KNN classifier	99.2
	12	Wavelet packet entropy with hierarchical EEG classification	99.449
	13	Permutation Entropy with SVM	93.55
	14	Multiwavelet transform based approximate entropy feature with artificial neural networks.	99.85
	17	clustering technique-based least square support vector machine	99.90
	Proposed	DWT with GWO-SVM	**100**
B vs E	8	Weighted Visibility Graph with SVM and KNN	97.25
	13	Permutation Entropy with SVM	82.88
	17	clustering technique-based least square support vector machine	96.30
	18	DWT based approximate entropy (ApEn) Artificial neural network and SVM	92.5
	Proposed	DWT with GWO-SVM	**99.577**
C vs E	8	Weighted Visibility Graph with SVM and KNN	98.25
	13	Permutation Entropy with SVM	88.83
	17	clustering technique-based least square support vector machine	96.20
	Proposed	DWT with GWO-SVM	**99.472**
D vs E	8	Weighted Visibility Graph with SVM and KNN	93.25
	13	Permutation Entropy with SVM	83.13
	17	clustering technique-based least square support vector machine	93.60
	18	DWT based approximate entropy (ApEn) Artificial neural network and SVM	95
	20	DWT based fuzzy approximate entropy and SVM	95.85
	Proposed	DWT with GWO-SVM	**99.232**

5.3. *Comparison with Existing Studies*

Many other methods are also proposed by different researchers for epileptic seizure detection. Table 6 compares the obtained results from the proposed method with those presented in literature in terms of accuracy. Only the methods using the same data for the same cases are incorporated because a comparison between the results is realistic. For case 1-4, the classification accuracy obtained by the developed GWO-SVM model with feature selection is 100%, 99.577%, 99.472% and 99.232% accuracy, respectively, which are the best presented for this data set.

6. Conclusion

Visually, epileptic seizure detection by a trained professional from the long-time EEG epochs is the costly and time-consuming procedure. The automatic detection of epileptic seizures in EEG is significant in the estimation of epileptic patients. In this chapter, the DWT is used to analyze EEG for detecting epilepsy. EEG epochs are analyzed into several sub-bands through DWT to get ten features entropy, Skewness, max, median, min, mean, energy, standard deviation, Relative Wave Energy (RWE) and variance from each sub-band to classify EEG signal. This chapter presents an approach using GWO for feature selection integrated with SVM for parameters optimization and the SVM classifier for automatic seizure detection in EEG signals. The 100% classification accuracies are obtained using GWO-SVM for case 1, 99.577% for case 2, 99.472% for case 3 and 99.232% for case 4. These results illustrate the effectiveness of using GWO and SVM classifier for seizure detection in EEG signals. Experimental results showed that the presented GWO-SVMs approach outperformed GA-SVM and the native SVMs classification algorithm for RBF kernel function.

References

1. Q. Yuan, W. Zhou, S. Li, and D. Cai, Epileptic eeg classification based on extreme learning machine and nonlinear features, *Epilepsy research.* **96**(1), 29–38 (2011).
2. L. Guo, D. Rivero, J. Dorado, C. R. Munteanu, and A. Pazos, Automatic feature extraction using genetic programming: An application to epileptic eeg classification, *Expert Systems with Applications.* **38**(8), 10425–10436 (2011).
3. U. R. Acharya, H. Fujita, V. K. Sudarshan, S. Bhat, and J. E. Koh, Application of entropies for automated diagnosis of epilepsy using eeg signals: a review, *Knowledge-Based Systems.* **88**, 85–96 (2015).
4. E. H. Houssein, A. E. Hassanien, and A. K. A. Ismaeel. Eeg signals classification for epileptic detection: A review. In *Second International Conference on Internet of Things and Cloud Computing, ICC17 Cambridge City, UK* (2017).
5. M. Kalaivani, V. Kalaivani, and V. A. Devi, Analysis of EEG signal for the detection of brain abnormalities, *International Journal of Computer Applications* (2014).
6. P. Gaspar, J. Carbonell, and J. L. Oliveira, On the parameter optimization of support vector machines for binary classification, *Journal of Integrative Bioinformatics (JIB).* **9**(3), 33–43 (2012).

7. G. Garšva and P. Danenas, Particle swarm optimization for linear support vector machines based classifier selection, *Nonlinear Analysis: Modelling and Control.* **19**(1), 26–42 (2014).

8. S. Supriya, S. Siuly, H. Wang, J. Cao, and Y. Zhang, Weighted visibility graph with complex network features in the detection of epilepsy, *IEEE Access.* **4**, 6554–6566 (2016).

9. A. Subasi and M. I. Gursoy, Eeg signal classification using PCA, ICA, LDA and support vector machines, *Expert Systems with Applications.* **37**(12), 8659–8666 (2010).

10. N. Ozdemir and E. Yildirim, Patient specific seizure prediction system using Hilbert spectrum and bayesian networks classifiers, *Computational and mathematical methods in medicine.* **2014** (2014).

11. L. M. Patnaik and O. K. Manyam, Epileptic EEG detection using neural networks and post-classification, *Computer methods and programs in biomedicine.* **91**(2), 100–109 (2008).

12. D. Wang, D. Miao, and C. Xie, Best basis-based wavelet packet entropy feature extraction and hierarchical eeg classification for epileptic detection, *Expert Systems with Applications.* **38**(11), 14314–14320 (2011).

13. N. Nicolaou and J. Georgiou, Detection of epileptic electroencephalogram based on permutation entropy and support vector machines, *Expert Systems with Applications.* **39**(1), 202–209 (2012).

14. L. Guo, D. Rivero, and A. Pazos, Epileptic seizure detection using multi-wavelet transform based approximate entropy and artificial neural networks, *Journal of neuroscience methods.* **193**(1), 156–163 (2010).

15. K. Sivasankari and K. Thanushkodi, An improved EEG signal classification using neural network with the consequence of ICA and STFT, *Journal of Electrical Engineering and Technology.* **9**(3), 1060–1071 (2014).

16. K.-C. Hsu and S.-N. Yu, Detection of seizures in eeg using subband nonlinear parameters and genetic algorithm, *Computers in Biology and Medicine.* **40** (10), 823–830 (2010).

17. Y. Li, P. P. Wen, *et al.*, Clustering technique-based least square support vector machine for eeg signal classification, *Computer methods and programs in biomedicine.* **104**(3), 358–372 (2011).

18. Y. Kumar, M. Dewal, and R. Anand, Epileptic seizures detection in EEG using dwt-based apen and artificial neural network, *Signal, Image and Video Processing.* **8**(7), 1323–1334 (2014).

19. D. of Epileptology University of Bonn, EEG time series data URL http://www.meb.uni-bonn.de/epileptologie/science/physik/eegdata.htmlAccessedOct2016.

20. Y. Kumar, M. Dewal, and R. Anand, Epileptic seizure detection using dwt based fuzzy approximate entropy and support vector machine, *Neurocomputing.* **133**, 271–279 (2014).

21. O. Faust, U. R. Acharya, H. Adeli, and A. Adeli, Wavelet-based EEG processing for computer-aided seizure detection and epilepsy diagnosis, *Seizure.* **26**, 56–64 (2015).

22. M. Li, W. Chen, and T. Zhang, Classification of epilepsy EEG signals using DWT-based envelope analysis and neural network ensemble, *Biomedical Signal Processing and Control.* **31**, 357–365 (2017).

23. A. E. Hassanien and E. Emary, *Swarm intelligence: principles, advances, and applications.* CRC Press (2016).

24. S. Mirjalili, S. M. Mirjalili, and A. Lewis, Grey wolf optimizer, *Advances in Engineering Software.* **69**, 46–61 (2014).

25. A. A. El-Gaafary, Y. S. Mohamed, A. M. Hemeida, and A.-A. A. Mohamed, Grey wolf optimization for multi input multi output system, *Universal Journal of Communications and Network.* **3**(1), 1–6 (2015).

26. E. Elhariri, N. El-Bendary, A. E. Hassanien, and A. Abraham. Grey wolf optimization for one-against-one multi-class support vector machines. In *Soft Computing and Pattern Recognition (SoCPaR), 2015 7th International Conference of*, pp. 7–12 (2015).

27. E. Emary, H. M. Zawbaa, C. Grosan, and A. E. Hassenian. Feature subset selection approach by gray-wolf optimization. In *Afro-European Conference for Industrial Advancement*, pp. 1–13 (2015).

28. C. Cortes and V. Vapnik, Support-vector networks, *Machine learning.* **20**(3), 273–297 (1995).

29. A. M. Andrew. An introduction to support vector machines and other kernel-based learning methods by Nello Christianini and John Shawe-Taylor, cambridge university press, cambridge, 2000, xiii+ 189 pp., isbn 0-521-78019-5 (hbk,£ 27.50) (2000).

30. R. Sharma, R. B. Pachori, and S. Gautam. Empirical mode decomposition based classification of focal and non-focal seizure EEG signals. In *Medical Biometrics, 2014 International Conference on*, pp. 135–140 (2014).

31. A. Hamad, E. H. Houssein, A. E. Hassanien, and A. A. Fahmy. Feature extraction of epilepsy EEG using discrete wavelet transform. In *Computer Engineering Conference (ICENCO), 2016 12th International*, pp. 190–195 (2016).

Chapter 9

Optimization of Recurrent Neural Networks Using Evolutionary Group-based Particle Swarm Optimization for Hexapod Robot Gait Generation

Chia-Feng Juang[*,†] and Yu-Cheng Chang

Department of Electrical Engineering, National Chung Hsing University
145 Xingda Road, South Dist., Taichung 402, Taiwan
[†] *cfjuang@dragon.nchu.edu.tw*

I-Fang Chung

Institute of Biomedical Informatics, National Yang-Ming University
No. 155, Sec. 2, Linong Street, Taipei 112, Taiwan
ifchung@ym.edu.tw

This chapter introduces the application of a hybrid metaheuristic algorithm to the optimization of recurrent neural networks (RNNs) in generating forward walking gait of a hexapod robot. The algorithm used is the evolutionary group-based particle swarm optimization (EGPSO), which creates new solutions through the hybrid of group-based genetic algorithm (GA) and particle swarm optimization (PSO). In this application, each leg of the robot is actuated by two motors with control signals generated from a fully connected RNN (FCRNN). The FCRNN is replicated over the six legs and the connection of these FCRNNs form a whole multiple-FCRNN (MFCRNN). The MFCRNN is learned through a data-driven evolutionary approach instead of a traditional model-based approach that explicitly uses the kinematic model of the hexapod robot. This chapter formulates the evolutionary gait learning approach as an optimization problem that optimizes the walking speed of the robot. The EGPSO optimizes all the free weights in the MFCRNN. Simulation of the evolutionary robot is performed using a robot simulator. Comparisons with various GA and PSO algorithms demonstrate the advantage of EGPSO. The MFCRNN optimized through the EGPSO in simulations is applied to generate the gait of a real hexapod robot for forward movement.

Keywords: Genetic algorithms, particle swarm optimization, hybrid metaheuristic algorithm, hexapod robot, recurrent neural networks.

*Corresponding author.

1. Introduction

Genetic algorithms (GAs) and particle swarm optimization (PSO) are well-known metaheuristic algorithms. GAs uses the operators of crossover and mutation to evolve new solutions [1]. PSO creates new solutions based on particle positions and velocities. The velocity of a particle is derived from its best-so-far position and the best position of the particles in its neighborhood [2]. The movement of the particles enables the PSO to expand a search space. PSO shows a fast convergence speed but may suffer from a premature convergence problem. A hybrid metaheuristic algorithm aims to combine the optimization characteristics of different metaheuristic algorithms. Based on this idea, a few metaheuristic algorithms based on the hybrid of the operators in GA and PSO have been proposed [3–12]. One category focuses on introducing the crossover or mutation operator into PSO [3, 5, 7]. In the PSO with time-varying acceleration coefficients and mutation (MPSO-TVAC) [3], the mutation operator in GA is introduced to mutate the velocity of a particle when the global optimum stagnates over a period of optimization iterations. A wavelet-based mutation operator is introduced into PSO in [7]. The PSO with recombination and dynamic linkage discovery (PSO-RDL) [5] integrates PSO with the dynamic linkage discovery and recombination operator in GA.

In another category of GA/PSO hybrid, a new population is partially generated from GA with the left part generated from PSO. The early work in this category is the hybrid of GA and PSO (HGAPSO) [4]. In the HGAPSO, half of the solutions in a new population are generated from PSO and the others are from GA. The HGAPSO has been shown to outperform GAs and PSO. Based on the HGAPSO framework, some GA/PSO hybrid algorithms have been proposed [6, 8–10]. In the genetical swarm optimization (GSO) [6], a self-adaptive strategy is proposed to determine the percentage of population at each iteration that is generated from GA or PSO. Likewise, in the hybrid of PSO and GA (HPSOGA) [10], the percentage of new solutions generated from GA or PSO is based on a hybrid probability P. In the GA/PSO-hybrid algorithm [8], each of the GA and PSO creates half the population as in the HGAPSO. This hybrid algorithm uses different GA and PSO operators from the HGAPSO to generate new GA and PSO solutions. A new group-based framework to generate partial solutions from GA and PSO was proposed in the evolutionary group-based PSO (EGPSO) algorithm [9]. The GA crossover operator in the EGPSO selects parents from different groups formed dynamically and newly evolved solutions replace the worst group in current population. The other solutions in a new population are generated from group-based PSO. The EGPSO has been successfully applied to fuzzy controller optimization with superior performance than HGAPSO and various advanced PSO. This chapter introduces the application of EGPSO to optimize recurrent neural networks (RNNs) for evolutionary hexapod robot gait generation.

RNNs have feedback connections from other nodes and/or self-feedback connections in their topologies, which are developed to handle sequential information. These feedback loops are used to capture information about what has been received so far. Different types of feedback topologies have been proposed [13]. A wide range of temporal/spatiotemporal problems have been successfully addressed using RNNs. Examples are machine translation [14], speech recognition [15], generation of image descriptions [16], and dynamic system control [17]. To optimize the parameters in RNNs, one popular category is using the gradient descent algorithm, such as the back propagation through time [18]. Another approach is using metaheuristic algorithms. GAs [19] and PSO algorithms [20] have been applied to optimize RNNs for different applications. These global search algorithms have shown their strength in optimizing RNNs. Therefore, this chapter applies EGPSO to optimize RNNs.

The application of RNNs to generate rhythmic walking gaits of legged robots has been proposed in several studies [21, 22]. In this application, different patterns of rhythmic waves are generated from RNNs to generate walking postures in different legged robots. For RNN-based bipedal robots, the determination of the connection weights in a RNN through manual tuning [23], reinforcement learning [24], or metaheuristic algorithms [25, 26] has been proposed. The manual deign is generally performed in a step-by-step manner to approximate a desired, specified motion pattern which may be suitable only for a specific robot structure. Reinforcement learning based on a central pattern generator (CPG)-actor-critic framework was previously proposed [24]. In this method, the connection weights in the RNN-based CPG are adopted from [23] and are fixed. An additional actor that receives feedbacks from robot states and CPG outputs is proposed for shaping the CPG outputs. Reinforcement leaning is applied only to the feedback weights connecting to the actor. For the metaheuristic algorithm-based approach, weights optimization using GAs [25] or continuous ant colony optimization [26] has been proposed.

Because of the high degrees of freedom of the six legs in a hexapod robot, the coordination of each leg for fast walking is a complex problem.

To mimic the learning of neuros in hexapod biological organisms, the use of a RNN as a CPG to automatically generate the gait of a hexapod has been proposed [27–31]. Different RNN structures have been proposed in this application. The multiple fully connected RNNs (MFCRNN) has been applied to evolve dynamic gaits of a hexapod robot in some studies [27, 29]. The parameters in the MFCRNN were evolved through GAs in [27], where only simulations were performed. To improve the evolution efficiency and walking speed, evolution of the MFCRNN using the symbiotic species-based particle swarm optimization (SSPSO) algorithm was proposed in [29]. This chapter also considers the optimization of the MFCRNN. The EGPSO-optimized MFCRNN is applied to generate the gait of a hexapod robot for fast walking. The advantage of using the EGPSO is shown through comparisons with GA, SSPSO, and various advanced PSO algorithms. The EGPSO-designed MFCRNN in simulations is also applied to generate the gait of a real hexapod robot for forward movement.

This chapter is organized as follows. Section 2 describes the GAs, PSO, and EGPSO. Section 3 describes the robot structure and the fully connected RNN (FCRNN) in controlling the movement of a single leg. Section 4 introduces the MFCRNN and EGPSO-based evolutionary learning configuration for robot gait generation. Section 5 presents simulations and experimental results. Finally, conclusions are summarized in Section 6.

2. Evolutionary Group-based Particle Swarm Optimization (EGPSO)

2.1. *Genetic Algorithms*

This section introduces the GA and PSO used in the EGPSO [9]. A typical GA evolves the individuals (solutions) in a population by using three operators: reproduction, crossover, and mutation [1]. Figure 1 shows the flowchart of a typical GA. The basic concepts of the three operators are described as follows.

2.1.1. *Reproduction operator*

In the reproduction operator, a better-performed individual in the current population has a higher probability to be reproduced to the next generation. The two widely used selection strategies are roulette wheel and tournament selections. The basic idea in the roulette wheel selection is creating and spinning a roulette wheel. The sizes of the slots in the roulette wheel

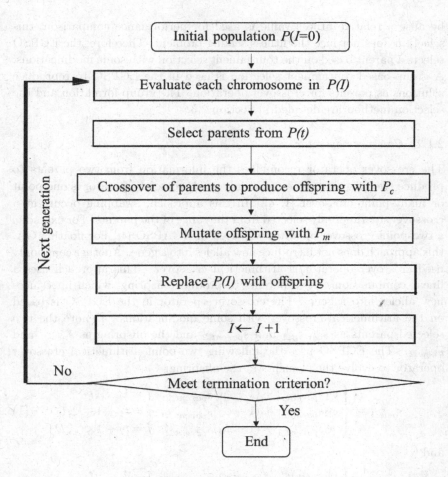

Fig. 1. Flowchart of a typical GA.

are different and are in proportion to the fitness values of individuals. A parent is selected by spinning the roulette wheel. In this selection strategy, proper fitness scaling may be necessary. This scaling operation is to avoid that a few super individuals with much larger fitness values than the others in the same population could take over nearly the whole population, leading to premature convergence to a local optimum. In the tournament selection, at least two individuals in a population are randomly and uniformly selected. Among the selected individuals, the best-performing one is selected. This selection method is easier in implementation. In addition, because a relative fitness value is used for performance comparison, this selection does not face the fitness scaling problem. Therefore, the EGPSO selects a parent based on the tournament selection with some modifications. A group-based tournament selection is used in the EGPSO to reproduce solutions as parents for crossover operation. The group formation and the selection method are detailed in Section 2.3.

2.1.2. *Crossover operator*

The crossover operator recombines the information from two parents to produce two offspring. One commonly used crossover operator is one-point or many-point crossover [1, 4]. In this approach, swapping occurs at a crossover site randomly selected from the range of the parents. For example, a two-point crossover operator was used in HGAPSO [4]. For floating GA, this approach does not introduce new alleles into a gene. Another commonly used crossover operator is arithmetical crossover. This approach uses a linear combination of two parents to produce offspring, which introduces new alleles into a gene. The crossover operator in the EGPSO is based on the arithmetical crossover with some modifications. Denote the two selected parents as $\vec{s}_{parent\_1}$ and $\vec{s}_{parent\_2}$ and the offspring as $\vec{s}_{new\_1}$ and $\vec{s}_{new\_2}$. The EGPSO uses the following two-point arithmetical crossover operator to evolve the elements in the offspring:

$$
s_{new\_1}^j = \begin{cases} \phi_1 s_{parent\_1}^j + (1 - \phi_1)s_{parent\_2}^j, & j = 1, \ldots, t_1 \\ \phi_2 s_{parent\_1}^j + (1 - \phi_2)s_{parent\_2}^j, & j = t_1 + 1, \ldots, t_2 \\ \phi_3 s_{parent\_1}^j + (1 - \phi_3)s_{parent\_2}^j, & j = t_2 + 1, \ldots, D \end{cases} \tag{1}
$$

and

$$
s_{new\_2}^j = \begin{cases} (1 - \phi_1)s_{parent\_1}^j + \phi_1 s_{parent\_2}^j, & j = 1, \ldots, t_1 \\ (1 - \phi_2)s_{parent\_1}^j + \phi_2 s_{parent\_2}^j, & j = t_1 + 1, \ldots, t_2 \\ (1 - \phi_3)s_{parent\_1}^j + \phi_3 s_{parent\_2}^j, & j = t_2 + 1, \ldots, D \end{cases} \tag{2}
$$

where t_1 and t_2 are randomly selected crossover sites and D is the vector dimension. The variable ϕ_i in (1), (2), and the following equations represents a uniform random number in $[0, 1]$.

2.1.3. *Mutation operator*

Mutation is an exploration operation that introduces new components into each individual in a population through a random operator. This operator randomly alters the allele of a gene to introduce new information at the gene level into a chromosome. The mutation operator is applied independently to each gene in a chromosome according to a mutation probability P_m. Because of the stochastic search property, the mutation probability is generally and sparingly set to a low value. A higher mutation probability will cause the mutation operator becoming more like a completely stochastic search. One simple mutation method is uniform mutation, as used in [4]. In this method, a gene in a real-coded chromosome is replaced by a mutated gene whose value is randomly and uniformly selected from its domain. Non-uniform mutation strategies have also been proposed [1]. The basic idea of non-uniform mutation is that the random search range decreases with the increase of iteration number. In the EGPSO, most offspring would function as particles in PSO at the next iteration, where an adaptive velocity-mutated operator (AVMO) for solution mutation is employed. Therefore, the traditional GA mutation operation is not applied to the offspring. The AVMO is detailed in the following section.

2.2. *Particle Swarm Optimization*

Like GAs, PSO is a population-based metaheuristic optimization algorithm [2]. Figure 2 shows the flowchart of a typical PSO algorithm. PSO consists of a swarm of solution vectors (called particles). PSO performs searches through a swarm of particles moving in a search domain. Each particle is associated with a position vector $\vec{s}_i$ and a velocity vector $\vec{v}_i$. For particle i, the best position it has passed so far is recorded as $\vec{p}_i(t)$. In addition, the best position among the neighborhood particles of a particle obtained so far is kept track. The definition of neighborhood can be divided into global and local versions. In the global version, the whole population is defined as as the neighborhood. In the local version, the neighborhood is defined as a smaller number of adjacent members of the population. In the EGPSO, the local version is used and the neighborhood of a particle in group z is defined to be all the particles that are also in the same group. For a particle i within group z, the best position among its neighborhood is defined as the group leader $\vec{p}_{z,i}^{Leader}$. The updated velocity of particle i at each iteration $I + 1$ is given as follows:

$$v_i^j(I+1) = \chi(v_i^j(I) + c_1\phi_4^j \cdot (p_i^j(I) - s_i^j(I)) + c_2\phi_5^j \cdot (p_{z,i}^{Leader,j}(I) - s_i^j(I))),$$
$$j = 1, \ldots, D$$

(3)

where c_1 and c_2 are positive acceleration coefficients. The constriction coefficient χ in (3) restricts the magnitude of velocity and so no explicit limit of the velocity has to be assigned in advance. This chapter sets $c_1 = 1$, $c_2 = 1$, and $\chi = 0.8$, as in [9]. The PSO in the EGPSO uses the AVMO with probability p_m to drive particles to possibly escape from local optima. The mutation operation mutates each element in the mutated velocity vector $\vec{v}_i = [v_i^1, \ldots, v_i^D]$ by the following equation:

$$v_i^j \leftarrow (1 - \phi_6^j)v_i^j + \phi_7^j v_{rand}^j, \, i = 1, \ldots, P_S, \, j = 1, \ldots, D \qquad (4)$$

where v_{rand}^j is a random velocity given as follows:

$$v_{rand}^j = g(I) \cdot b \cdot [\phi_8^j \cdot 2\Delta^j - \Delta^j], \, j = 1, \ldots, D \qquad (5)$$

where $0 < b < 1$ is a constriction coefficient and $\Delta^j := s_{max}^j - s_{min}^j$, where $[s_{min}^j, s_{max}^j]$ denotes the domain of s^j in $\vec{s}$. The function $g(I)$ in (5) is given as follows:

$$g(I) = max\left(exp\left\{-\left(\frac{I}{T_{end}}\right)^2\right\}, 0.1\right) \qquad (6)$$

where T_{end} is the termination iteration number. The value of $g(I)$ decreases with iteration number I to emphasize the exploration search at the early optimization stage and to emphasize the exploitation search at the final stage. Given the particle velocity, the equation used to update the new position of particle i is

$$\vec{s}_i(I + 1) = \vec{s}_i(I) + \vec{v}_i(I + 1). \qquad (7)$$

2.3. *Evolutionary Group-based Particle Swarm Optimization (EGPSO)*

The basic concept of the EGPSO algorithm and its implementation details are described in this section. Figure 3 shows the flowchart. The evolutionary process in the EGPSO employs the crossover and mutation operators in GA to create new solutions. Therefore, the EGPSO algorithm belongs to the framework of GA/PSO hybrid, which was proposed to enhance the optimization ability of GA and PSO based on the fusion of their optimization characteristics. Individuals in the population are formatted into different groups based on their performances and locations in the search space. The group formation is used in the operators of GA and PSO. The motivation is to improve search diversity and reduce the chance of being got stuck in a local optimum at the early optimization stage.

The details of the algorithm are described as follows. The population size is denoted as P_S. At each new iteration, the EGPSO incorporates the

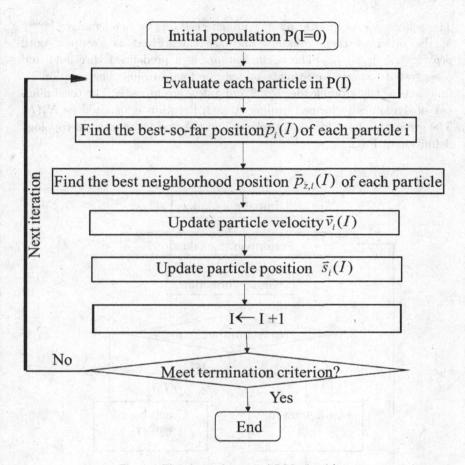

Fig. 2. Flowchart of a typical PSO algorithm.

technique of group formation into GA and PSO in the generation of P_S new solutions. In the group formation, solutions are ranked from the best (minimum cost value) to the worst (maximum cost value) according to their cost function values. The best solution $\vec{p}_z^{Leader}$ in group z is called a group leader. The similarity degree, ρ, between a solution $\vec{s}_i$ and $\vec{p}_z^{Leader}$ is found by

$$\rho(\vec{p}_z^{Leader}, \vec{s}_i) = \sqrt{\frac{\| \vec{p}_z^{Leader} - \vec{s}_i \|_2^2}{D}}. \tag{8}$$

The solutions ranked after $\vec{p}_z^{Leader}$ are checked one by one against $\vec{p}_z^{Leader}$ in the order of their rankings and are categorized as group z until $\rho(\vec{p}_z^{Leader}, \vec{s}_{i*}) > \rho_{th}$. The coefficient ρ_{th} is a predefined threshold and a suggested formula to estimate ρ_{th} can be found in [9]. The solution $\vec{s}_{i*}$ functions as the group leader $\vec{p}_{z+1}^{Leader}$ of a new group $z+1$. The total number of dynamically formed groups at each iteration is denoted as $N_g(I)$. The groups are used for parent selection in GA and neighborhood topology definition in PSO.

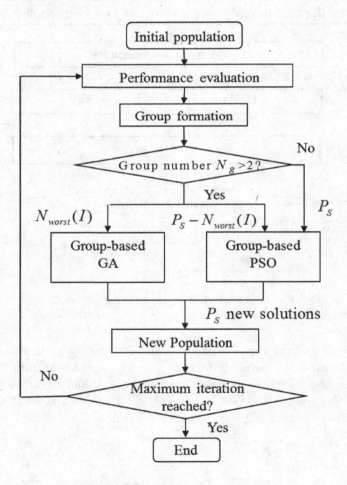

Fig. 3.   Flowchart of the EGPSO.

Parts of the new solutions are generated by the group-based GA described in Section 2.1 when the group number $N_g(I)$ is greater than one. Based on the group formation, the GA uses a tournament scheme to select parents for crossover. In this selection, two parents are randomly selected from the groups with the sole except of the worst-performing one. First, $\frac{N_g(I)}{2}$ groups are randomly and uniformly selected from the population. Among them, the best group is reserved. Then, a parent is randomly and uniformly selected from the individuals in this group. The same process applies to the selection of the other parent. The selected parents perform the crossover operation in (1) and (2) to generate new solutions (offspring). The number of solutions generated from the GA is identical to the number of solutions, $N_{worst}(I)$, in the worst-performing group. That is, these GA evolved solutions replace the worst-performing group in the current population. These solutions function as particles in the next iteration. The initial velocity $\vec{v}_{new}$ of each new particle $\vec{s}_{new}$ is assigned as follows. Among the $N_g - 1$ group leaders, the leader z^* that shows the maximum similarity degree $\rho(\vec{p}_{z^*}^{Leader}, \vec{s}_{new})$ to $\vec{s}_{new}$ is found. The particle $\vec{s}_{new}$ is categorized into group z^*. The vector $\vec{v}_{new}$ is assigned according to the directions from the two parents and the group leader to $\vec{s}_{new}$ and is given as follows:

$$
\begin{aligned}
v_{new}^j = \gamma_8^j \cdot (p_{z^*}^{leader,j} - s_{new}^j) + \gamma_9^j \cdot (s_{parent\_1}^j - s_{new}^j) \\
+ \gamma_{10}^j \cdot (s_{parent\_2}^j - s_{new}^j), \quad j = 1, \ldots, D
\end{aligned}
\tag{9}
$$

The group-based PSO in Section 2.2 generates the left $P_S - N_{worst}(I)$ solutions in a new population. In this PSO, the top $P_S - N_{worst}(I)$ ranked solutions in the current population are regarded as particles. The $P_S - N_{worst}(I)$ new solutions are created using (7). These new solutions replace the original top $P_S - N_{worst}(I)$ ranked solutions. The whole algorithm ends when the predefined iteration number T_{end} is reached.

3. Fully Connected Recurrent Neural Network (FCRNN) for Single Leg Control

Two actuators drive the movement of each leg in the hexapod robot. Figure 4 shows the body model and the locations of the two joint actuators in each leg of the robot. One actuator drives the knee of the leg to move the foot up or down, while the other drives the hip of the leg to swing forward or backward. In a stance phase, a foot touches the ground and the hip swings to move the body. In a swing phase, a foot lifts up and the leg swings in the air.

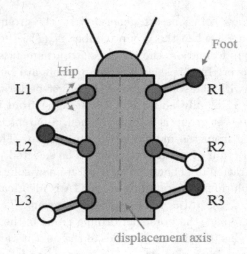

Fig. 4. Hexapod body model, where white foots are lifting-up foots and black foots are supporting foots.

The FCRNN is used to control the forward/background swing and up/down of a single leg. Figure 5 shows the structure of the FCRNN. In the FCRNN, all nodes are connected with self-feedbacks. In a typical FCRNN, a node may function as an input node, an output node, neither (a hidden node) or both. Let x_i and y_i denote the input and output of node i, respectively. The input-output function of node i is

$$\tau_i \dot{y}_i = -y_i + a \left(\sum_j w_{ij} y_j - b_i \right) + x_i \tag{10}$$

where τ_i is a relaxation time scale, b_i is a bias, and w_{ij} is a connection weight. The bipolar sigmoid function a defined as

$$a(m) = \frac{1 - exp(-m)}{1 + exp(-m)} \in [-1, 1] \tag{11}$$

is selected as the activation function. In digital implementation, the differential equation in (10) is implemented by the following difference equation

$$y_i(t + \Delta t) = \left(1 - \frac{\Delta t}{\tau_i} \right) y_i(t) + \frac{\Delta t}{\tau_i} a(m_i(t)) + \frac{\Delta t}{\tau_i} x_i(t) \tag{12}$$

where $m_i(t) = \sum_j w_{ij} y_j(t) - b_i$ is the net input to node i and the time step interval Δt is set to 0.1. This paper uses a five-node FCRNN to control a single leg, as shown in Fig. 6. In the five-node FCRNN, there are no input nodes (i.e., $x_i = 0$), two hidden nodes, and three output nodes. The output y_1 is sent to the knee actuator to control the up/down of a leg. If y_1 is greater or smaller than zero, then the foot lifts up or touches the ground, respectively. The difference $y_2 - y_3$ of the other two outputs controls the hip actuator. If $y_2 - y_3$ is greater or smaller than zero, then the leg swings forward or backward, respectively. The switching between the two phases of stance and swing (i.e., the walking speed) is thus determined by the three network outputs. The 5-node FCRNN is evolved to find the 25 optimal feedback weights w_{ij}, 5 biases b_i, and 5 relaxation time scales τ_i to obtain an optimal walking gait. Therefore, a total of 35 parameters in the FCRNN have to be optimized.

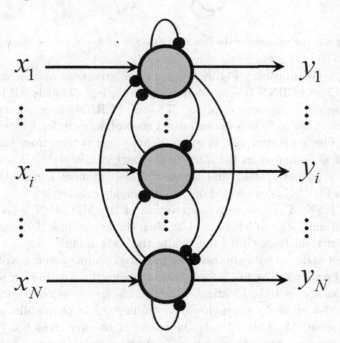

Fig. 5. The FCRNN structure, where all nodes are connected with self-feedbacks.

4. Evolutionary Hexapod Robot Gait Generation

This section introduces the architecture of the MFCRNN for the evolutionary hexapod robot gait generation and the EGPSO-based evolutionary

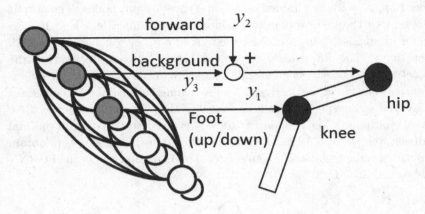

Fig. 6. Architecture of the five-node FCRNN used to control a single leg.

learning configuration. Figure 7 shows the structure of the MFCRNN [27, 29]. The FCRNN is replicated over the six legs. That is, all FCRNNs share the same parameter values. The six FCRNNs have to coordinate with each other to form a decentralized control network for forward movements. The generated gait is set to exhibit symmetries from the left to the right sides and from the front to the back of the body. Based on the symmetry property along and across the displacement axis of the robot body, an FCRNN is connected only to its neighboring replications, forming an MFCRNN. The order of computation of the MFCRNN is as follows: the left-front (L1) and left-back (L3), then the left-middle (L2), right-front (R1), and right-back (R3), and finally the right-middle (R2) leg. These computed node outputs are then sent to corresponding actuators of legs for foreword walking. The five intersegmental connections on the left and right body sides are set to be identical. Likewise, the five cross body connections between the left and right nodes in controlling the front, middle, and back legs are identical. That is, only the values of the five cross body weights $cw_1, \ldots, cw_5$ and five intersegmental connection weights $sw_1, \ldots, sw_5$ have to be determined. These ten weights coordinate the timing of the six legs for forward walking and have to be optimized as well.

The MFCRNN is evolved through a data-driven evolutionary learning configuration without explicit usage of the the kinematic model of the robot. Figure 8 shows the evolutionary learning configuration. In the evolutionary hexapod robot application, the objective is that the hexapod robot successfully learns the coordination of its legs for fast forward walking using only

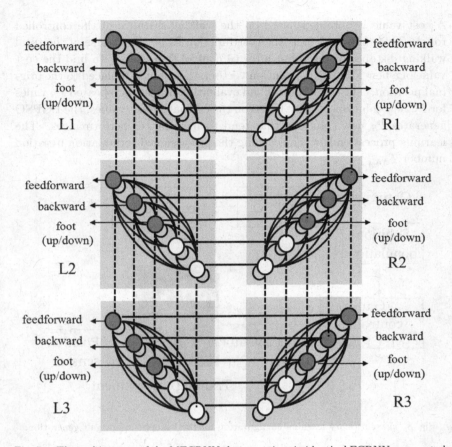

Fig. 7. The architecture of the MFCRNN that contains six identical FCRNNs connected by dashed and dash-dot lines.

reinforcement signal. The reinforcement signal for performance evaluation is the total walking distance of the robot. This chapter formulates the evolutionary gait learning configuration as an optimization problem with the objective of walking a long distance. The EGPSO is applied to optimize the MFCRNN. The dimension of a solution in the EGPSO is thus $D = 35 + 10 = 45$. The EGPSO contains a population of solutions, with each corresponding to an MFCRNN. Each solution vector $\vec{s}$ is represented as follows:

$$\vec{s} = [w_{11}, \ldots, w_{55}, b_1, \ldots, b_5, \tau_1, \ldots, \tau_5, cw_1, \ldots, cw_5, sw_1, \ldots, sw_5] \quad (13)$$

An MFCRNN with the solution vector in (13) is applied to control a robot.

A cost value is obtained based on the walking distance of the controlled robot. This chapter defines the cost function to be the inverse of the total walking distance of the robot after t_S control time steps. To find the cost value of a new MFCRNN (solution vector), the robot is replaced to the original position. The same control and evaluation process is repeated P_S times for P_S new solutions. Then, based on the evaluated cost values, the EGPSO generates P_S new solutions that tend to have better performances. The learning process ends when reaching the pre-assigned termination iteration number T_{end}.

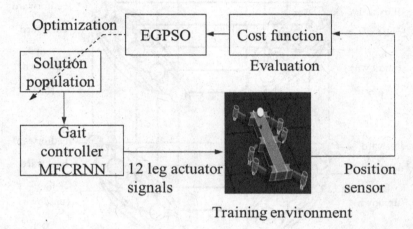

Fig. 8.   Evolutionary learning configuration for the hexapod robot gait generation.

5. Simulations and Experiments

5.1. *Simulations*

This section presents the forward walking gait of the hexapod robot learned through the EGPSO-deigned MFCRNN. Simulation of the evolutionary robot was performed using the Webots simulator software [32]. Figure 9 shows the simulation model of the hexapod robot with each leg controlled by two motors. The hip motor drives the leg to swing forward or backward and the knee motor drives the foot to lift up or step down, as described in Section 2. The robot learns to walk forwards with an MFCRNN controller evolved for fast walking. In (12), the $x_i(t)$ and $y_i(t)$ values were all initially set to zero. The control chip in controlling the real hexapod robot in the subsequent experiments does not provide the execution of the exponential function in implementing the bipolar sigmoid function in (11). Therefore, a piecewise linear function was proposed to approximate the bipolar sigmoid function and was given as follows:

$$a(m) = \begin{cases} 1, & 5 \leq m \\ 0.35 + 0.013m, & 1 \leq m \leq 5 \\ 0.01 + 0.47m, & -1 \leq m \leq 1 \\ -0.3284 + 0.0132m, & -5 \leq m \leq -1 \\ -1, & m \leq -5 \end{cases} \tag{14}$$

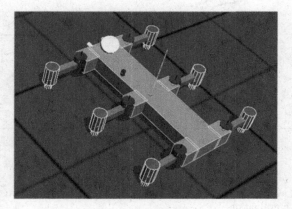

Fig. 9. The simulated hexapod robot in the Webots.

The swarm size P_S was set to 50. All the individuals in the initial population were randomly generated. The mutation probability p_m in AVMO was set to 0.05. The termination iteration number T_{end} was set to 1000, which corresponded to $1000 \times 50 = 5 \times 10^4$ evaluations (trials) in a single run. In the evaluation of the performance of an MFCRNN, the distance between the start and final positions of the robot in 145 time steps was measured. A longer distance indicated a better designed MFCRNN. The objective is to minimize a cost function C_f defined to be the inverse of the walking distance. Fig. 10 shows shows the average best-so-far values of C_f for each evaluation over 10 runs. Table 1 shows the average and standard deviation (STD) of C_f and the corresponding average walking distance (m) as well.

Figures 11 and 12 show two examples of unsatisfied gaits during the evolutionary learning process. In Fig. 11, the swing amplitude of each leg

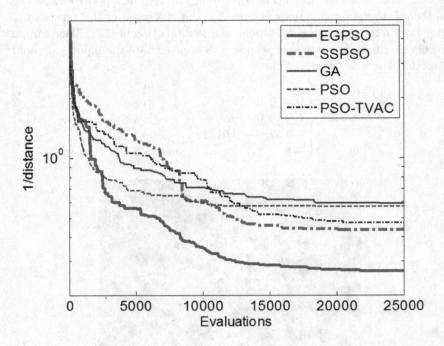

Fig. 10. The average best-so-far cost values of GA, PSO, PSO-TVAC, SSPSO, and EGPSO at each evaluation.

is small and the switching between the stance and swing phases is fast. The left legs generate a stronger net, forward force than the right legs, so the robot rotates clockwise instead of walking forward. In Fig. 12, the generated gait is irregular and so that robot walks forward and backward in different states. To see the finally evolved gait, Fig. 13 shows the control signal of each leg using a successfully designed MFCRNN after the learning process in a run. The solid and dashed lines represent the outputs of a foot node and the difference between the forward and backward swing nodes, respectively. Control signals to legs L1, R2, and L3 are almost identical. Likewise, control signals to leg R1, L2, and R3 are almost identical. Figure 14 shows the successful simulated leg control results. The result shows the periodic walking states of the legs. The gait consists of four states and the control actions in the periodic four states are explained as follows.

Table 1. Performances of EGPSO, SSPSO, PSO-TVAC, PSO and GA.

Methods		GA	PSO	PSO-TVAC	SSPSO	EGPSO
Iteration number		1000	1000	1000	200	1000
Evaluation number		50000	50000	50000	50000	50000
1/distance (m^{-1})	Average	0.5891	0.5704	0.4831	0.4341	0.2659
	STD	0.14	0.0882	0.0865	0.0814	0.0316
distance (m)	Average	1.7655	1.795	2.1317	2.3717	3.8142

State one. L1, R2, and L3: swing forward and move up. R1, L2, and R3: swing backward and move down. The robot moves forward in this state.

State two. L1, R2, and L3: swing forward and move down. R1, L2, and R3: swing backward and move up. As shown in Fig. 13, the time period of this transition state is short.

State three. L1, R2, and L3: swing backward and move down. R1, L2, and R3: swing forward and move up. The robot moves forward in this state as well.

State four. L1, R2, and L3: swing backward and move up. R1, L2, and R3: swing forward and move down. Like state two, the time period of this transition state is short, as shown in Fig. 13.

With the assumption of front-back symmetry in the MFCRNN output signals, it is observed that the obtained gait imitates the real hexagonal insect walking, with three legs on the ground at each state, followed by the other three legs on the ground at the next state. The switching of the legs forms tripod stability when the robot walks forward.

For comparison, optimization of the same MFCRNN using the elite GA [33], constriction PSO [34], PSO with time-varying acceleration coefficient (PSO-TVAC) [3], and SSPSO [29] was performed. The algorithms used for comparison are briefly described as follows.

In the elite GA, the top-half ranked individuals (called elites) in the old population are directly reproduced to the new population. The others in the new population are generated via applying the crossover operations to the elites. The tournament selection is employed to selected two elites at a time. Of the two selected elites, the better one is selected as a parent. The two-point crossover followed by the uniform mutation operations are applied to the selected parents. The newly produced offspring constitute the other half of the new population.

In the constriction PSO, a constriction factor χ is used for velocity update. The velocity update equation is similar to (3) except that the global

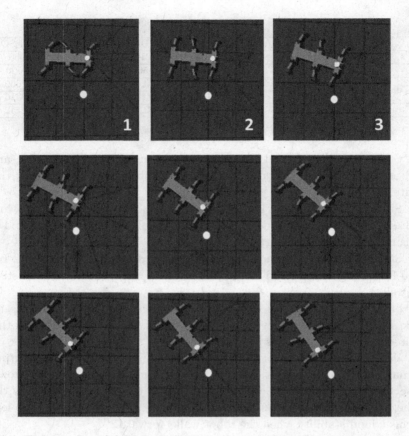

Fig. 11.   One of the generated gaits in the evolutionary learning process.

version is used in defining the neighborhood of a particle. The coefficients $c_1 = 1$, $c_2 = 1$, and $\chi = 0.8$ were selected as in [9].

In the PSO-TVAC, the constriction factor is not used. Instead, a linearly time varying inertia weight that decreases with the iteration number is used to control the weight of current velocity. That is, $v_i^j(I)$ in (3) is changed to $w(I) \cdot v_i^j(I)$. The two coefficients c_1 and c_2 are not fixed at constant values. The coefficients c_1 and c_2 decrease and increase with the iteration number, respectively. The global version of neighborhood is used in velocity update.

In the SSPSO, multiple swarms are created, with the number of swarms set to be the number of nodes in an FCRNN. Five swarms are created, where a swarm only optimizes the weights connected to a single node. The particles from the five swarms cooperatively form a full solution vector.

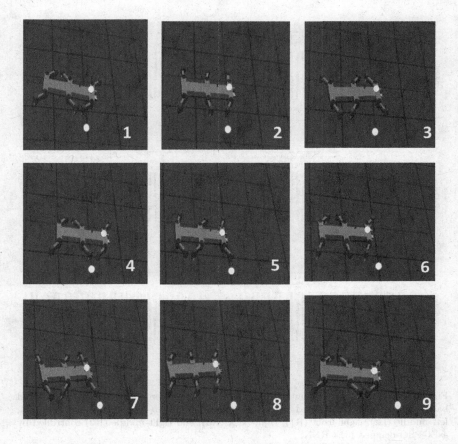

Fig. 12.   Another example of the generated gait in the evolutionary learning process.

In each swarm, specialization is formed and is used to define the neighborhood of a particle. That is, the local version of neighborhood for velocity update is used. The coefficients $c_1 = 1$, $c_2 = 1$, and $\chi = 0.8$ were selected as in [9, 29].

For a fair comparison, the population size and the total evaluation number of all algorithms were set to be identical. The termination iteration number T_{end} in the GA, PSO, and PSO-TVAC was identically set to 1000 so that the total evaluation number was 5×10^4 as well. For the SSPSO, an iteration took 50×5 (swarms) evaluations because of its multiple swam structure. Therefore, T_{end} was set to 200 so that the total evaluation number in a single run was $200 \times 50 \times 5 = 5 \times 10^4$ as well.

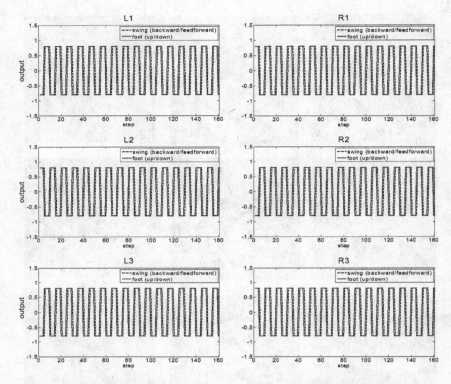

Fig. 13. The foot node outputs (solid lines) and the differences between forward and backward swing nodes (dotted lines) for the six legs of left-front (L1), left-back (L3), left-middle (L2), right-front (R1), right-back (R3), and right-middle (R2) controlled by a EGPSO-deigned MFCRNN.

Fig. 10 shows the optimization curves of the algorithms used for comparison. Table 1 shows the performances of the algorithms used for comparison. Both the average and STD of the EGPSO were smaller than the algorithms used for comparison. That is, the average forward walking distance of the robot controlled by the EGPSO-designed MFCRNN is longer than those of the other algorithms. The result shows the better optimization ability of the EGPSO over the other algorithms in this application.

5.2. *Experiments*

The EGPSO-designed MFCRNN from the simulator was practically applied to generate the gait of a real hexapod robot for forward movement.

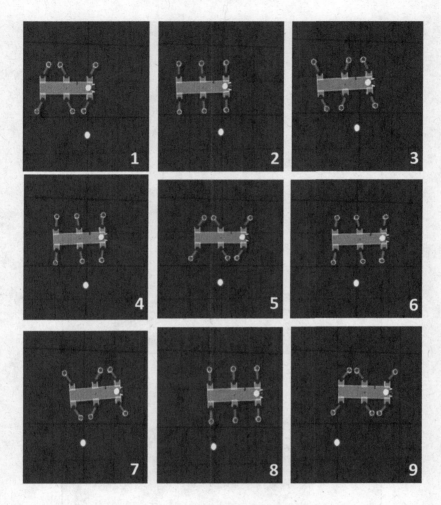

Fig. 14. The gait of the hexapod robot in the simulation environment, where the legs are controlled using the EGPSO-designed MFCRNN and the gait in images 5 and 9 repeat that in image 1.

Figure 15 shows different views of the real robot and its dimension. The robot is controlled by a 32-bit Motorola 68332 chip running at the speed of 25 MHz. The robot is driven by 12 motors, with each leg driven by two. The maximum swing distance and foot-up height of each leg are 9 cm and 3.6 cm, respectively. Figure 16 shows the motors used to control the

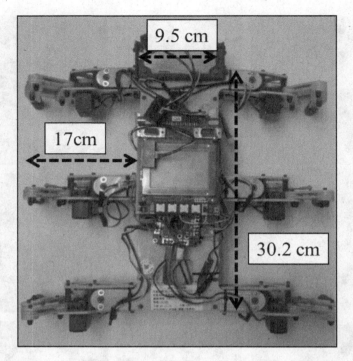

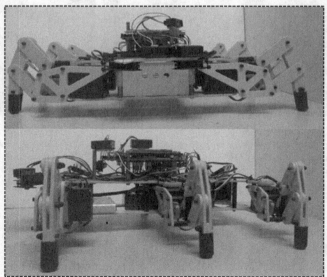

Fig. 15.   Top view and side views of the real hexapod robot.

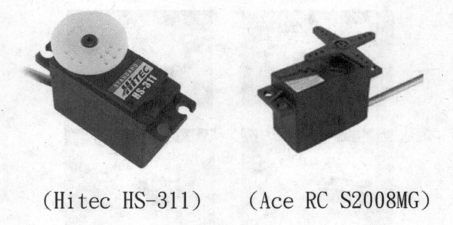

(Hitec HS-311)　　　(Ace RC S2008MG)

Fig. 16.　The two motors used to control a leg.

Fig. 17.　A complete foot set.

knee and the hip. The motor Ace RC S2008MG is selected to control the up/down motion of each leg. The specification of the motor is described as follows. The torque (4.8V) is 7.8 kg-cm. The speed (48 V) is 0.21 sec./60^0. The weight is 48.5 g. The dimension is length×width×height = 40.4 mm×20.1 mm×37.8 mm. This motor is selected because of its metal

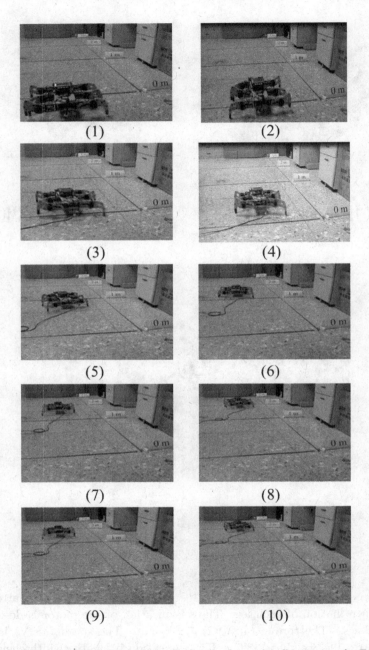

Fig. 18. Screenshots of the real hexapod robot for forward walking using the EGPSO-designed MFCRNN controller.

shaft gear, which sustains a higher force to support the weight of the robot. The motor Hitec HS-311 is selected to control the forward/backward of a leg. The specification of the motor is described as follows. The torque (4.8V) is 3.02 kg-cm. The speed (48 V) is 0.19 sec./60^0. The weight is 43.0 g. The dimension is length$\times$width$\times$height $= 39.9$ mm$\times 19.8$ mm$\times 36.3$ mm. The motor is equipped with a shaft plastic gear. Because this motor does not need to support the robot, this motor is selected for cost reduction. Figure 17 shows a complete set of a leg. Figure 18 shows screenshots the successful gait control result for forward movement using the EGPSO-designed MFCRNN. The MFCRNN drove the robot to walk 2.2 meters in 25 seconds.

6. Conclusion

This chapter introduces the application of a hybrid metaheuristic algorithm, the EGPSO, to evolutionary robot gait optimization for fast forward walking. In this application, an MFCRNN functions as a pattern generator and controls not only the movement of each leg but also the coordination of the six legs in the hexapod robot. Because the desired outputs of the MFCRNN are unknown, the traditional supervised learning configuration based on the gradient descent algorithm cannot be directly applied to optimize the MFCRNN. In the presented evolutionary learning configuration, the EGPSO is employed to optimize the parameters in the MFCRNN using the walking distance as a reinforcement signal for performance evaluation. The simulation result shows the EGPSO-designed MFCRNN successfully evolves the forward gait of the hexapod robot. The optimization ability of the EGPSO is also shown to outperform various advanced GA and PSO algorithms. Furthermore, the experimental result shows that the successful transforming of the optimized MFCRNN in the simulation to the control of a real hexapod robot.

References

[1] Z. Michalewicz, *Genetic algorithms + data structures = evolution programs*, Springer, 1999.
[2] J. Kennedy, R. C. Eberhart, and Y. Shim, *Swarm intelligence*, Morgan Kaufmann, 2001.
[3] A. Ratnaweera, S. K. Halgamuge, and H. C. Watson, Self-organizing hierarchical particle swarm optimizer with time-varying acceleration coefficients,

IEEE Trans. Evolutionary Computation, vol. 8, no. 3, pp. 240-255, June 2004.

[4] C. F. Juang, A hybrid of genetic algorithm and particle swarm optimization for recurrent network design, *IEEE Trans. Syst., Man, and Cyber., Part B: Cybernetics*, vol. 34, no. 2, pp. 997-1006, April 2004.

[5] Y. P. Chen, W. C. Peng, and M. C. Jian, Particle swarm optimization with recombination and dynamic linkage discovery, *IEEE Trans. Syst., Man, and Cyber., Part B- Cyber.*, vol. 37, no. 6, pp. 1460-1470, December 2007.

[6] F. Grimaccia, M. Mussetta, and R. E. Zich, Genetical swarm optimization: self-adaptive hybrid evolutionary algorithm for electromagnetics, *IEEE Trans. Antennas Propag.*, vol. 55, no. 3, pp. 781-785, March 2007.

[7] S. H. Ling, H. H. C. Iu, F. H. F. Leung, and K. Y. Chan, Improved hybrid PSO-based wavelet neural network for modeling the development of fluid dispensing for electronic packaging, *IEEE Trans. Ind. Electron.*, vol. 55, no. 9, pp. 3447-3460, September 2008.

[8] S. Jeong, S. Hasegawa, K. Shimoyama, and S. Obayashi, Development and investigation of efficient GA/PSO-hybrid algorithm applicable to real world design optimization, *IEEE Trans. Comput. Intell. Mag.*, vol. 4, no. 3, pp. 36-44, August 2009.

[9] C. F. Juang and Y. C. Chang, Evolutionary group-based particle swarm optimized fuzzy controller with application to mobile robot navigation in unknown environments, *IEEE Trans. Fuzzy Syst.*, vol. 19, no. 2, pp. 379-392, April 2011.

[10] H. Duan, Q. Luo, Y. Shi, and G. Ma, Hybrid particle swarm optimization and genetic algorithm for multi-UAV formation reconfiguration, *IEEE Computational Intelligence Magazine*, vol. 8, no. 3, pp. 16-27, August 2013.

[11] J. Zhang, H. Wang, L. Chen, C. Tan, and Y. Wang, Multi-objective optimal design of bearingless switched reluctance motor based on multi-objective genetic particle swarm optimizer, *IEEE Trans. Magnetics*, vol. 54, no. 1, sn. 8100113, pp. 1-13, January 2018.

[12] Y. J. Gong, J. J. Li, Y. Zhou, Y. Li, H. S. H. Chung, Y. H. Shi, and J. Zhang, Genetic learning particle swarm optimization, *IEEE Trans. Cybernetics*, vol. 46, no. 10, pp. 2277-2290, 2016.

[13] J. hertz, A. Krogh, and R. G. Palmer, *Introduction to the theory of neural computation*, Addiso-Wesley Publishing Company, USA, 1991.

[14] S. Liu, N. Yang, M. Li, and M. Zhou, A recursive recurrent neural network for statistical machine translation, *Proc. 52nd Annual Meeting of the Association for Computational Linguistics*, pp. 1491-1500, Maryland, USA, 2014.

[15] C. F. Juang, C. T. Chiou, and C. L. Lai, Hierarchical singleton-type recurrent neural fuzzy networks for noisy speech recognition, *IEEE Trans. Neural Networks*, vol. 18, no. 3, pp. 833-843, May 2007.

[16] A. Karpathy and F. F. Li, Deep visual-semantic alignments for generating image descriptions, *IEEE Trans. Pattern Analysis and Machine Intelligence*, vol. 39, no. 4, pp. 664-676, April 2017.

[17] C. F. Juang and J. S. Chen, Water bath temperature control by a recurrent fuzzy controller and its FPGA implementation, *IEEE Trans. Industrial Electronics*, vol. 53, no. 3, pp. 941-949, June 2006.

[18] D. E. Rumelhart, G. E. Hinton, and R. J. Williams, Learning internal representations by error propagation, *Parallel Distributed Processing*, Cambridge, MA: MIT Press, vol. 1, pp. 318-362, 1986.

[19] R. Chandra, Competition and collaboration in cooperative coevolution of Elman recurrent neural networks for time-series prediction, *IEEE Trans. Neural Networks and Learning Systems*, vol. 26, no. 12, pp. 3123-3136, 2015.

[20] R. Xu, D. C. Wunsch, and R. L. Frank, Inference of genetic regulatory networks with recurrent neural network models using particle swarm optimization, *IEEE Trans. Computational Biology and Bioinformatics*, vol. 4, no. 4, pp. 681-692, October-December 2007.

[21] A. J. Ijspeert, Central pattern generators for locomotion control in animals and robots: A review, *Neural Netw.*, vol. 21, no. 4, pp. 642-653, 2008.

[22] J. Yu, M. Tan, J. Chen, and J. Zhang, A survey on CPG-inspired control models and system implementation, *IEEE Trans. Neural Networks and Learning Systems*, vol. 25, no. 3, pp. 441-456, March 2014.

[23] G. Taga, Y. Yamaguchi, and H. Shimizu, Self-organized control of bipedal locomotion by neural oscillators in unpredictable environment, *Biol. Cybern.*, vol. 65, no. 3, pp. 147-159, 1991.

[24] Y. Nakamuraa, T. Moria, M. Sato, and S. Ishii, Reinforcement learning for a biped robot based on a CPG-actor-critic method, *Neural Networks*, vol. 20, no. 6. pp. 723-735, August. 2007.

[25] J. Santos and A. Campo, Biped locomotion control with evolved adaptive center-crossing continuous time recurrent neural networks, *Neurocomputing*, vol. 86, no. 1, pp. 86-96, June 2012.

[26] C. F. Juang and Y. T. Yeh, Multi-objective evolution of biped robot gaits using advanced continuous ant-colony optimized recurrent neural networks, *IEEE Trans. Cybernetics*, vol. 48, no. 7, pp. 1910-1922, June 2018.

[27] R. D. Beer and J. C. Gallagher, Evolving dynamical neural networks for adaptive behavior, *Adapt. Behavior*, vol. 1, no. 1, pp. 92-122, 1992.

[28] R. Reeve and J. Hallam, An analysis of neural models for walking control, *IEEE Trans. Neural Netw.*, vol. 16, no. 3, pp. 733-742, May 2006.

[29] C. F. Juang, Y. C. Chang, and C. M. Hsiao, Evolving gaits of a hexapod robot by recurrent neural networks with symbiotic species-based particle swarm optimization, *IEEE Trans. Industrial Electronics*, vol. 58, no. 7, pp. 3110-3119, July 2011.

[30] X. Xiong, F. Wrgtter, and P. Manoonpong, Adaptive and energy efficient walking in a hexapod robot under neuromechanical control and sensorimotor learning, *IEEE Trans. Cybernetics*, vol. 46, no. 11, pp. 2521-2534, 2016.

[31] P. Cizek, P. Milicka, and J. Faigl, Neural based obstacle avoidance with CPG controlled hexapod walking robot, *Proc. 2017 Int. Joint Conf. Neural Networks (IJCNN)*, pp. 650-656, 2017.

[32] O. Michel, Webots: Professional mobile robot simulation, *Int. J. Adv. Robot. Syst.*, vol. 1, no. 1, pp. 39-42, 2004.

[33] C. F. Juang, A TSK-Type recurrent fuzzy network for dynamic system processing by neural network and genetic algorithms, *IEEE Trans. Fuzzy Systems*, vol. 10, no. 2, pp. 55-170, 2002.

[34] M. Clerc and J. Kennedy, The particle swarm-Explosion, stability, and convergence in a multidimentional complex space, *IEEE Trans. Evol.Comput.*, vol. 6, pp. 58-73, 2002.

Chapter 10

Load Optimization using Hybrid Metaheuristics in Power Generation with Transmission Loss

Dipankar Santra

RCC Institute of Information Technology, Kolkata, India
santra.dipankar@gmail.com

Krishna Sarker

Saroj Mohan Institute of Technology, Guptipara,
West Bengal, India
krishna80sarker@gmail.com

Anirban Mukherjee

RCC Institute of Information Technology, Kolkata, India
anirbanm.rcciit@gmail.com

Subrata Mondal

Jadavpur University, Kolkata, India
sub.mondal@gmail.com

This paper presents an application of a hybrid optimization technique combining particle swarm optimization (PSO) with ant colony optimization (ACO) in finding economic load dispatch (ELD) of large scale thermal power system. The proposed PSO-ACO algorithm is tested on standard 40- generator system simulated in MATLAB. The test results in terms of total cost of power generation, transmission loss and convergence characteristics strongly attests the viability of the algorithm for addressing large scale economic dispatch in actual power generation scenario. One significant contribution of this study is that the hybrid approach has been tested with 40-generator ELD problem considering transmission loss in combination with other non-linear constraints namely, valve point loading, ramp rate limits and prohibited operating zones. Though PSO has been extensively used in ELD problems for its flexibility, robustness and fast convergence, it often produces not so good solution due to its premature convergence to local optima. ACO, on the contrary, known for its good global exploration feature, strikes good balance between local and global search for optimum solution when combined with PSO. This aspect has been exploited for the first time in large scale ELD problems in this study to mark its another significant contribution.

Keywords: Ant colony optimization, Economic load dispatch, Particle swarm optimization, Prohibited operating zone, Ramp rate limits, Transmission loss, Valve point loading.

1. Introduction

Economic load dispatch (ELD) is one of the most important challenges for power generation industry. It directly affects the suppliers and the consumers of electricity as ELD impacts the cost of generation and transmission of electricity. Basically, ELD is the optimum distribution of load or power generation schedule among the various committed generating units in a way that minimizes the overall power generation cost and transmission loss while satisfying various operational constraints. The fuel cost is the prime component of the total cost of power generation, hence the fuel cost function is considered as the objective function of the ELD optimization problem. This chapter presents an approach to solve complex ELD problem of 40-generator system with transmission loss and smooth and non-smooth fuel cost function (i.e. without or with valve point loading (VPL) effect) combined with some or all of generator constraint, ramp rate limit (RRL) and prohibited operating zone (POZ).

Over last few decades researchers have been investigating optimal or near optimal solutions of small to large scale ELD problems with non-smooth and non-linear characteristics. The classical methods [1] are not quite useful in dealing with such type of ELD problems. The solutions given by them are mostly sub-optimal. Wood and Wollenberg [2] proposed dynamic programming approach without restraining the cost curves, but it bears the problems of dimensionality and lengthy simulation. Since late 20th century different meta-heuristic algorithms are being increasingly used to solve complex ELD problems. Such algorithms include Neural Network (NN) [3], Firefly Algorithm (FA) [4], Bacterial Foraging Optimization (BFO)[5], Particle Swarm Optimization (PSO)[6][7], Ant Colony Optimization (ACO) [8], Differential Evolution (DE) [9], Evolutionary Programming (EP)[10]. But each meta-heuristic method suffers from weakness in some form or other that prevents them from finding the best possible solutions.

Predominantly in the 21st century, a new trend has been the development and application of different hybrid or modified heuristic or meta-heuristic methods to overcome the weaknesses of the original methods thereby yielding better or high quality ELD solutions. A detailed account of research on various original and hybrid optimization techniques to solve ELD problems of different complexity and for small to large power generation systems has been provided in [11] by the present authors. As the focus of the present study is hybrid methods applied in 40-generator ELD problems, it appears from literature review that most researchers have considered 40-generator ELD problems without transmission loss. Some of the hybrid methods developed to this end are: Chaotic DE and Sequential Quadratic Programming (DEC-SQP) [12], GA tuned DE [13], Fuzzy Controlled Parallel PSO (FCP-PSO) [14], DE-BBO [15], Interior Point Assisted DE (IPM-DE) [16], GA-Pattern Search-SQP (GA-PS-SQP) [17], DE-Harmony Search (DE-HS) [18], Hybrid Chemical Reaction Optimization-DE (HCRO-DE) [19], Chaotic Teaching Learning Based Optimization with Lvy Flight (CTLBO) [20]. In contrary to this very few studies and methods are found that deals with 40-generator system with transmission loss; a brief overview of such hybrid methods reported in the recent literature is given below.

Ciornei *et al.* [21], in 2012, proposed GA-API, a new hybrid of Real Coded GA (RCGA) by combining it with a special class of Ant Colony Optimization called API to successfully test with convex and non-convex ELD where RRL, POZ and Spinning Reserve constraints were considered along with transmission loss. In this method, the good spreading of GA in the solution space is complemented with good search capability of API around the global solution.

In 2013, Reddy *et al.* presented a hybrid Shuffled Differential Evolution (SDE) [22] algorithm which blended the strong features of Shuffled Frog Leaping Algorithm (SFLA) and DE to find ELD considering VPL effect and transmission loss. SDE, characterized by a novel mutation operator, combines the exploration and exploitation capabilities of DE and thus helps overcome the intrinsic limitation of DE and SFLA in solving large scale non-convex ELD.

Roy P K and Bhui S [23] introduced in 2013 Quasi-Oppositional Teaching Learning based Optimization (QOTLBO) technique that successfully optimized load dispatch problem with VPL and transmission loss. The authors employed Opposition Based Learning (OBL) concept (proposed by Tizhoosh [24]) in original Teaching Learning Based Optimization (TLBO) algorithm [25] to step up the convergence rate achieved by original TLBO algorithm.

Quasi-Oppositional Gravitational Search Algorithm (QOGSA) reported in 2014 by Bulbul A and Roy P K [26] combined OBL with GSA to effectively achieve higher convergence speed of GSA. Opposition-based population initialization and generation jumping is exploited in QOGSA to yield reasonably good solution of ELD problem considering VPL effect and transmission loss.

In 2014 Bhattacharjee *et al.* [27] proposed the Oppositional Real Coded Chemical Reaction Optimization (ORCCRO) by incorporating the concept of Quasi-Opposition Based Learning (QOBL) in RCCRO motivated by the computational efficiency of QOBL. The fitness of a candidate solution and its opposite are measured and the fitter solution is retained in the population set. ORCCRO has been successfully tested on large scale ELD problems considering RRL and POZ along with VPL and transmission loss.

In 2015, Hazra *et al.* [28] have presented Oppositional Chemical Reaction Optimization (OCRO) algorithm where OBL is integrated with the Chemical Reaction Optimization (CRO) algorithm (developed by Lam *et al.* in 2010 [29]) based on dynamics of chemical reaction. OCRO is characterized by the fitness (or closeness to the global optima) of an opposite candidate solution and also an improved diversity among the population. In effect better convergence is achieved as OCRO is applied to ELD problem involving VPL and transmission loss.

In 2015, Barisal *et al.* [30] introduced Oppositional Invasive Weed Optimization (OIWO) by hybridizing IWO, characterized by the encompassing nature of weeds, and OBL that features quasi-opposite numbers. IWO is a novel, population based stochastic, derivative-free optimization algorithm developed by Mehrabian and Lucas [31]. The algorithm exploits some characteristic features of weeds namely, fast replication and spreading, distribution and self adjustment to the climatic changes. OBL helps improve the convergence rate of IWO thereby producing satisfying results of large scale ELD problem that takes into account VPL effect and transmission loss.

With the background of limited hybrid optimization methods applied in large scale ELD with transmission loss and motivated by the success of PSO-ACO hybrid applied earlier in small scale ELD [32], the PSO-ACO hybrid approach has been taken up in the present study with 40-generator system.Invented by Kennedy and Eberhartin in 1995, PSO produces good quality solution in reasonably short time satisfying all the constraints for both convex and non-convex ELD. It is found that execution of PSO is very fast towards the convergence point (local optima), so number of iterations is less compared to other meta-heuristic techniques. But due to large accumulation of particles at gbest position, PSO [6][7] gives unsatisfactory result in terms of achieving global optimal solution.

ACO [8] is another probabilistic optimization technique that was introduced by Marco Dorigo in 1992. It is observed that ACO is a powerful yet flexible heuristic algorithm with a good downhill behaviour to better explore around the global solution region than PSO. Again for complex problems, ACO suffers from stagnation and slow convergence. In the hybrid PSO-ACO approach proposed by the authors [11] for solving ELD problems, the global exploration feature of ACO has been exploited along with local search capability of PSO. This has, in effect, mitigated the weaknesses of both the algorithms.

The superiority of PSO-ACO over PSO and ACO and few other hybrid methods in solving non-convex ELD problem for 6-generator system has been experimentally established in [32]. The present study considers following six different cases of non-convex smooth and non-smooth ELD problem for large scale power system involving 40 generating units:

(i) With transmission loss only
(ii) With transmission loss and RRL only
(iii) With transmission loss, RRL and POZ only
(iv) With transmission loss, VPL effect only
(v) With transmission loss, VPL effect and RRL only
(vi) With transmission loss, VPL effect, RRL and POZ

This study has two significant contributions. One is that the PSO-ACO hybrid optimization method applied by the present authors for solving 40-generator ELD problem has not been experimented before. The other contribution is that all the six cases of ELD problem studied here includes transmission loss and the cases cover all possible combinations of non-linear constraints and non-smooth characteristics that models the actual power generation scenario. Similar study and that too considering transmission loss is quite limited as evident from the literature. Interestingly, the results of the present study are found to be even better than that of the existing methods.

The paper is organized as follows. Section 2 of the paper provides mathematical formulation of standard ELD problem along with its different associated constraints and their brief description. The standard PSO and ACO algorithms followed by the PSO-ACO hybrid approach are described in Sections 3, 4 and 5 respectively. Experiment, Result & Analysis of simulation are presented and discussed in Section 6 & 7 respectively. Finally the conclusion in Section 8 highlights the salient points of this study and indicates future scope of research.

2. ELD Formulation

The ELD problem is generally formulated as a nonlinear optimization problem as shown in Eq. (1) where $C_i(P_i)$ is the ith generators cost function expressed as a quadratic polynomial in P_i. The total generation cost F is the arithmetic sum of the individual generators cost function. The objective (function) of ELD is to minimize the total cost F.

$$F = C_i(P_i) = \sum_{i=1}^{n}(a_i + b_iP_i + c_iP_i^2) \tag{1}$$

In Eq. (1) a_i, b_i and c_i are the cost coefficients of the ith generator; n is the number of committed generators, in our study $n = 40$; P_i is the power output of the ith generator.

ELD problem comes with following constraints out of which power balance with transmission loss and generator capacity constraints are linear in nature while the rest are non-linear.

2.1. *Power Balance Constraint*

$$\sum_{i=1}^{n}P_i = P_D + P_L \tag{2}$$

For a given i^{th} unit, the power output (P_i) must equal the total load demand (P_D) and the transmission loss (P_L).

2.2. *Transmission Loss*

The loss P_L is expressed in terms of the B-coefficients as:

$$P_L = \sum_{i=1}^{n}\sum_{j=1}^{n}P_iB_{ij}P_j + \sum_{i=1}^{n}P_iB_{0i} + B_{00} \tag{3}$$

Here B_{ij}, B_{0i} and B_{00} are the B-coefficients of power loss in transmission network; B_{ij} is the ij^{th} element of the loss coefficient matrix, B_{0i} is the ith element of the loss coefficient vector and B_{00} is the loss coefficient constant.

2.3. Generator Capacity Constraint

The power generated by each generator should be within their respective lower P_i^{min} and upper limits P_i^{max} of active power generation as expressed in Eq. (4).

$$P_i^{min} \leq P_i \leq P_i^{max} \tag{4}$$

2.4. Ramp Rate Limit (RRL)

The power output P_i of the ith generator should not exceed any previous power output P_{i0} by more than UR_i, (the up-ramp limit) for increase in generation and should not be less than P_{i0} by more than DR_i (the down-ramp limit) for decrease in generation. Mathematically expressing,

For increase in generation:

$$P_i - P_{i0} \leq UR_i \tag{5}$$

For decrease in generation:

$$P_{i0} - P_i \leq DR_i \tag{6}$$

Combining Eqs. (5) and (6) in Eq. (4) we get,

$$max(P_i^{min}, P_{i0} - DR_i \leq P_i \leq min(P_i^{max}, P_{i0} + UR_i) \tag{7}$$

2.5. Prohibited Operating Zone (POZ)

A prohibited operating zone of a generator is the span of output power where the procedural operation causes undue disturbance. Normally power adjustment is not allowed in such spans. The allowable operating zones of a generator can be described as follows:

$$P_i^{min} \leq P_i \leq P_{i,1}^{lower}$$
$$P_{i,j}^{upper} \leq P_i \leq P_{i,j}^{lower}$$

$$P_i, {n_i}^{upper} \leq P_i \leq P_i^{max} \tag{8}$$

Where, $i \in \phi$ and $j = 2, 3, \ldots\ldots n_i$

2.6. Valve Point Loading (VPL)

The VPL effect is the ripples added to the characteristic curve of the generating units when steam admission valves in steam turbines are released. To account this realistic effect, the objective function F is formulated as

the superposition of sinusoidal functions and quadratic functions as shown
in Eq. (9). In ELD with VPL, the objective function F is represented by a
more complex formula, as in Eq. (9), in contrast to F for ELD without valve
point loading as expressed by Eq. (1). A non-smooth curve corresponds to
Eq. (9), unlike a smooth quadratic polynomial curve representing Eq. (1).

$$Minimize F = C_i(P_i) = \sum_{i=1}^{n}(a_i + b_i P_i + c_i P_i^2) + \mid e_i \sin(f(P_i^{min} - P_i)) \mid \quad (9)$$

e_i and f_i are the valve point coefficient of ith generating unit reflecting
valve point effects and P_i^{min} is the minimum power output of unit i.

3. Particle Swarm Optimization (PSO)

PSO is a swarm intelligence based heuristic search algorithm that emulates
the collective behaviour of a colony of insects; a flock of birds; or a school
of fish. The particle represents, for example, a bird in a flock. If a flock of
birds randomly search for a food item in a particular area then it is least
likely that all the birds at a time locate the food. If one bird discovers a
good path and comes closer to the food, the best strategy of the other birds
is simply following the same path even if their position is far from the food.
PSO follows this natural phenomenon of swarm movement and uses it to
optimize non-linear discontinuous problems.

In PSO, each "particle" represents a potential solution in the search
space. Each particle has fitness, position and velocity. The fitness of each
particle is assessed by the fitness function (i.e. the fuel cost function in case
of ELD problem). Initially a random velocity is assigned to the particles
which then makes parallel searches for optima while dynamically updating
their velocity and position vide expressions Eqs. (10) and (11) respectively.
At any iteration, the updating is done through particles own experience of
best found solution i.e. pbest or personal best and neighbors experience of
best found solution so far i.e. gbest or global best. Each particle progresses
in the search space by judging its next position using the current velocity
and distance with respect to pbest and gbest position. This process is
continued till the maximum iteration or the minimum fitness is reached.

$$V_i^{t+1} = wV_i^t + c_1 rand_1()(pbest_i - X_i^t) + c_2 rand_2()(gbest_i - X_i^t) \quad (10)$$

$$X_i^{t+1} = X_i^t + V_i^{t+1} \quad (11)$$

Here, X_i^t and V_i^t are respectively the position and velocity of ith particle
at i^{th} iteration, where $V_{min} \leq V_i \leq V_{max}$; w is the inertia weight factor,

where $w_{max} \leq w \leq w_{min}$; c_1, c_2 are the acceleration coefficients; $rand_1$, $rand_2$ are random numbers between 0 and 1; the term $rand_1(\ )(pbest_i-X_i^t)$ concerns individual particles experience while $rand_2(\ )(gbest_i - X_i^t))$ represents swarm or group influence.

Generally, the inertia weight w that carries the exploration property of PSO is given by Eq. (12):

$$w = w_{max} - \frac{w_{max} - w_{min}}{t_{max}} \times t \qquad (12)$$

Here t_{max} is the maximum number of iterations.

Again the acceleration coefficients c_1 and c_2 are set by following two expressions:

$$c_1 = c_{1max} - \frac{c_{1max} - c_{1min}}{t_{max}} \times t \qquad (13)$$

$$c_2 = c_{2max} - \frac{c_{2max} - c_{2min}}{t_{max}} \times t \qquad (14)$$

If $c_1 > c_2$, the particle approaches pbest or the local optima, else it converges to gbest or the global optima.

4. Ant Colony Optimization (ACO)

ACO is another swarm intelligence based search technique which, in search of best solution, follows the strategy of movement of an ant colony towards the source of food through the shortest path. It is found that during movement, each ant leaves behind a trail of chemical substance, called pheromone. The other ants are attracted by this chemical essence and breaking their random motion they trace the pheromone trail along the path used by the predecessor ants. Now in search of food, the ant which finds food earlier following the shorter path causes more pheromone deposit on this path compared to the longer path. This is because, the longer the path the more the pheromone trail gets evaporated, thus reducing its strength. Once a shorter route is found by an ant, the other ants are likely to follow that route as the chemical essence is more in this route. In doing so, they will reconstruct the existing pheromone trail by spreading additional amount of pheromone on the way. Conversely, less traveled path will have its pheromone layer evaporated, thus reducing its attraction.

During search the ants use two types of information. The private or local information concerns the ants own experience of visited nodes and the public or global information concerns other ants experience accessed through pheromone trail. Based on solution found by individual ant, better solutions are yielded by exchanging experience with other ants through the public source (pheromone). Thus, analogous to an ant, the ACO algorithm constructively builds or improves a solution by progressing through nodes (or states) of a neighborhood graph. The ACO process comprises initialization, transition rule, and pheromone trail update rule.

4.1. *Initialization*

In this phase the parameters like number of ants, relative importance of the pheromone trail, visibility, quantity of pheromone deposited on a path, evaporation factor, tuning factor etc. are initialized with suitable values.

4.2. *Transition Rule*

The probability of transition of an ant k from state i to j is given by:

$$P_{ij}^k(t) = \frac{[\tau_{ij}]^\alpha [\eta_{ij}]^\beta}{\sum\limits_{l \in N_i^k} [\tau_{il}(t)]^\alpha [[\eta_{il}]^\beta]} \tag{15}$$

if $l \in N_i^k$

Here, N_i^k is the feasible neighborhood of ant k at position i, l is the unvisited state or node, η_{ij} is a heuristic function given by the inverse of distance traveled, τ_{ij} is the pheromone trail intensity on edge (i,j), α is the relative importance of the trail, β is the relative importance of the visibility; $\alpha \geq 0, \beta \geq 0$.

4.3. *Pheromone Trail Update Rule*

4.3.1. *Local update rule*

An ant changes the pheromone level τ_{ij} of a visited edge (i,j) according to Eq. (16).

$$\tau_{ij} = (1 - \zeta)\tau_{ij} + \tau_0 \tag{16}$$

Here ζ is a heuristically defined parameter for initial pheromone level.

4.3.2. *Global update rule*

After all the ants build their individual solutions, global pheromone-update rule Eq. (17) is applied only to those paths that are visited by more ants and each ant tends to deposit more pheromone.

$$\tau_{ij} = (1 - \rho)\tau_{ij} + \Delta\tau_{ijk} \tag{17}$$

Here, ρ is the pheromone decay factor or evaporation rate ($0 < \rho < 1$). Δ τ_{ijk} is the amount of pheromone deposited on edge (i,j) by best ant k and is given by $\Delta \tau_{ijk} = Q/L_k$, where Q is a constant and L_k is the length of path traversed by k^{th} ant.

5. PSO-ACO Hybrid

Considering the flexibility of both PSO and ACO in combining with other methods and also their mutually complementary strength and weakness, the PSO-ACO hybrid algorithm [11] has been taken up in this study to experiment with multi-constraint ELD problem of 40-generator system.

PSO is good in processing ELD problems with multiple non-linear constraints but it has its limitations as well. It has a tendency to get confined to local optima if, for a number of iterations, the global and local best positions remain equal to the particles position. If the global best position does not change with iteration, other particles are driven towards that position. Again, if velocity is very high, particles might fly past good solutions in search of global optima. On the contrary, if velocity is very less, the search is confined locally and particles may not explore globally beyond local good regions.

ACO when applied in ELD suffers from the disadvantage of slow convergence. The pheromone trail of ACO can potentially help diversification and avoid stagnation if ACO can be fed with the global best solution found by PSO after a good number of iterations. Taking as input the gbest particles, the ants response functions are evaluated, compared and information is exchanged with the best ant to finally arrive at the optimal solution. Again the pheromone trail intensity in ACO decreases (evaporates) over time which helps avoid faster convergence of the hybrid to a sub-optimal region.

The general algorithm of the PSO-ACO method is given below and flowchart is shown in Fig. 1.

Input data for PSO
Initialize particles position and velocity with random values
  While (terminal condition not satisfied)
  Find local and global fitness values,pbestandgbest

          Update inertia weight
          Update positions and velocities
     If gbest solution improves Then
          Save the solution for ACO
     End if
     End while
     Initialize ACO with the gbest found by PSO
     While (terminal condition not satisfied)
          Generate ants and make path for each ant
          Evaluate and Compare response function
     If response function does not improve Then
          Exchange information with best ant
          Generate path from local position to best ant
     Else
     If response function improves Then
          Repeat While Else
          Wait for Exchange with best ant
     End if
     End if
     End while

The values of different parameters of PSO-ACO algorithm as used in the MATLAB simulation programs are given below. Through trial and error method some of the parameters to which PSO, in particular, is sensitive are fine tuned to obtain better results.

For PSO: Population Size=100, Generations=500, Inertial constant(w)=0.3 ,t_{max}=1000, c_1=2, c_2=2, w_{max}=0.9, w_{min}=0.4

For ACO: No. of iterations=500, No. of ants=50, Initial pheromone value (τ_0)=0.0088, Pheromone update constant(Q)=20, Exploration constant(q_0)=1,ρ= 0.05, α=1, β=5.

6. Experiment

Proposed PSO-ACO algorithm has been applied to solve simulated 40-generator ELD problems for six different test cases by varying the constraints and fuel cost function. The program has been written in MATLAB-7.8 and executed on a 64-bit PC with Intel Core i3 2.7 GHz processor, 1 TB HDD, 8 GB RAM and Windows 7 operating system.

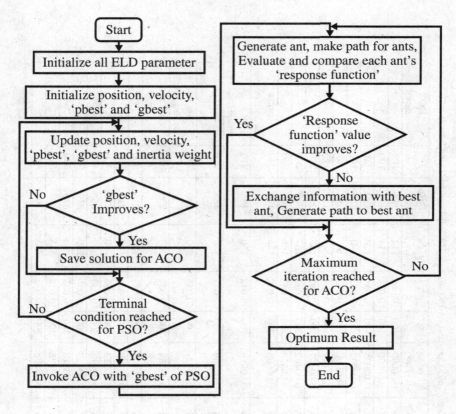

Fig. 1.   Flowchart of hybrid PSO-ACO

6.1. *Test Case 1: Smooth Cost Curve with Transmission Loss and Linear Constraints*

The values of basic ELD modeling parameters like cost coefficients a_i, b_i, c_i, and generator capacity constraints (P_{min}, P_{max}) for each generator are given in Table 1 in the Appendix. The objective function to be optimized in this case is Eq. (1) and the linear constraints considered are given by Eqs. (2) and (4).

The values of the transmission loss B coefficients according to Eq. (3) are given in the Appendix. The B-loss coefficients are obtained by replicating row and column wise loss coefficient data of 6 unit system [30] as given below.

Table 1. Values of Cost Coefficients and Constraints Parameters [33][34] Used in Test Cases 1-6

Unit	P_i^{min} (MW)	P_i^{max} (MW)	a_i	b_i ($/MW)	c_i ($/MW^2)	e_i	f_i	UR_i (MW/h)	DR_i (MW/h)	P_i^0	POZ (MW)
1	36	114	94.705	6.73	0.00690	100	0.084	114	114	100	-
2	36	114	94.705	6.73	0.00690	100	0.084	114	114	100	-
3	60	120	309.54	7.07	0.02028	100	0.084	120	120	90	-
4	80	190	369.03	8.18	0.00942	150	0.063	100	150	150	-
5	47	97	148.89	5.35	0.0114	120	0.077	97	97	80	-
6	68	140	222.33	8.05	0.01142	100	0.084	80	125	120	-
7	110	300	287.71	8.03	0.00357	200	0.042	165	200	280	-
8	135	300	391.98	6.99	0.00492	200	0.042	165	200	200	-
9	135	300	455.76	6.60	0.00573	200	0.042	165	200	230	-
10	130	300	722.82	12.9	0.00605	200	0.042	155	190	240	[130,150] [200,230][270,299]
11	94	375	635.20	12.9	0.00515	200	0.042	150	185	210	[100,140] [230,280][300,350]
12	94	375	654.69	12.8	0.00569	200	0.042	150	185	210	[100,140] [230,280][300,350]
13	125	500	913.40	12.5	0.00421	300	0.035	206	235	230	[150,200] [250,300][400,450]
14	125	500	1760.4	8.84	0.00752	300	0.035	260	290	355	[200,250] [300,350][450,490]
15	125	500	1728.3	9.15	0.00708	300	0.035	186	215	350	-
16	125	500	1728.3	9.15	0.00708	300	0.035	186	215	350	-
17	220	500	647.85	7.97	0.00313	300	0.035	240	270	460	-
18	220	500	649.69	7.95	0.00313	300	0.035	240	268	470	-
19	242	550	647.83	7.97	0.00313	300	0.035	290	315	500	-
20	242	550	647.81	7.97	0.00313	300	0.035	290	315	500	-
21	254	550	785.96	6.63	0.00298	300	0.035	335	360	510	-
22	254	550	785.96	6.63	0.00298	300	0.035	335	360	520	-

(Continued)

Table 1. (Continued)

Unit	P_i^{min} (MW)	P_i^{max} (MW)	a_i	b_i ($/MW)	c_i ($/MW^2)	e_i	f_i	UR_i (MW/h)	DR_i (MW/h)	P_i^0	POZ (MW)
23	254	550	794.53	6.66	0.00284	300	0.035	335	362	520	-
24	254	550	794.53	6.66	0.00284	300	0.035	350	378	450	-
25	254	550	801.32	7.10	0.00277	300	0.035	350	380	400	-
26	254	550	801.32	7.10	0.00277	300	0.035	350	380	520	-
27	10	150	1055.1	3.33	0.52124	120	0.077	95	145	20	-
28	10	150	1055.1	3.33	0.52124	120	0.077	95	145	20	-
29	10	150	1055.1	3.33	0.52124	120	0.077	98	145	25	-
30	47	97	148.89	5.35	0.01140	120	0.077	97	97	90	-
31	60	190	222.92	6.43	0.00160	150	0.063	90	145	170	-
32	60	190	222.92	6.43	0.00160	150	0.063	90	145	150	-
33	60	190	222.92	6.43	0.00160	150	0.063	90	145	190	-
34	90	200	107.87	8.95	0.0001	200	0.042	105	150	190	-
35	90	200	116.58	8.62	0.0001	200	0.042	105	150	150	-
36	90	200	116.58	8.62	0.0001	200	0.042	105	150	180	-
37	25	110	307.45	5.88	0.0161	80	0.098	110	110	60	-
38	25	110	307.45	5.88	0.0161	80	0.098	110	110	40	-
39	25	110	307.45	5.88	0.0161	80	0.098	110	110	50	-
40	242	550	647.83	7.97	0.00313	300	0.035	290	315	512	-

$$
B_{6X6}=
\begin{bmatrix}
0.0017 & 0.0012 & 0.0007 & -0.0001 & 0.0005 & -0.0002 \\
0.0012 & 0.0014 & 0.0009 & 0.0001 & 0.0006 & -0.0001 \\
0.0007 & 0.0009 & 0.0031 & 0.0000 & -0.0010 & -0.0006 \\
-0.0001 & 0.0001 & 0.0000 & 0.0024 & -0.0008 & -0.0006 \\
-0.0005 & -0.0006 & -0.0010 & -0.0006 & 0.0129 & -0.0002 \\
-0.0002 & -0.0001 & -0.0006 & -0.0008 & -0.0002 & 0.0150
\end{bmatrix}
$$

The simulation result i.e. the optimized output power generation schedule, power loss and generation cost for all the 40 generating units for Test Case 1 is given in Table 2 in the Appendix. The convergence characteristics for Test Case 1 is shown in Fig. 2.

6.2. *Test Case 2: Smooth Cost Curve with Transmission Loss, and RRL*

In this case cost coefficients (a_i, b_i, c_i), and generator capacity constraints (P_{min}, P_{max}) for each generator are same as that used in Test Case 1. This case is tested by considering RRL as a constraint in addition to the linear constraints given by Eq. (2) and Eq. (4). The upper and lower RRLs namely, UR_i and DR_i (refer Eq. (5)-Eq.(7)) are different for each generator and are listed in Table 1. The objective function to be optimized is again Eq. (1) as valve point loading is not considered. The transmission loss B coefficients are same as that in Test Case 1. The simulation result is given in Table 2. The convergence characteristics for Test Case 2 is shown in Fig. 3.

6.3. *Test Case 3: Smooth Cost Curve with Transmission Loss, RRL and POZ*

This test case considers POZ in addition to the other non-linear constraint RRL. The POZ (refer Eq. (8)) falls in the power output zones of 10th to 14th generating units as in Table 1. These prohibited zones produce three or four operating zones for each of these units. Hence, POZ result in a non-convex search space for the cost function curve which is smooth otherwise. The values of other constraints, ELD modeling parameters and loss coefficients are same as that of Test Case 2. The simulation result is shown in Table 2. The convergence characteristics for Test Case 3 is shown in Fig. 4.

Table 2.   Summary of Optimum Power Generation Schedule (MW), Loss (MW) and Total Generated Cost (\$/hr) for 40-generator ELD Test Cases with P_D = 10500 MW using PSO–ACO hybrid method; POZ regions corresponding to output of P_{10} - P_{14} are shaded

Unit (MW)	With Loss, POZ and RRL	With Loss and RRL	With Loss, RRL and POZ	With Loss and VPL	With Loss, VPL and RRL	With Loss, VPL, RRL and POZ
P_1	105.011	112.529	108.349	109.431	111.783	112.155
P_2	114.000	114.000	114.000	114.000	114.000	114.000
P_3	120.000	120.000	107.639	120.000	120.000	111.910
P_4	190.000	186.732	190.000	190.000	190.000	190.000
P_5	97.000	97.000	97.000	97.000	97.000	97.000
P_6	140.000	140.000	140.000	111.235	140.000	140.000
P_7	300.000	300.000	300.000	300.000	300.000	300.000
P_8	300.000	300.000	284.527	300.000	300.000	300.000
P_9	300.000	300.000	300.000	300.000	298.537	300.000
P_{10}	300.000	194.235	300.000	194.404	262.921	300.000
P_{11}	155.637	107.906	95.806	102.669	215.472	96.372
P_{12}	94.591	94.217	97.402	166.888	95.059	166.520
P_{13}	500.000	500.000	393.601	500.000	213.970	218.162
P_{14}	485.376	500.000	492.470	500.000	485.017	500.000
P_{15}	391.329	500.000	500.000	485.512	500.000	500.000
P_{16}	500.000	500.000	500.000	500.000	500.000	500.000
P_{17}	500.000	500.000	500.000	500.000	500.000	500.000
P_{18}	314.130	404.380	402.852	377.208	500.000	500.000
P_{19}	550.000	550.000	550.000	550.000	550.000	550.000
P_{20}	550.000	550.000	519.433	502.321	550.000	550.000
P_{21}	515.452	550.000	550.000	550.000	522.179	550.000
P_{22}	550.000	550.000	550.000	550.000	550.000	550.000
P_{23}	550.000	550.000	550.000	509.187	526.781	550.000
P_{24}	550.000	445.234	533.152	550.000	550.000	550.000
P_{25}	550.000	550.000	550.000	550.000	550.000	550.000
P_{26}	550.000	550.000	550.000	550.000	550.000	537.711
P_{27}	13.453	20.461	12.780	12.157	13.597	12.700
P_{28}	10.880	11.995	19.096	12.876	28.871	17.093
P_{29}	20.190	19.644	28.149	10.965	10.313	11.710
P_{30}	97.000	97.000	97.000	97.000	97.000	97.000
P_{31}	190.000	190.000	190.000	190.000	190.000	190.000
P_{32}	190.000	190.000	190.000	190.000	190.000	190.000
P_{33}	190.000	190.000	190.000	190.000	190.000	190.000
P_{34}	200.000	200.000	200.000	200.000	200.000	200.000
P_{35}	170.563	200.000	200.000	200.000	200.000	200.000
P_{36}	200.000	200.000	147.267	188.227	200.000	165.229
P_{37}	104.018	110.000	110.000	110.000	110.000	110.000
P_{38}	110.000	110.000	110.000	110.000	110.000	110.000
P_{39}	110.000	110.000	110.000	110.000	110.000	110.000
P_{40}	550.000	517.839	550.000	550.000	550.000	550.000
P_{loss} (MW)	928.629	933.171	930.519	951.0813	992.499	987.562
Total Cost(\$/h)	136237.497	136350.061	136374.557	136423.400	136502.704	136530.953

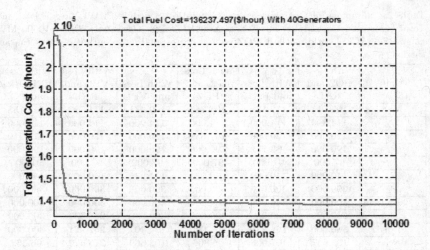

Fig. 2.   Convergence characteristics for PSO-ACO of Test Case 1

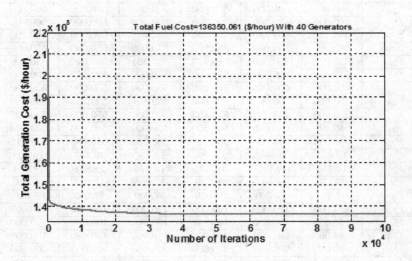

Fig. 3.   Convergence characteristics for PSO-ACO of Test Case 2

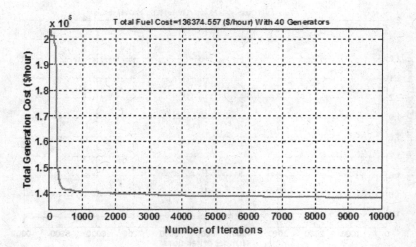

Fig. 4.   Convergence characteristics for PSO-ACO of Test Case 3

6.4. *Test Case 4: Non-smooth Cost Curve with Transmission Loss and Linear Constraints*

This test case considers valve point loading effect implying non-smooth cost function curve. The objective function to be optimized in this case is (9) and only the linear constraints given by Eqs. (2) and (4) are considered. The basic modeling parameters include the valve point coefficients e_i and f_i in addition to a_i, b_i, c_i, as listed in Table 1. The values of linear constraints and loss coefficient are same as that of Test Case 1. The simulation result is shown in Table 2. The convergence characteristics for Test Case 4 is shown in Fig. 5.

6.5. *Test Case 5: Non-smooth Cost Curve with Transmission Loss and RRL*

This test case considers valve point loading effect coupled with non-linear constraint RRL specified with UR_i and DR_i. pairs of values for each generating unit as used in Test Case 2 and 3. The objective function to be optimized in this case is Eq. (9). The values of linear constraints, ELD modeling parameters and loss coefficients are same as used in Test Case 4. The simulation result is shown in Table 2. The convergence characteristics for Test Case 5 is shown in Fig. 6.

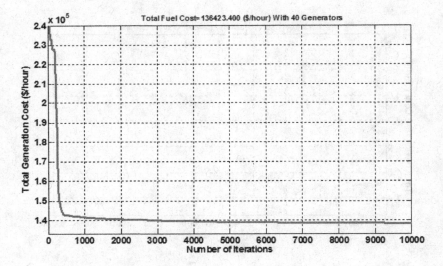

Fig. 5.　Convergence characteristics for PSO-ACO of Test Case 4

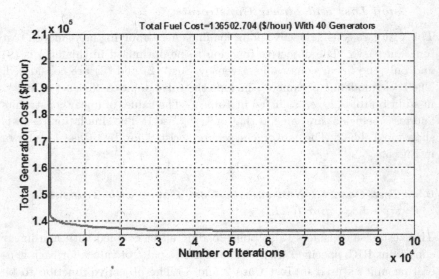

Fig. 6.　Convergence characteristics for PSO-ACO of Test Case 5

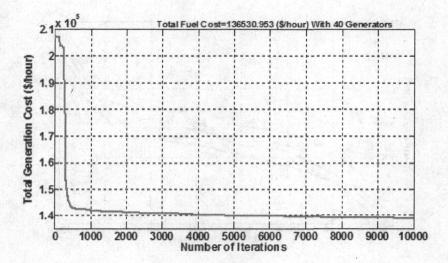

Fig. 7.   Convergence characteristics for PSO-ACO of Test Case 6

6.6. *Test Case 6: Non-smooth Cost Curve with Transmission Loss, RRL and POZ*

This test case is similar to Test Case 3 that considers all linear and non-linear constraints (including RRL and POZ). The only difference is, unlike Test Case 3, valve point loading effect is considered here. Hence this represents the most complex and realistic case out of the six cases taken up in this study. The values of RRL and linear constraints, ELD modeling parameters and loss coefficients are same as used in Test Case 5. The simulation result is shown in Table 2. The convergence characteristics for Test Case 6 is shown in Fig. 7. Test Case 6 being the most complex one, PSO-ACO handles it well as the convergence is achieved in relatively lesser time.

7. Result and Analysis

From Table 2, where the simulation result for all the test cases for P_D=10500 MW for all 40 generating units is summarized, it is seen that the total cost is minimum (136237.497 $/hr)for Test Case 1 which is the simplest of the ELD cases considered here, whereas the maximum cost(136530.953 $/hr) corresponds to Test Case 6, which is the most complex and realistic case. There is a distinct positive shift in cost as valve point

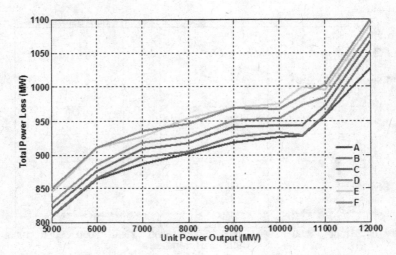

Fig. 8.   Variation of Total Power Loss (MW) with Power Output for six Test Cases: Curves marked A, B, C, D, E, F stands for Test Case 1, 2, 3, 4, 5, 6 respectively

loading effect i.e. non-smooth cost function is introduced in the ELD problem pertaining to Test Case 4. Again for smooth as well as non-smooth curves, the generation cost increases as non-linear constraints RRL and POZ are added (in Test Cases 2 are 3 respectively and also in Test Cases 5 are 6 respectively). As far as loss is concerned, Test Case 1 yields the minimum value (928.629MW) closely followed by Test Case 3 (930.519MW) and then Test Case 2 (933.171MW). The maximum value of loss (992.499MW) again corresponds to Test Case 5.

Variations of total loss (MW) and total generation cost ($/hr) with generator power output for different cases have been depicted in Figs. 8 and 9 respectively.

The total generation cost and power loss P_{loss} outputted by the PSO-ACO hybrid in Test Case 4 corresponding to $P_D = 10500$ MW have been compared (in Table 3 in the Appendix) with those obtained under same test condition for different other hybrid methods discussed in Section 1. The generation cost in $/hr as obtained for hybrids OIWO [30], OCRO [28], ORCCRO [27], QOGSA [26], QOTLBO [23], SDE [22], GAAPI [21] are 136452.677, 136563.48, 136855.19, 136758.768, 137329.86, 138157.46 and 139864.96 respectively whereas the generation cost for PSO-ACO is 136423.400 $/hr. Considering also power loss and generation schedule, it is evident from Table 3 that PSO-ACO yields the most optimum and economic

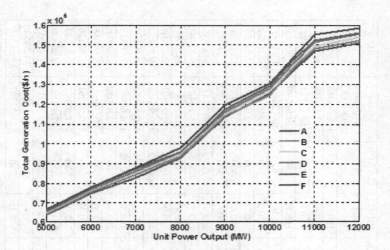

Fig. 9. Variation of Total Generation Cost($/hr)with Power Output for 6 Test Cases: Curves marked A, B, C, D, E, F stands for Test Case 1, 2, 3, 4, 5, 6 respectively

solution as f ar as 40-generator convex ELD problem with transmission loss and valve point loading is concerned. The performance of PSO-ACO could not be compared for other test cases as no other hybrid method has been found to have reported their performance for 40-generator ELD problem with transmission loss with or without valve point loading and with non-linear constraints RRL and/or POZ. The ability of PSO-ACO hybrid to handle such variations of large scale ELD problem strongly attests the potential of the method and uniqueness of the present study.

The standard deviations (SD) of optimized power output given by different hybrid methods (including PSO-ACO) for each of the 40 generators corresponding to Test Case 4 are calculated in Table 3. Taking the means of the generator output (and also power loss) for the other hybrid methods (excluding PSO-ACO) and comparing (by t test) the means with the corresponding generator output for PSO-ACO , we find p = 0.485959, t = 0.03531, which is not statistically significant at $p < 0.05$.

Table 2 and 3 indicates high solution quality and computational efficiency of the PSO-ACO method applied in large scale ELD problem representing actual power generation scenario. Again, since initialization of population is performed using random numbers in PSO-ACO algorithm like other stochastic search algorithms, hence the performance of the algorithm should be judged over a number of trials. Several trials with varying

Table 3. Comparison of Optimum Power Generation Schedule (MW), Loss (MW) and Total Generated Cost ($/hr) for 40-generator ELD Test Case 4 with Loss and VPL but without POZ and RRL and with $P_D = 10500$ MW PSO–ACO hybrid vs other hybrid methods

Unit (MW)	PSO-ACO	OIWO [30]	OCRO [28]	ORCCRO [27]	QOGSA [26]	QOTLBO [23]	SDE [22]	GAAPI [21]	Mean without PSO-ACO	SD
P_1	109.431	113.9908	113.5367	111.68	111.2855	114.0000	110.06	114	112.65043	1.88259
P_2	114.000	114.0000	113.6954	112.16	114.0000	114.0000	112.41	114	113.46649	0.78039
P_3	120.000	119.9977	120.0000	119.98	120.0000	107.8221	120.0	120	118.25711	4.30442
P_4	190.000	182.5131	180.7326	182.18	180.1647	190.0000	188.72	190	184.90149	4.50783
P_5	97.000	88.4227	88.4359	87.28	88.4666	88.3702	85.91	97	89.12649	4.34199
P_6	111.235	140.0000	140.0000	139.85	140.0000	140.0000	140.0	140	139.97857	10.16252
P_7	300.000	299.9999	300.0000	298.15	300.0000	300.0000	250.19	300	292.61999	17.52901
P_8	300.000	292.0654	299.5611	286.89	285.9981	300.0000	290.68	300	293.59923	6.17596
P_9	300.000	299.8817	300.0000	293.38	300.0000	300.0000	300	300	299.03739	2.33492
P_{10}	194.404	279.7073	279.9786	279.34	281.2029	211.2071	282.01	205.25	259.8137	40.0308
P_{11}	102.669	168.8149	243.9604	162.35	318.2088	317.2766	180.82	226.3	231.10439	76.31752
P_{12}	166.888	94.0000	100.0889	94.12	95.4202	163.7603	168.74	204.72	131.54	44.6787
P_{13}	500.000	484.0758	483.5532	486.44	483.4532	481.5709	469.96	346.48	462.21901	49.35198
P_{14}	500.000	484.0477	482.9409	487.02	485.6648	480.5462	484.17	434.32	476.95851	19.31152
P_{15}	485.512	484.0396	483.8711	483.39	481.7678	483.7683	487.73	431.34	476.55811	18.80309
P_{16}	500.000	484.0886	483.7963	484.51	481.0551	480.2998	482.30	440.22	476.60997	17.06572
P_{17}	500.000	489.2813	489.7968	494.22	487.8277	489.2488	499.64	500	492.85923	5.39801
P_{18}	377.208	489.2966	489.3228	489.48	490.3429	489.5524	411.32	500	479.9021	45.99088
P_{19}	550.000	511.3219	511.1120	512.20	510.8762	512.5482	510.47	550	516.93261	17.87116
P_{20}	502.321	511.3350	511.8301	513.13	511.0289	514.2914	542.04	550	521.95077	16.89624
P_{21}	550.000	549.9412	523.4767	543.85	523.2121	527.0877	544.81	550	537.48253	12.25389
P_{22}	550.000	549.9999	528.3479	548.00	524.5515	530.1025	550	550	540.14311	11.47205
P_{23}	509.187	523.2804	524.2743	521.21	523.4272	524.2912	550	550	530.92616	14.3353
P_{24}	550.000	523.3213	523.1350	525.01	523.9441	524.6512	528.16	550	528.31737	11.81315

(Continued)

Table 3. (Continued)

Unit (MW)	PSO-ACO	OIWO [30]	OCRO [28]	ORCCRO [27]	QOGSA [26]	QOTLBO [23]	SDE [22]	GAAPI [21]	Mean without PSO-ACO	SD
P_{25}	550.000	523.5804	523.7182	529.84	523.8473	525.0586	524.16	550	528.60064	11.73554
P_{26}	550.000	523.5847	524.3740	540.04	530.9198	524.4654	539.10	550	533.21199	11.09882
P_{27}	12.157	10.0086	10.1471	12.59	10.2810	10.8929	10	11.44	10.76566	1.0191
P_{28}	12.876	10.0068	10.6337	10.06	10.1583	17.4312	10.37	11.56	11.46	2.53706
P_{29}	10.965	10.0123	10.6496	10.79	10.6544	12.7839	10	11.42	10.90146	0.89092
P_{30}	97.000	87.8664	87.8463	89.70	87.9125	88.8119	96.10	97	90.74816	4.33493
P_{31}	190.000	190.0000	190.0000	189.59	190.0000	190.0000	185.33	190	189.27429	1.63669
P_{32}	190.000	189.9983	190.0000	189.96	190.0000	190.0000	189.54	190	189.92833	0.16113
P_{33}	190.000	190.0000	190.0000	187.61	190.0000	190.0000	189.96	190	189.65286	0.84309
P_{34}	200.000	199.9940	200.0000	198.91	200.0000	200.0000	199.90	200	199.82914	0.3816
P_{35}	200.000	200.0000	171.2759	199.98	170.8313	168.0873	196.25	200	186.63207	15.18375
P_{36}	188.227	164.8283	164.8722	165.68	166.1489	165.5072	185.85	200	173.26951	14.03503
P_{37}	110.000	110.0000	110.0000	109.98	110.0000	110.0000	109.72	110	109.95714	0.09823
P_{38}	110.000	109.9940	110.0000	109.82	110.0000	110.0000	110	110	109.97343	0.06337
P_{39}	110.000	110.0000	110.0000	109.88	110.0000	110.0000	95.71	110	107.94143	5.04639
P_{40}	550.000	550.000	549.9970	548.50	513.3504	511.5313	532.43	550	536.5441	17.00835
Total power (MW)	11451.0813	11,457.2965	11468.9607	11458.75	11484.15	11508.96	11,474.43	11,545.06	11485.37246	31.70278
P_{Loss} (MW)	951.0813	957.2965	968.9607	958.75	984.15	1008.96	974.43	1045.06	985.37246	31.70278
Total Cost ($/h)	136423.400	136452.677	136563.48	136855.19	136758.768	137329.86	138,157.46	139864.96	137426.05643	1185.31361

initial population have been carried out to check the consistency of the PSO-ACO hybrid. The frequency of attaining optimum cost for the different test cases out of 50 independent trials is quite high. Thus experimentally PSO-ACO emerges as a robust method to deal with large scale ELD problem.

8. Conclusion

In this study, the hybrid swarm intelligence-based search algorithm PSO-ACO is applied for the first time in finding optimal solution of 40-generator ELD problem.Though the performance of the method is quite encouraging, it is still in the experimental stage and more studies are needed to further improve its performance.The number of iterations required to arrive at the optimal solution is on the higher side and needs to be brought down further. More trials are required to confirm that the set of parameter values used are the optimum ones or need to be adjusted more.

PSO-ACO is a combination of two powerful optimization algorithms. In PSO, the decision of each particle for selecting the best path is strengthened with introduction of the ACO method. This combination can provide a scope for all individuals and particularly the most-fit particle to search the neighboring area better. The experimental result justify that the PSO-ACO algorithm is a realistic, reliable and an efficient soft computing approach to find optimal solutions for large-scale multi-constraint smooth and non-smooth ELD problem. It is observed that PSO-ACO hybrid has the ability to converge to a high quality, robust ELD solution and possess good convergence characteristics and successfully avoids the traps of local optima. In future PSO-ACO hybrid can be tried for ELD solution for larger scale and more complex power system optimization problems like Dynamic Economic Dispatch (DED) problem and Combined Economic and Emission Dispatch (CEED) problem.

References

1. L. L.Grigsby,*Power System Stability and Control*. CRC Press, Second Edition (2007).
2. A. J. Wood and B. F. Wollenberg, *Power Generation,Operation and Control*. John Wiley & Sons (1996).
3. T. Yalcinoz and M. J. Short, Neural networks approach for solving economic dispatch problem with transmission capacity constraints, *IEEE Trans. on Power Systems.* **13**(2), 307–313 (1998).

4. X. S. Yanga, S. S. S. Hosseinib and, A. H. Gandomic, Firefly algorithm for solving non-convex economic dispatch problems with valve loading effect, *Applied Soft Computing.* **12**, 1180-1186 (2012).

5. K. M. Passino, Biomimicry of bacterial foraging for distributed optimization and control, *IEEE Control Systems Magazine*, **22**(3), 52–67 (2002).

6. J. Kennedy and R. C. Eberhart, Particle swarm optimization, *In proc. of IEEE International Conference on Neural Networks*, Perth, Australia, (1995), 1942–1948.

7. J. Kennedy and R. Eberhart, Swarm Intelligence, *Morgan Kaufman Publishers*, Inc., San Francisco, CA (2001).

8. M. Dorigo and L. Ganbardella, Ant colony system: a cooperative learning approach to the traveling salesman problem, *IEEE Transactions on Evolutionary Computation*, **1**(1), 53–66 (1997).

9. N. Nomana and H. Iba, Differential evolution for economic load dispatch problems, *Electric Power Systems Research.* **78**, 1322–1331 (2008).

10. T. Jayabarathi, G. Sadasivam and V. Ramachandran, Evolutionary programming based economic dispatch of generators with prohibited operating zones, *Electric Power Systems Research*, **52**(3), 261–266 (1999).

11. D. Santra, A. Mondal and A. Mukherjee, Study of economic load dispatch by various hybrid optimization techniques, *In S. Bhattacharyya, editor. Hybrid Soft Computing: Research and Applications*, Springer India (2014), 37–74.

12. L. D. S. Coelho and V. C. Mariani, Combining of chaotic differential evolution and quadratic programming for economic dispatch optimization with valve-point effect, *IEEE Trans on Power Systems*, **21**(2), 989–996 (2006).

13. N. Sinha, Y Ma, and Loi Lei Lai, GA tuned Differential Evolution for economic load dispatch with non-convex cost function, *In Proc. IEEE(ICSMCSA) International Conference on Systems*, Man, and Cybernetics, San Antonio, TX, USA , Oct. (2009), 4183–4188.

14. B. Mahdad, K. Srairi, T. Bouktir and M. E. Benbouzid, Fuzzy controlled parallel pso to solving large practical economic dispatch, *IEEE ENERGYCON*, Manama, Bahrain, 34–40 (2010).

15. A. Bhattacharya, and P. K. Chattopadhyay, Hybrid differential evolution with biogeography-based optimization for solution of economic load dispatch, *IEEE Trans on Power Systems*, **25**(4), 1955–1964 (2010).

16. N. Duvvuru, and K. S.Swarup, A hybrid interior point assisted differential evolution algorithm for economic dispatch, *IEEE Trans. on power systems*, **26**(2), 541–549 (2011).

17. J. S.Alsumait, J. K. Sykulski and A. K. Al-Othman, A hybrid GAPSSQP method to solve power system valve-point economic dispatch problems, *Applied Energy*, **87**, 1773-1781 (2010).

18. L. L. Dinh, D. V. Ngoc, T. H. Nguyen and D. L. Anh, A hybrid differential evolution and harmony search for nonconvex economic dispatch problems, *In Proc. PEOCO*, (2013), 238–243.

19. P. K. Roy, S. Bhui and C. Paul, Solution of economic load dispatch using hybrid chemical reaction optimization approach, *Applied Soft Computing*, **24**, 109-125 (2014).

20. X. He, Y. Rao and J. Huang, A novel algorithm for economic load dispatch of power systems, *Neurocomputing*, **171**, 1454–1461 (2016).
21. I. Ciornei and E. Kyriakides, A GA-API solution for the economic dispatch of generation in power system operation, *IEEE Trans. on Power System*, **27**, 233–242 (2012).
22. A. S. Reddy and K. Vaisakh, Shuffled differential evolution for large scale economic dispatch, *Electr. Power Syst. Res*, **96**, 237-245 (2013) .
23. P. K. Roy and S. Bhui, Multi-objective quasi-oppositional teaching learning based optimization for economic emission load dispatch problem, *Int. J Electr. Power Energy Syst.*, **53**, 937–948 (2013).
24. H. Tizhoosh, Opposition-based learning: a new scheme for machine intelligence, *In Proc. of the international conference on computational intelligence for modelling control and automation*, Austria, 28-30 Nov., (2005) 695–701.
25. R. V. Rao, V. J. Savsani and D. P. Vakharia, Teaching-learning-based optimization: an optimization method for continuous non-linear large scale problems, *Inform Sci.*, **183**(1), 1–15 (2012).
26. S. M. A. Bulbul and P. K. Roy, Quasi-oppositional gravitational search algorithm applied to complex economic load dispatch problem, *In Proc. ICONCE*, Kalyani, India, 16 - 17 Jan., (2014) 308–313.
27. K. Bhattacharjee, A. Bhattacharya and S. H. Dey, Oppositional real coded chemical reaction optimization for different economic dispatch problems, *Int. J. Electr. Power Energy Syst.*, **55**, 378-391 (2014).
28. S. Hazra, P. K. Roy and A. Sinha, An efficient evolutionary algorithm applied to economic load dispatch problem, *In Proc. CCC and IT*, Hooghly, India, 7-8 Feb, (2015) 1–6.
29. A. Y. S. Lam and V. O. K. Li, Chemical-reaction-inspired meta heuristic for optimization, *IEEE Trans. Evol. Comput.*, **14**, 381-399 (2010).
30. A. K. Barisal, R. C. Prusty, Large scale economic dispatch of power systems using oppositional invasive weed optimization, *Applied Soft Computing*, **29**, 122–137 (2015).
31. A. R.Mehrabian and C. Lucas, A novel numerical optimization algorithm inspired from weed colonization, *Ecol. Inform.*, **1**(4), 355–366 (2006).
32. D. Santra, A. Mondal, A. Mukherjee and K. Sarker, Hybrid PSO-ACO technique to solve economic load dispatch problem, *In Proc. ICRCICN*, Kolkata, India, (2015) 187–191.
33. N. Sinha, R. Chakrabarti and P. K.Chattopadhyay,Evolutionary programming techniques for economic load dispatch, *IEEE Trans on Evolutionary Computation*, **7**(1), 83–94 (2003).
34. S. K.Wang, J. P. Chiou and C. W. Liu, Non-smooth /non-convex economic dispatch by a novel hybrid differential evolution algorithm, *IET Gener. Transm. Distrib.*, **1**(5), 793-803 2007.

Appendix A. B Loss Coefficient and Tables

B LOSS COEFFICIENT

B loss coefficients as obtained by replicating the B coefficients of 6 Unit system [30]

$$
B_{40,40} = \begin{bmatrix} B_1 \\ B_2 \\ \cdot \\ \cdot \\ B_{40} \end{bmatrix} = \begin{bmatrix} b_{1,1} & b_{1,2} & \cdot\cdot & b_{1,40} \\ \cdot & & \cdot\cdot\cdot & \cdot \\ \cdot & & \cdot\cdot\cdot & \cdot \\ \cdot & & \cdot\cdot\cdot & \cdot \\ b_{40,1} & \cdot & \cdot\cdot & b_{40,40} \end{bmatrix} \Big/ 100
$$

$B_1 =$
[0.0017 0.0012 0.0007 −0.0001 −0.0005 −0.0002 0.0017 0.0012
0.0007 −0.0001 −0.0005 −0.0002 0.0017 0.0012 0.0007 −0.0001
−0.0005 −0.0002 0.0017 0.0012 0.0007 −0.0001 −0.0005 −0.0002
0.0017 0.0012 0.0007 −0.0001 −0.0005 −0.0002 0.0017 0.0012
0.0007 −0.0001 −0.0005 −0.0002 0.0017 0.0012 0.0007 −0.0001];

$B_2 =$
[0.0012 0.0014 0.0009 0.0001 −0.0006 −0.0001 0.0012 0.0014
0.0009 0.0001 −0.0006 −0.0001 0.0012 0.0014 0.0009 0.0001
−0.0006 −0.0001 0.0012 0.0014 0.0009 0.0001 −0.0006 −0.0001
0.0012 0.0014 0.0009 0.0001 −0.0006 −0.0001 0.0012 0.0014
0.0009 0.0001 −0.0006 −0.0001 0.0012 0.0014 0.0009 0.0001];

....

....

$B_{40} =$
[−0.0001 0.0001 0.0000 0.0024 −0.0006 −0.0008 −0.0001 0.0001
0.0000 0.0024 −0.0006 −0.0008 −0.0001 0.0001 0.0000 0.0024
−0.0006 −0.0008 −0.0001 0.0001 0.0000 0.0024 −0.0006 −0.0008
−0.0001 0.0001 0.0000 0.0024 −0.0006 −0.0008 −0.0001 0.0001
0.0000 0.0024 −0.0006 −0.0008 −0.0001 0.0001 0.0000 0.0024];

$B_{0,40} = 1.0e^{-03}x$
[−0.3908 −0.1297 0.7047 0.0591 0.2161 −0.6635 −0.3908 −0.1297
0.7047 0.0591 0.2161 −0.6635 −0.3908 −0.1297 0.7047 0.0591
0.2161 −0.6635 −0.3908 −0.1297 0.7047 0.0591 0.2161 −0.6635
0.3908 −0.1297 0.7047 0.0591 0.2161 −0.6635 −0.3908 −0.1297
0.7047 0.0591 0.2161 −0.6635 −0.3908 −0.1297 0.7047 0.0591];

$B_{00} = 0.0056$;

Chapter 11

Conclusion

Siddhartha Bhattacharyya

Department of Computer Application,
RCC Institute of Information Technology,
Kolkata-700 015, India
dr.siddhartha.bhattacharyya@gmail.com

The interest in the field of metaheuristics for the application to various optimization problems is rapidly growing. Thanks are due to the constantly evolving algorithms which find widespread use in different disciplines of engineering and technology. A metaheuristic algorithm is a higher-level procedure designed to select a heuristic (partial search algorithm) that may lead to a sufficiently good solution to an optimization problem, especially with incomplete or imperfect information.[1-4] The main principle of operation of a metaheuristic algorithm is based on exploration and exploitation of the feature space. The two very important concepts which determine the behavior of the metaheuristics are intensification and diversification. These concepts are somewhat not conflicting and complementary to each other.

The basic objective of a metaheuristic algorithm is to exploit the search space by exploring all possible solutions.[5,6] As such, these algorithms often require a starting set of solutions for the problem at hand. During course of time, the algorithm improves upon the seed solutions to achieve the desired optimized set of solutions. Usually, the success of metaheuristics mainly depends on the encoding of candidate solutions and thus the search space. It is worthy of note that the improvement of the solutions is also dependent on the right choice of the parameters and the objective function.

Most of the optimization problems may have more than one local solutions. In these circumstances, choosing of the optimization method is very much important. The optimization method must not be greedy and the searching process will not be localized in the neighborhood of the best solution as it may stuck at a local solution and that will misguide the search process. It should be observed that the optimization algorithm should made a balance between global and local search. Both the mathematical and combinatorial types optimization problems can be solved by different methods. The optimization problems that have large search space or more complex in nature will become difficult to solve using conventional mathematical optimization algorithms. Here is the utility of the meta-heuristic algorithms. Different meta-heuristic optimization algorithms, present in the research arena are very much capable to solve difficult optimization problems.

It may be noted that the operation as well as the behavior of a meta-heuristic algorithm is also dependent on whether it is applied to a single-objective problem or a multi-objective one.[7] In a single-objective meta-heuristic, the aim of the algorithm is centered on optimizing a single objective function and hence the operation is quite simple and trivial. On the other hand, when more than one objective functions need to be optimized, the corresponding metaheuristic algorithm produces a set of pareto-optimal solutions instead of a single unique optimal solution. Hence, one needs to further select the best solution among the pareto-optimal set to achieve the desired objective.

Notable among the well-known meta-heuristic algorithms are Genetic algorithm (GA),[4] simulated annealing(SA),[8] 5 Tabu search (TS)[9-11] and different types of swarm intelligence algorithms. The operation of the genetic algorithm (GA) is inspired by the evolutionary process exhibited in nature. While the Tabu search applies the memory structure in living beings, the simulated annealing imitates the annealing process in crystalline solids. The widely used swarm intelligence algorithms include particle swarm optimization (PSO),[12] ant colony optimization (ACO),[13] artificial bee colony optimization (ABC),[14] differential optimization (DE)[15,16] and cuckoo search algorithm,[17] to name a few. Of late, several other swarm intelligence algorithms have been evolved. These include Egyptian Vulture Optimization Algorithm,[18,19] Rats herds Algorithm (RATHA),[20] Bat algorithm,[21] Crow search algorithm,[22] Glowworm Swarm Optimization (GSO),[23] Spider Monkey Algorithm,[24] to name a few.

A well designed heuristic method can usually provide a solution that is nearly optimal or can conclude that no solution exists, be it a single-objective trait or a multi-objective trait. Be that as it may, although these algorithms are efficient in solving complex optimization problems, yet they suffer from several disadvantages. one of the disadvantages of heuristic methods is that it is usually designed to fit a specific problem type rather than a variety of applications. Moreover, it has been observed that most of the algorithms suffer from high time complexity and often yield degenerate solutions.

Keeping in mind these disadvantages, scientists have invested a lot of efforts to evolve hybrid metaheuristic algorithms. Hybrid metaheuristics result from the coupling of different individual metaheuristics so that one algorithm can complement the other in the set thereby evolving more robust and failsafe solutions. This book is targeted to report the latest findings in the evolution of hybrid metaheuristics and their applications to several application areas.

Hybrid metaheuristic algorithms have been found to be proficient in solving complex optimization problems as well as real life optimization problems. Notable application areas include biometric authentication from a large database, optimized pattern recognition and image analysis, feature selection, power system optimization, robotics, to name a few. The inherent advantages offered by the hybrid metaheuristic algorithms when applied to different real life problems are time efficiency and robustness. In addition, researchers have also coupled other soft computing paradigms like neural networks and fuzzy logic to evolve variants of hybrid metaheuristics.[4,8,25,26]

References

1. D. E. Goldberg, *Genetic Algorithms in Search, Optimization and Machine Learning*. Kluwer Academic Publishers (1989).
2. F. Glover and G. A. Kochenberger, *Handbook of metaheuristics*. Springer, International Series in Operations Research & Management Science (2003).
3. E.-G. Talbi, *Metaheuristics: From Design to Implementation*. Wiley (2009).
4. J. H. Holland, *Adaptation in Natural and Artificial Systems*. University of Michigan Press (1975).
5. L. Bianchi, M. Dorigo, L. M. Gambardella, and W. J. Gutjahr, A survey on metaheuristics for stochastic combinatorial optimization, *Natural Computing*. **8**(2), 239–287 (2009).
6. C. Blum and A. Roli, Metaheuristics in combinatorial optimization: Overview and conceptual comparison, *ACM Computing Surveys*. **35**(3), 268–308 (2003).
7. T. Ganesan, I. Elamvazuthi, K. Shaari, K. Zilati, and P. Vasant, Swarm intelligence and gravitational search algorithm for multi-objective optimization of synthesis gas production, *Applied Energy*. **103**, 368–374 (2013).

8. S. Kirkpatrick, C. D. G. Jr., and M. P. Vecchi, Optimization by simulated annealing, *Science*. **220**(4598), 671–680 (1983).

9. F. Glover and M. Laguna, *Tabu Search*. Kluwer, Boston, MA (1997).

10. F. Glover, Tabu search, part i, *ORSA Journal on Computing*. **1**, 190–206 (1989).

11. F. Glover, Tabu search, part ii, *ORSA Journal on Computing*. **2**, 4–32 (1990).

12. K. Kennedy and R. Eberhart. *Particle Swarm Optimization*. vol. 4, pp. 1942–1945 (1995).

13. M. Dorigo, V. Maniezzo, and A. Colorni, The ant system: Optimization by a colony of cooperating agents, *IEEE Transactions on Systems, Man, Cybernetics - Part B*. **26**(1), 29–41 (1996).

14. D. Karaboga, *An idea based on honey bee swarm for numerical optimization*. Technical Report TR06, Erciyes University, Engineering Faculty, Computer Engineering Department (2005).

15. R. Storn and K. Price, Differential evolution-a simple and efficient heuristic for global optimization over continuous spaces, *Journal of Global Optimization*. **11**(4), 341–359 (1997).

16. U. K. Chakraborty, *Advances in Differential Evolution*. Springer-Verlag, Heidelberg (2008).

17. X.-S. Yang and S. Deb, Cuckoo search via lévy flights, *World Congress on Nature & Biologically Inspired Computing (NaBIC 2009)*. IEEE Publications. pp. 210–214 (2009).

18. C. Sur, S. Sharma, and A. Shukla, *Solving Travelling Salesman Problem Using Egyptian Vulture Optimization Algorithm: A New Approach*, In eds. M. A. Klopotek, J. Koronacki, M. Marciniak, A. Mykowiecka, and S. T. Wierzchon, *Language Processing and Intelligent Information Systems*, vol. 7912, *Lecture Notes in Computer Science*, pp. 254–267. Springer, Berlin, Heidelberg (2013).

19. C. Sur, S. Sharma, and A. Shukla, Egyptian Vulture Optimization Algorithm — A New Nature Inspired Meta-heuristics for Knapsack Problem. In *9th International Conf. on Computing and Information Technology (IC2IT2013)*, pp. 227–237 (2013).

20. J. A. Ruiz-Vanoye, O. Diaz-Parra, F. Cocòn, A. Soto, M. D. los À. B. Arias, G. Verduzco-Reyes, and R. Alberto-Lira, Meta-Heuristics Algorithms based on the Grouping of Animals by Social Behavior for the Traveling Salesman Problem, *International Journal of Combinatorial Optimization Problems and Informatics*. **3**(3), 104–123 (2012). ISSN 2007-1558.

21. X.-S. Yang, A new metaheuristic bat-inspired algorithm. In *Nature Inspired Cooperative Strategies for Optimization (NICSO 2010)*, vol. 284, *Studies in Computational Intelligence*, pp. 65–74 (2010).

22. A. Askarzadeh, A novel metaheuristic method for solving constrained engineering optimization problems: Crow search algorithm, *Computers & Structures*. **169**, 1–12 (2016).

23. K. Krishnanand and D. Ghose, Detection of Multiple Source Locations using a Glowworm Metaphor with Applications to Collective Robotics. In *Swarm Intelligence Symposium*, pp. 84–91 (2005).

24. J. C. Bansal, H. Sharma, S. S. Jadon, and M. Clerc, Spider monkey optimization algorithm for numerical optimization, *Memetic Computing*. pp. 1–17 (2013).
25. F. Glover, Heuristics for integer programming using surrogate constraints, *Decision Sciences*. **8**(1), 156–166 (1977).
26. F. Glover, Future paths for integer programming and links to artificial intelligence, *Computers and Operations Research*. **13**, 533–549 (1986).

Index

Printed in the United States
By Bookmasters